Introduction to Social Media Investigation

Introduction to Social Media Investigation
A Hands-on Approach

Jennifer Golbeck

Judith L. Klavans, Technical Editor

AMSTERDAM • BOSTON • HEIDELBERG • LONDON
NEW YORK • OXFORD • PARIS • SAN DIEGO
SAN FRANCISCO • SINGAPORE • SYDNEY • TOKYO

Syngress is an imprint of Elsevier

Executive Editor: Steven Elliot
Editorial Project Manager: Benjamin Rearick
Project Manager: Punithavathy Govindaradjane
Designer: Mark Rogers

Syngress is an imprint of Elsevier
225 Wyman Street, Waltham, MA 02451, USA

ISBN: 978-0-12-801656-5

British Library Cataloguing in Publication Data
A catalogue record for this book is available from the British Library

Library of Congress Cataloging-in-Publication Data
A catalog record for this book is available from the Library of Congress

For information on all Syngress publications,
visit our website at store.elsevier.com/Syngress

Working together
to grow libraries in
developing countries

www.elsevier.com • www.bookaid.org

For Gram
Thank you for a lifetime of encouraging my scientific pursuits,
including countless shark teeth and hours in the Planetarium.

Contents

Acknowledgments

Living in Washington, DC, gives me the opportunity to interact with people who have a lot of very cool jobs. My friends in federal law enforcement inspired me to write this book, although its audience has grown to be much larger.

Thanks to HARO (helpareporter.com) for helping me find amazing sources of case studies and anecdotes for the book, and thanks to everyone who responded to those queries and shared your tales of intrigue. Thanks also to my friend and colleague Scott Paquette for pointing me to *Flash Boys*, a great book with stories that made it in here.

Big thanks to Tony Rogers who edited all the chapters in this book. This is the second book of mine he has edited, and once again he has improved it dramatically over my awkward first drafts.

Appreciation also goes to my dogs Hopper and Venkman who patiently watched me write this whole thing and whose need for walks gave me excuses to take a break from the writing. Thanks also to Carly, our foster dog, who plays a role as Malcom's dog "Barley" throughout this book.

Thanks also to Ingo, who was my boyfriend when I started writing this book and my husband when I finished, for patiently listening to all my stories without once accusing me of being creepy for investigating so many people online.

And finally, thanks to the reviewers of this book who sent comments from the proposal stage through the final draft stage.

Introduction

In the fall of 2014, a social worker made two posts on her Facebook account. Before heading into court, she wrote "I'm in court tomorrow for a case where there is a high level of domestic violence amongst many things...." The next day, when she came out of the trial, she said "It's powerful to know that ... children's lives have just massively changed for the better and now they are safe and protected from harm and have every hope for the future...."

The mother of the child in the case found these posts after looking up the social worker online. Although the social worker thought her posts were private, they were not. They also included a map showing the location of the courthouse from which the last message had been posted. The mother filed a complaint, claiming the posts were a violation of confidentiality rules, and the social worker was sanctioned.[1]

This is an example of a social media investigation by a private citizen that led to real consequences. Although the outcome itself might be debated further, it nevertheless shows the power of social media as an investigative tool.

This book will show you how to find people on social media, what types of data are available on different sites, how to access the information on the most popular social media sites, and introduce some advanced techniques for understanding people that you may choose to learn more about.

Social media can connect people and help them maintain and support relationships from all parts of their lives. It lets us share and interact with one another in countless ways. People can use social media to build up and portray their online identity—sharing everything from major life events to what they ate for breakfast this morning. All that sharing and interaction leaves behind a long, complicated, and informative trail about a person's personality, motivations, friends, activities, patterns of behavior, and actions. That makes social media a powerful tool for investigators.

Just what do people share? Almost everything about themselves. Social media sites are full of:

- demographic information;
- lists of friends, family, and associates;
- logs of activities, preferences, and favorites;
- maps showing places a person goes and how frequently;
- time-stamped posts that indicate where a person was and when; and
- the content of the posts themselves, where people detail their thoughts, feelings, and ideas.

Why might you do an "investigation" online? Law enforcement and lawyers in civil suits certainly want to gather information on suspects or the opposing side of a dispute. Journalists may want to learn more about sources or subjects of their reporting. Businesses want to learn about the people they might hire or how well their current employees are representing the company. Parents may want to check up on their children to be sure they are interacting safely, though, just as frequently, adult children may want to check up on older parents to be sure they are not getting scammed.

This book is intended for all these groups. Professional investigators will find guidance for extending their skills into the social media arena. People who are new to investigating will find tips and examples that will help them get started with basic investigations while also mastering new online skills.

Individuals have countless reasons for wanting to find out more about others. They may worry about stalking. They may desperately want to get in touch with someone for whom they have very little information. Or, they may want to run their own background checks on people they let into their lives.

During the process of writing this book, I spoke to dozens of lawyers, investigators, law enforcement officials, journalists, and others who have used social media in their investigations. They provided a wealth of stories and examples of how it could be used. But without any prompting, all of them talked about how useful social media was as a source of information.

Lisa Helfend Meyer, of Los Angeles-based family law firm Meyer, Olson, Lowy & Meyers, uses all kinds of social media on a regular basis. "Social media can be a very valuable tool in your arsenal of weapons in family law." I heard the same from every family law attorney I spoke to. The information that people reveal online is valuable both as evidence and as preemptive information that can guide the direction of a case.

The open, public nature of social media makes all this possible.

Dusty Lefdal, an investigator at Employers Investigative Services, issues an important warning. He says:

> Social media has helped us during all kinds of investigations. Always be wary of using the information, especially if you are not sure it belongs to the individual you are looking for. You would be surprised at similarities between people. A trained professional should always be consulted and social media should never, ever be used solely and upon itself. It's simply a tool in a box full of investigative tools.

He's right. It quite easy to mistake one person for another online, and information needs to be analyzed carefully. A photo of someone at a party that was posted today might have been taken years ago; one cannot assume that all the information is current or evidence of present behavior. Furthermore, there are no guarantees that what someone posts online is true. Altered photographs, exaggerations, and straight-up lies can be expected.

This book will explain many of the pitfalls you might face while conducting an online investigation. It will help you be wary of what you see and show you how to verify information that is important to your investigation. In short, this book's purpose is to teach you how to use social media to successfully find individuals and information about them.

A few notes about the scope of this book....

The social media sites and services discussed here are the most popular in the world. However, the book does have a focus on sites more common in North America and Western Europe. Russia and the former Soviet republics, Asia, and South America all have sites that are particularly popular in those places, but are not widely used elsewhere. We do not address those sites in depth in this book, but readers are encouraged to visit this text's accompanying website, where more details will be available.

Social media is a huge part of the internet, and on each site, there is a tremendous amount to learn about how to use it. This book focuses on features of each site that are relevant to finding and learning about individuals. This book will *not* provide a full tutorial for each social media site; features that aren't useful investigative goals are omitted.

Except for one chapter at the end of this book, we also won't focus on investigating groups (although many of the same techniques apply). Similarly, we won't discuss techniques for investigating people based around some shared characteristics (like race, religion, gender, being a fan of a particular sports team, and reading a specific book). Again, many techniques discussed here could be used for that end, but we don't discuss them specifically.

The techniques described here are all ways to access information without deception or violation of sites' terms of service. While it would be possible to access more information by creating fake accounts, making deceptive social connections, or writing programs to collect data, this book focuses on what can be obtained by anyone with a legitimate account on the social media website or by publicly accessible information. Each chapter will detail a specific website's privacy restrictions and the issues an investigator might face when collecting information about a target.

Examples in this book focus on more serious situations—firings, law suits, and arrests. Anecdotes in these kinds of cases are more memorable and easier to find. But as an investigative tool, social media is also useful for general background information that would be hard to get otherwise. There are also a few examples from my own online investigative work that are more "typical." They center around finding background information or contact information for a particular target.

When you finish this book, you will have the skills you need to search, navigate, and collect information from many sources. Along the way, I hope that you will learn lessons for your use of social media: being mindful of what you put online, what to expect (or not) in terms of privacy, and how to manage your own online identity.

NOTE

1 Stevenson, Luke. 2014. "Social Worker given Conditions of Practice Order after 'disrespectful' Facebook Posts." CommunityCare. http://www.communitycare.co.uk/2014/09/10/social-worker-given-conditions-practice-order-disrespectful-facebook-posts/.

Background and basics

Before jumping in to all the details of social media, it's useful to know the types of websites and services, to have a vocabulary of common features, and to understand the origins and landscape of the area. This chapter introduces those basics that will be used throughout the rest of the book.

INVESTIGATING ON SOCIAL MEDIA

This book is intended to show investigators how to find information on social media. It covers the basics of social media, but not the very basics of investigative techniques. With that said, there are some tips on running social media investigations that are worth discussing up front. Many people will recognize these as standard investigation techniques but may not have thought about how to translate that into an online environment.

Investigator Dusty Lefdal describes a technique that was commonly used among many people I spoke with. "Often times, we locate a target, not by trying to find the target themselves, but by finding their associates. This will then lead us to the target."

Attorney Lisa Helfend Meyer agrees. In her family law practice, they often look at the social media accounts of clients' (and opposing parties') children to see what they are posting. While parents may try to keep a low social media profile, the kids often don't worry about this and may not even be aware that their posts can be used. The same is true of friends of the targets of investigation.

People also tend to be reliably uncreative in their profiles. They use the same email addresses, same usernames, and same profile photos over and over. In future chapters, we will look at techniques that you can use to take information you learn on one site and find information about a person on many other sites, including ones you have never heard of.

A BRIEF HISTORY OF SOCIAL MEDIA

The history of social media is a topic that deserves its own book, but understanding the major motivations and points of development in the timeline will help in understanding the current landscape and uses of these technologies.

GENESIS OF THE INTERNET

The internet has been a social place since its invention. Work began on the internet in the 1960s, and the modern internet was in place by the early 1980s. In 1980, Usenet was created. This was an online discussion system where people could find discussion boards on a topic they were interested in and then read messages from others and post replies.

New methods of finding community and social connection arose as the internet evolved to include services like CompuServe and America Online. But the biggest shift came with the invention of the World Wide Web, which went online in 1991.

THE EARLY WORLD WIDE WEB

The web was originally a place where a person needed a number of technical skills to post content. Creating a web page required knowledge of the language for writing web pages (HTML), space on a server to store the web pages, and the ability to upload the coded version. As such, the web's first decade was a time when people mostly browsed content created by others. The (relatively) small number of content creators consisted mostly of technically skilled individuals or organizations with teams that could put pages online.

GROWING POPULARITY

The late 1990s saw the development and release of several tools designed to make creating web content easier. One of the most important of these in terms of the rise of social media was the blog. Blogs (short for web logs) are a type of online diary. While it was technically possible for anyone to have created a frequently updated journal on the web since its invention, blog software made this much easier. Instead of writing code, people could author "posts" (like diary entries) using a graphical interface similar to a word processor's. The blog software would convert the post into code for the web, handle the organization of the site, sort posts by date, and format them.

Blogs helped millions of people to create online presences. As blogging software improved, it became possible for people to comment on the blog entries of others. In time, this created *de facto* communities around people's posts.

SOCIAL NETWORKS APPEAR

In the early 2000s, as blog numbers continued growing dramatically, a new kind of site started to appear. These sites were focused less on creating online diaries and more on creating online profiles. At the time, the ability to create a page about yourself, your skills, and your interests was difficult. Blogs had empowered the masses to create sites in a specific category, but creating web content belonging to another category still required all the technical skills mentioned above. This new breed of site allowed people to create personal pages by simply completing a form. But it went one step further: people could also find any friends who were also members of the same system and connect to them.

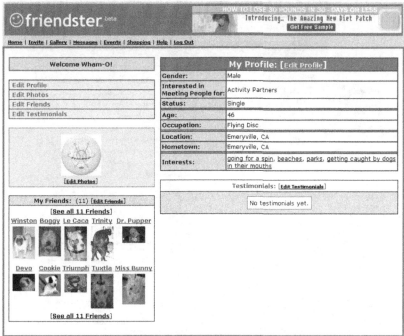

FIGURE 2.1

An example of how the social networking website Friendster appeared in 2003.

There were a handful these new social networking sites in the earliest generation, but the most popular was Friendster. Figure 2.1 shows an image of Friendster, as it appeared in the early 2000s. Basic profile information appears on the right, and toward the bottom left is a list of friends.

This general structure—a static profile with a list of friends—was the standard among social networking sites for many years. Figure 2.2 shows a 2005 Myspace profile page, with very similar organization.

These types of sites began to gain popularity in the early to mid-2000s. By 2005, there were already hundreds of social networking websites, and many had over 1 million members—quite a large number for the time.

WEB 2.0 AND THE RISE OF SOCIAL NETWORKS

Part of the reason social networks were so popular is because they made it easy for people to put information online. As social network sites continued to gain popularity, this technology started appearing elsewhere on the web. Photo-sharing websites (like Photobucket and Flickr) began in 2003-2004. Soon after followed video sharing, exemplified by YouTube's launch in 2005.

FIGURE 2.2

A Myspace profile page from 2005. Information about the user, Tom, appears near the top left, while friends are shown at the bottom right.

Sites that let people organize other types of content (like bookmarks to sites they liked) also appeared. Appearing in 2003, del.icio.us let people share links, add labels to make finding them easier, and browse the shared links of others. Digg, appearing in 2004, also let people share links but introduced the ability for others to "vote" links "up" or "down." This feature helped people find new, popular content as a result of voting.

Countless websites started integrating tools to allow users to comment on shared content, vote them up or down, and post reviews. By 2005, there was a dramatic shift well under way in how people used the web. No longer were they simply browsing others' content. Instead, they were actively creating profiles, interacting, making connections, and generating their own content.

This behavioral shift—often described as a transition from consumer to producer—came to be recognized by the nickname "Web 2.0." Despite criticism centered around the fact that the use of "2.0" implied that the web itself had supposedly undergone a software upgrade, the name stuck. Regardless, the fact remains that this was recognized as a paradigm shift in people's behavior on the web.

Noticing the change, social networks added what is now a fundamental part of many people's online experience: the status update.

At first inspection, it might seem that status updates were hardly something new; after all, blogs had allowed people to publish their lives' current events for years. But status updates were real time, (usually) brief, and almost always about what people were doing, thinking, reading, and watching.

In 2006, Facebook introduced the News Feed. This collected all the status updates of someone's friends and displayed them on one page in chronological order. Visiting several friends' blogs for news seemed incredibly tedious by comparison. Figure 2.3 shows the early version of the News Feed on Facebook.

FIGURE 2.3

The early version of Facebook's News Feed, showing all of a person's friends' updates.

Since then, posting updates has been a central feature of many new social media websites. The self-described "microblogging" site Twitter was introduced in 2007. It limited the length of status updates to a maximum of 140 characters.

The membership of these sites has continued to grow as well. Facebook now has over 1.2 billion active users—nearly half of the world's internet-using population. Twitter has 300 million active users but possibly as many as 850 million registered users. Social features are now the norm on websites and offer the ability to review items, to share links through social media sites, and to log in using social media accounts.

TYPES OF CONTENT

People can post basically anything on social media, but there are a few terms that are used across sites that are important to know:

- *Updates/posts*—An update is a general term for something a user posts. It tends to be a stand-alone piece of content, as opposed to a message in a discussion or a review. Often, these are short bits of text that say something a person has done, links to interesting content (sometimes with a comment), or photos or videos. They may also be called "status updates" or "posts," or they will have names specific to the platform. For example, updates on Twitter are called "tweets." We will cover these terms as the relevant websites are discussed in greater detail.
- *Comment/reply*—A common type of social interaction online is to comment on or reply to an update that someone else has posted. These are often grouped along with the original update so others can view the updates and comments together.
- *Photos and videos*—Sharing this kind of media is common online. Photos and videos are often shared as part of updates, but they can be uploaded separately. For example, many social network sites have sections where users can create albums and upload many photos at once.
- *Social networks/friends/contacts*—Social interaction is the heart of social media, and this often occurs because people have the ability to create connections with people they know. These may be friends, business associates, family members, or a mix. The connections between people form a social network.
- *Metadata*—The updates, comments, photos, and social connections people have form the data of social media websites. The information about those posts, photos, and connections is *metadata*. This often includes the date and time of the update and may include the location from which the person was posting or the platform (e.g., standard web browser vs. a mobile phone app) used to post.

CATEGORIES OF SOCIAL MEDIA

There are many types of social media: social networks, forums, photo sharing, review sites, and more.

A first distinction to make is between social media *websites* or *sites* and social media *services*. Essentially all social media can be accessed over the web with a traditional browser. For some, this is the only way to access them. However, some companies offer other services. For example, Facebook and Google allow people who have accounts with them to use those accounts to log in to other websites. Figure 2.1 shows the log-in screen on a website called ask.fm that allows people to log in with Facebook, Twitter, or VK (a European social network). When a company provides other services, like allowing people to use their accounts across the web, they are sometimes referred to as a social media *service*.

Generally, people use these terms interchangeably. In this book, we will generally use the term "social media site" since we are concerned primarily with the information that can be gathered by looking at the websites in a normal web browser. If we look at other services that these companies offer, we will use the broader term "social media service."

There are also many types of social media services based on the features they offer. The distinctions we draw here are a bit artificial in the sense that there is really a continuum of features across sites. Deciding what category a site fits into is not always easy. Given that, knowing the different general categories and which sites are good examples of each can be useful when you are trying to understand what information you may be able to collect about a person on a specific site:

- *Social networks*—In general, the term social network refers to people and their connections. This applies off-line and online. Online social networks allow users to create accounts and form connections with one another. Most social media sites have this feature, but for some, the ability to make connections and share with friends is the core feature.

  A social networking website will have a strong emphasis on connecting with other people (*friending* them or forming a social connection). Most modern social network sites also allow people to post status updates, photos, and other contents. The goal behind this is usually to help people engage with their friends by sharing updates about their lives and links to things online they find interesting.

  Popular sites in this category include Facebook and LinkedIn.

- *Photo and video sharing*—Sharing photos and videos is a common part of social media. The ability to share these types of media is built into most social media sites, but some sites are dedicated to this task. When you visit a photo or video-sharing website, the images and videos are featured, and there tends to be a limited amount of text.

  YouTube is an extremely popular video-sharing website. Newer sites like Instagram, Vine, and others are also drawing populations of users.

- *Microblogging*—Blogs were created in the late 1990s as a way for people to easily post text online without a lot of technical knowledge. These resembled online diaries, and blogging is still extremely popular. *Microblogging* came about in the late 2000s. The key feature of microblogs is that people are limited in how much text they can share. On Twitter, the most popular microblogging website, people's updates are limited to 140 characters. Other sites have different limits, but the core idea is that people are posting very short updates.

In addition to Twitter, Tumblr is a popular microblogging site.

- *Social bookmarking*—These sites are set up so people can collect links to pages they like online and share them with their friends. They can usually add annotations or captions to the links and organize them into categories. Currently, Pinterest is one of the most popular social bookmarking sites.
- *Social gaming*—Video games used to be played alone or by people who were in the same place. With the internet, games can be played by friends in different locations. Social gaming has become very popular, and the games range from very simple competitions to intensive military-style team game playing. Major game consoles, like PlayStation and Xbox, have social features that let players create friend lists and play games online with those friends. There are also many websites and apps for mobile devices that let people play together.
- *Apps*—The term "app" is short for "application." These are (often) small programs that run alone or within other social media sites. They can have their own social experiences. For example, apps that run in Facebook allow users to connect with some of their Facebook friends within the game, but it may support its own types of posts and interactions.

CURRENT SOCIAL MEDIA LANDSCAPE

Because the landscape of social media changes so quickly, in one sense, parts of this book are outdated before they are written. However, the core lessons about what information is available and how to find it are accurate for much longer. We also focus on major sites, which are likely to be around for years because they have large, active user bases. The structure and features of these sites may go through changes, and the companion website for this book will offer updates to highlight these tweaks as well as new content.

At the time of writing in spring 2014, the ten most popular social media sites (by number of users) are as follows:

1. *Facebook*—they report having 1.2 billion active users. It is primarily a social networking website but has many features, from gaming to chat to email, which make it the main destination for many people online.
2. *Twitter*—a microblogging website with around 300 million users. People create social connections by following people whose content they are interested in. Posts are called "tweets."
3. *YouTube*—the most popular video-sharing website. YouTube is owned by Google, which in turn has a single sign-in for all of their services. Also, people

can use YouTube to watch videos even if they don't have an account; thus, an estimate of users does not make as much sense here.

4. *LinkedIn*—A business-oriented network frequently used in the job market with 250 million users.

5. *Pinterest*—a social bookmarking site centered around sharing images from the web, with 150 million users.

6. *Google+*—Google's social networking site designed to be a competitor of Facebook. As with YouTube, Google users have a single sign-in for all Google products (including Gmail, YouTube, and Google+). However, Google+ user totals around 120 million.

7. *Tumblr*—a microblogging website that allows sharing text, photos, and other media with no strict limit on the length of content (unlike Twitter). Tumblr has around 110 million users.

8. *Instagram*—A photo-sharing website especially popular among teens and young adult audiences. It is not owned by Facebook and is not integrated into the Facebook platform. Instagram has around 85 million users.

9. *VK*—This is the only website that isn't extremely popular in the United States. It is a social networking site similar to Facebook but oriented toward European users. It has roughly 80 million members.

10. *Flickr*—The oldest site on this list, Flickr was one of the early, popular social media tools. It is a photo-sharing site with 65 million users.

SOME VOCABULARY

To make the descriptions of these investigations easier, we will use some specific vocabulary throughout this book.

Since our focus is on finding information about individuals, we will refer to the individual under investigation as a *target*.

There are also a number of technical terms that we will use throughout the discussion. These are all addressed in the glossary, but some will benefit from further explanation here. First, we will look at the basics of the internet and the web. The internet is a system of computers networked together, which allows communication around the world. Every computer on the internet has to be uniquely identified so information can be sent directly to it. This unique identifier is called an internet protocol (IP) address, and it comprises four numbers between 0 and 255 separated by dot, for example, 192.168.0.1. IP addresses can almost always be tracked to a general location and, with assistance from internet service providers, can even be tracked to a specific address. While not all social media sites display IP addresses, some do. Others have access to the IP address of users, which can sometimes be obtained by request or subpoena.

A user's computer connects to the internet through an internet service provider, like a cable company. When a person requests a web page, their computer sends a request through the internet to a *server*. A server is a computer that has web pages and code stored on it, and it sends these to a user's computer in response to a request. For example, if a user goes to twitter.com, their computer sends a request to Twitter's server, which processes the request, generates the appropriate page, and then sends it back to the user's computer (identified by its IP address).

When a user signs up for a social media site, they usually create a name to log in with. This is called a *username* or *screen name*. Usernames are usually one word, similar to the part of an email address that comes before the "@" sign. They then create a profile, which is a collection of personal information, often generated by filling out questionnaires and forms or writing short biographical paragraphs.

OUR OWN TARGET

It will be useful to practice the techniques we cover in this book on your own. To do that, it helps to have a target with lots of information online that you can investigate without worrying about privacy. To that end, we have created a fake personality who is very active on social media.

Our example user is Malcom Conroy-Smith. He uses the same profile picture on all of his accounts (see Figure 2.4). His common username is "malcomcsmith" though, like many people, he has a few variations on this name depending on the site.

Malcom is obviously not a real person, and all the information you will find on his social media profiles has been made up and posted by this book's author. However, it is also designed to let you find patterns in his behavior, much like you could find on a real target.

You are encouraged to investigate Malcom deeply. Look at his information on all his accounts. Search for him on Google. Read things he has posted online. It will be good practice for finding actual targets without worrying about invading anyone's privacy.

FIGURE 2.4

The profile picture of our example target, Malcom Conroy-Smith.

PRIVACY: YOURS AND OTHERS'

Privacy is important on social media, both for people who have profiles there and for people who are searching.

Most sites provide users with privacy options that allow them to make all their information public or to restrict access. Most sites allow information to be restricted so that only friends can view it. Some allow much more complex and fine-grained privacy settings. Posts can be limited to specific groups of friends or even individual people.

You also have privacy protections when you visit people's profiles. Some sites let anyone browse users' profiles, photos, or other posts, even if the browser does not have an account. Other sites will require you to register before you can see users' information. Either way, most sites do not show any information to a user about who views their profile. Some sites are exceptions, though. Dating websites and some professionally oriented websites reveal the identity of each person who has viewed a user's profile. These exceptions are noted throughout the book, since, as an investigator, it is important to know when your searches are private.

CONCLUSIONS

Social media is a rapidly evolving space that now touches most of the web as we know it. As interaction moves from something we do primarily on desktops to mobile devices, these sites and services have evolved to operate in a number of different ways and on various platforms.

Though the sites have different features that encourage users to share and allow them to interact in various ways, this chapter has introduced a basic taxonomy of purposes that can be used to categorize most sites. We have also covered basic social media vocabulary that will be useful in understanding all the sites we will discuss in the rest of the book.

Types of personal information

Social media sites provide such vast amounts of information about people that it can be overwhelming at times. Depending on your investigation, you may want different types of information. One helpful way to deal with everything that's available is to divide the information into different types.

This chapter will define the major categories of information that are available on social media and show examples of how it appears on various sites. Later in the book, we will see specifically how to access this data on some of the most popular social media sites.

BASIC DEMOGRAPHICS

Nearly every social media site has some profile page for its users, and that page has some essential demographic information. Age, gender, location, and a short personal description are all very common. Some sites have very long personal profiles, while others have very brief personal profiles.

Figure 3.1 shows the "About" page on Facebook, which contains the background information for users. The figure shows the overview, but on the left-hand site is a list of subcategories. On Facebook, you will often find a user's current location and a list of all the other places they have lived. You can get education history, work history, contact information, family members, political preferences, relationship status, religion, and more.

On the other hand, the microblogging site Twitter has very limited demographic information. Figure 3.2 shows all of what is available on Twitter: a name, city, and a short self-written bio.

Dating sites offer a third example where demographic information is especially plentiful. Figure 3.3 shows only a small fraction of the information provided on OkCupid. You can see data about Malcom's height, weight, build, diet, smoking and drinking habits, exercise regimen, religion, personal preferences for dozens of things, and so on. This makes sense in a dating site where people often want to quickly make decisions about what they share in common with a stranger. If you want as much straightforward background as possible, your best bet is to locate your target on a dating site.

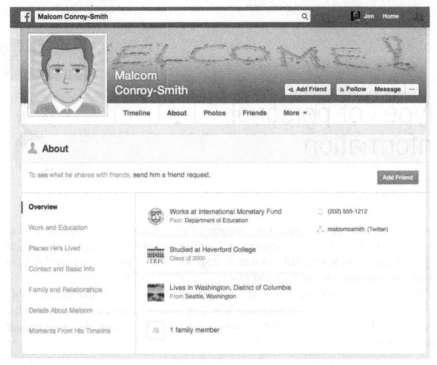

FIGURE 3.1

The "About" page on Facebook has a lot of demographic information.

FIGURE 3.2

The biographical information available on Twitter is very brief.

FIGURE 3.3

Dating sites like OkCupid have extensive demographic information for users.

SOCIAL CONNECTIONS AND ASSOCIATES

The "social" part of social media implies that people are interacting with others and, indeed, social media profiles can be an excellent tool for identifying a person's friends, family members, and associates. Most sites support the creation of explicit social connections with other people. These tend to come in two forms: *friending* and *following*.

When one person *friends* another, a request is sent from the person to the potential friend. If the potential friend approves the request, then the two people are linked to one another. Friending generally implies a mutual relationship, and it requires both people to acknowledge the relationship.

Following, on the other hand, can be a one-way relationship. A person follows someone on social media when they are interested in what that person posts. The person being followed does not have to approve the relationship in most cases, nor is there a requirement or expectation that the follow is reciprocated. Certainly, two people may choose to follow one another, but unlike "friending," it is not required.

A person's social connections, regardless of how they are created, are often visible on social media. Usually, a list of friends or followers is linked from a user's profile. This list tends to have a profile photo and name for the person. Figure 3.4 shows a user's friend list from Facebook. Clicking on the names of these friends will take you to their profile page.

Twitter uses a follower system. For any given user, you can see lists of who he follows and who is following him back. Figure 3.5 shows the list of people that Malcom

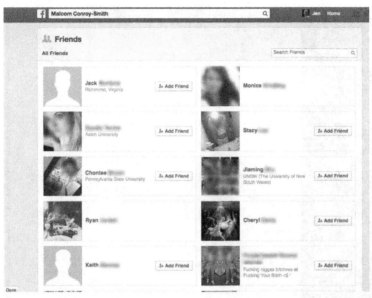

FIGURE 3.4

A friend list on Facebook (names and faces are blurred for privacy).

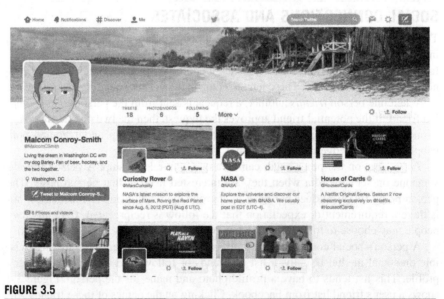

FIGURE 3.5

On sites where people follow each other, like Twitter, lists for "Following" and "Followers" are often available.

is following. Twitter uses a more extensive set of information for each person on this list, including their name, bio, profile picture, and "cover" image (a background photo).

Aside from the lists of social connections, a person's photos can reveal who they spend time with. Many sites support photo sharing and allow you to browse a person's photos. If you are interested in a person's social habits, you may find success in looking at who appears frequently in photos with the target.

Similarly, most sites allow people to like or comment on posts. When you read a target's posts, look at who frequently likes them or offers a reply. This can be an indicator of who the target is especially close with (not only online but also offline).

LOCATION DATA

One interesting development in social media is geotagging, which allows people to associate GPS coordinates or other location data with their posts. Many networks support this, and later chapters in this book will explain when and how to access this information on each site. In addition, there is an entire chapter dedicated to explaining location information.

In this section, we will look at just a few examples of how this data appears. In Figure 3.6, which shows a Twitter post, the location information appears under the text of the post. "Washington, DC" indicates the location.

Figure 3.7 shows how location information appears on Facebook. In this case, it has the name of a place (Whole Foods Market Georgetown). Moving the mouse over the place name brings up a preview of the Facebook page for that place.

FIGURE 3.6

A Twitter post with location information underneath the text of the post (Washington, DC).

FIGURE 3.7

A Facebook post with location information.

Some social media sites are dedicated to sharing location information, including Foursquare (discussed in depth in a future chapter). Figure 3.8 shows the profile for a Foursquare user. This lists every place the user has logged as somewhere he has visited. While we only see the top of the list in this figure, the interface allows you to scroll through the full list of everywhere the user has ever logged in.

There are also sites that will aggregate location information for a given user and show it on a map. Figure 3.9 shows a heat-map produced by the site GeoSocial Footprint.[1] When given a person's Twitter username, this site collects GPS coordinates from every available post and plots it on a map. Red areas are visited more often than green ones. The small red flags on the map can be clicked to bring up the actual Twitter post that was made at each location.

There is so much that can be done with location information. It can tell you where a person claimed to be, when, and what they were doing there. It can also help you establish patterns of behavior, which is discussed more in the next section.

BEHAVIOR PATTERNS

During investigations that run deeper than collecting demographic information or photos, discovering behavior patterns can be important. That may be what a person does, when, and with whom. It could be the way they interact with others or the tone of voice they use. Ultimately, your questions will drive the investigation you do; but in this section, we will look at a few examples of how you can find behavior patterns in social media.

Consider our example user Malcom. His Facebook profile shows a map of all the locations he visits (more detail on accessing this is available in the Facebook chapter of this book). Figure 3.10 shows us a map of those locations and the number of times he has posted from each. There are four posts from *Elephant & Castle*, a bar and restaurant near his office. Clicking on that location brings up a list of posts he has made

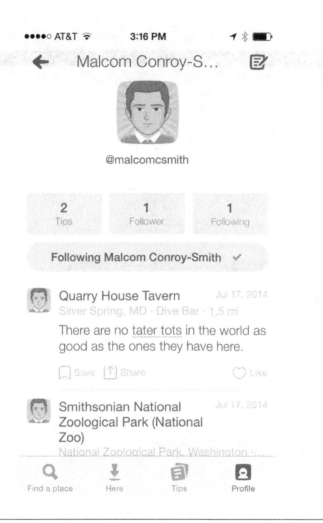

FIGURE 3.8

The beginning of a user's list of places he has visited, along with dates, comments, and address information for each place.

from there. You can click through those posts, and what you will notice if you try this yourself is that he posts from this location every Friday after work.

Turning to Malcom's Instagram feed, which is made up entirely of photos he has taken, we can see a few things in the pictures he has posted. He likes to go out and tell people about it, and he seems to really like his dog. The biographical descriptions from a number of his social media profiles mention his dog, Barley. She is clearly a big part of his life (Figure 3.11).

Discovering a man loves his dog is not an earth-shattering revelation, but it is an insight nonetheless. As we will see in many stories throughout this book, one will often discover that a man loves his girlfriend, or his guns, or his drugs, or is lying

FIGURE 3.9

A map generated by GeoSocial Footprint, showing the locations Malcom visits most often.

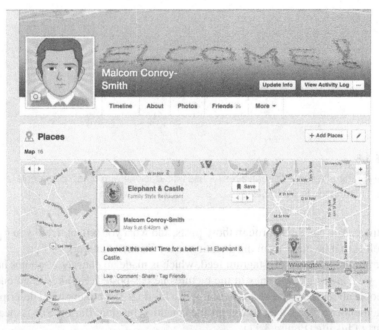

FIGURE 3.10

Malcom posts from *Elephant & Castle* every Friday after work.

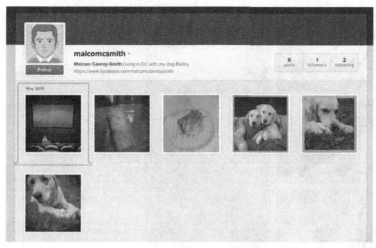

FIGURE 3.11

Malcom's Instagram feed, where half the pictures are of his dog.

to his boss and then is taking off work to play volleyball. Depending on your goals, those revelations can be quite important.

POSTED CONTENT

Last, but not least, is the category that encompasses *most* of what people share. The content of people's posts—that is, the text they write, what it says, the content of their photos and videos, and the ratings they assign—is really the most valuable thing you can find in a deep social media investigation. It tells you what people are doing, what they care about, who they interact with, and why. It not only can provide deep insight into the psyche but also can be useful simply because people tell you exactly what they think or what they do.

Indeed, when we hear stories of people being sued, fired, questioned, or arrested because of social media, it's almost always because of the content of their posts.

Let's look at a few examples.

SOCIAL MEDIA POSTS THAT BACKFIRE

Taylor Harrison

A Florida man posted frequently on Facebook about his drug dealing.[2] It turns out police were checking his page and collected a lot of information about him from it. He was arrested and charged, and the Martin County Sheriff's Office made its own Facebook post about him (see Figure 3.12 for the actual Facebook post).

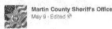

FIGURE 3.12

A post from the Martin County Sheriff's Office about a suspect's selfies gone wrong.

WHEN SELFIES BACKFIRE

These are photos of 21-year old Taylor Harrison of Port St. Lucie bragging on his Facebook page about his life as a drug dealer and how easy it is for him to sell drugs in front of our deputies.

The first photo Taylor took himself as he pulled alongside one of our deputies. The second photo is a selfie of Taylor with stacks of drug cash and drugs that he says he sells. Notice next to his car, is a patrol car.

The third shot is a MCSO undercover camera capturing Taylor selling drugs to one of us. He tells us, he is the best around!

The photo to the right is Taylor's booking photo at Martin County Jail after being arrested for…you guessed it, selling drugs to our undercover narcotics detectives.

Since Taylor was kind of enough to share photos of us on his Facebook page, we thought we would share these photos of Taylor on our page.

In a similar case, another man was arrested for stealing several guns from a pawnshop when he asked for ammunition[3] to go with them on Facebook.

Justine Sacco

One of the most high-profile cases of someone being fired for a tweet was that of PR executive Justine Sacco.[4] In December 2013, she tweeted "Going to Africa. Hope I don't get AIDS. Just kidding. I'm white!" (Figure 3.13). She made the post before

FIGURE 3.13

"The tweet heard round the world" that got Justine Sacco fired.

FIGURE 3.14

The racist tweets that got Gov. Walker aide Taylor Palmisano fired.

boarding a 12-hour flight to South Africa. While she was disconnected during the flight, Twitter erupted with angry replies. Upon her arrival, she was fired.

Scott Walker

She is *far* from the only one, though. An aide for Wisconsin Governor Scott Walker's 2012 campaign tweeted a series of racist tweets against Hispanics[5] (Figure 3.14 shows a couple), and when they came to light in the media, she was also fired.

Katie Duke

Less obviously offensive posts can also lead to bad results. Nurse Katie Duke was fired from New York-Presbyterian Hospital after posting this photo on Instagram with the caption "Man Vs 6Train… the After. #lifesaving #EMS #NYC #ER #Nurses

FIGURE 3.15

This Instagram post with its caption led to the firing of the nurse who shared it.

#Doctors #nymed #trauma #realLife" (Figure 3.15). While her post did not violate any rules, her supervisors said the post was "insensitive."

THE IMPORTANCE OF CONTENT

The point of looking at all these examples is not to say "bad things happen when you misbehave online." Rather, you have to look at the *content* of the posts people are making. What people actually say reveals the most about them and their actions. These examples demonstrate that some of the greatest insights that come from investigating people on social media do not come from canned profile fields or analysis of travel locations (although they can also be useful, too).

WHAT YOU (PROBABLY) WON'T FIND

There is so much you can get from social media, but there are some things you should not expect to be able to access as someone approaching the websites as a normal user (as opposed to approaching the social media companies with a court order, which is outside the scope of this book).

First, you will not have access to truly private conversations. Email, instant messaging, and private or direct messages sent on social media simply cannot be accessed by third parties. You may see some people having conversations in public parts of social media. For example, they may have discussions on Twitter or through comments on a post on Facebook. These are visible to anyone and are indeed quite common. However, when people use explicitly private channels to communicate, you will generally not be able to get access.

You also won't be able to see things a user has deleted. Sometimes, social media companies keep copies of deleted content. As a regular user, though, you simply won't be able to see or bring back these deleted posts.

CONCLUSION

There are many types of information that come from social media. Major categories include basic demographic information, social connections, location information, patterns of behavior, and the content of the posts themselves. Future chapters will detail where and how to find all this data, but keeping in mind what type of information will help your investigation can guide your searches in the social media space.

NOTES

1 Weidermann, Chris. 2013. "GeoSocial Footprint." http://geosocialfootprint.com.
2 Gibson, Travis. 2014. "Man Posts Drug Dealing Selfie Online, Gets Arrested." First Coast News. http://www.firstcoastnews.com/story/news/crime/2014/05/11/drug-dealing-selfie-arrested/8969705/.
3 Seiler, Lucas. 2014. "Teen Arrested after Making Facebook Post about Stolen Guns—NBC-2.com WBBH News for Fort Myers, Cape Coral & Naples, Florida." NBC 2 News. http://www.nbc-2.com/story/24697174/teen-arrested-after-making-facebook-post-about-stolen-guns#.VB8JHb5nKpY.
4 Stelter, Brian. 2013. "Ex-PR Exec Justine Sacco Apologizes for AIDS in Africa Tweet." CNN. http://www.cnn.com/2013/12/22/world/sacco-offensive-tweet/.
5 Bice, Daniel. 2013. "Scott Walker Campaign Aide Fired after Tweets Demeaning Hispanics." Journal Sentinel. http://www.jsonline.com/watchdog/noquarter/scott-walker-campaign-aide-fired-after-tweets-demeaning-hispanics-b99155734z1-234291761.html.

Privacy controls

WHAT ARE PRIVACY CONTROLS?

The "social" part of "social media" means that people are sharing with one another. Sometimes, it's with a very small and carefully controlled group. But more often, it's with large groups of people. Many social media services make users' posts available to anyone on the internet by default.

In some cases, someone may be perfectly fine with their online post being shared broadly. It might even be desirable: someone searching for a job may want their professional profile to be widely viewed. The same is true of public figures, celebrities, and others who make their living from gaining public attention in some way. Plenty of people also like the attention they get from sharing things publicly; it can be exciting if a stranger likes a video or photo you posted.

But not everyone wants to share that publicly or in all contexts. Someone who wants to share their professional profile for a job search may prefer to keep more personal information (like photos of their kids and their travel schedule) limited to a more select group.

Privacy controls allow users the power to limit who can see their posts. Depending on the site, the controls vary greatly. Throughout this book, chapters about specific social media sites will detail their privacy settings. In this chapter, we will overview the major categories of privacy control options.

PRIVACY CONTROLS
PUBLIC/PRIVATE

The simplest privacy control is the public/private setting. On sites that use this, posts are usually public by default and visible by anyone online. Users have one option to restrict visibility of their posts, and that is to make them private. This generally restricts them to be visible by only the user's friends or another approved list of people. For example, Figure 4.1 shows the Twitter privacy options. Next to "Tweet privacy" is the one option for protecting posts: "Protect my Tweets." If the user selects this, the user has to approve anyone who wants to follow their posts.

Many social media sites use some variant of this model. As one other example, Pinterest allows users to create boards (basically an organized collection of posts with a common theme) that are either public or restricted to a specific list of approved viewers.

Privacy

Photo tagging   ⦿ Allow anyone to tag me in photos

       ○ Only allow people I follow to tag me in photos

       ○ Do not allow anyone to tag me in photos

Tweet privacy   ☐ Protect my Tweets

If selected, only those you approve will receive your Tweets. Your future Tweets will not be available publicly. Tweets posted previously may still be publicly visible in some places. Learn more.

FIGURE 4.1

The privacy settings on Twitter. Note that the only option to keep tweets private is with the "Protect my Tweets" option next to "Tweet privacy."

ITEMIZED PRIVACY

On the more complex end of the spectrum, some sites give users fine-grained control over who can see every post. Facebook is one of these sites. Users can set the privacy level for each post. Facebook provides a default set of options, including Public (visible to anyone on the internet), Friends, Friends except Acquaintances (the latter being a list of casual friends that the user maintains), Only Me (which prevents anyone else from seeing the post), or Custom. Figure 4.2 shows these basic options.

The user can also create custom lists of friends and restrict the post to be visible to only people on a specific list. Examples of lists could be high school friends, fellow Chicago Cubs fans, coworkers, etc. The advantage of these lists is that they can be used to avoid bothering people with certain posts they might not be interested in. For example, you may want to share a link about your profession with your work friends, even though you know your high school friends would not have any interest in it.

Users can also create custom settings for each post. This lets the user pick a default group to share with (e.g., Friends) and then selectively remove others from

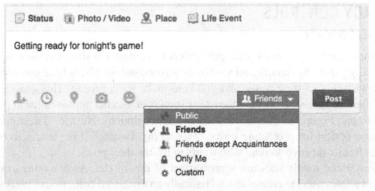

FIGURE 4.2

Facebook's privacy options for a given post.

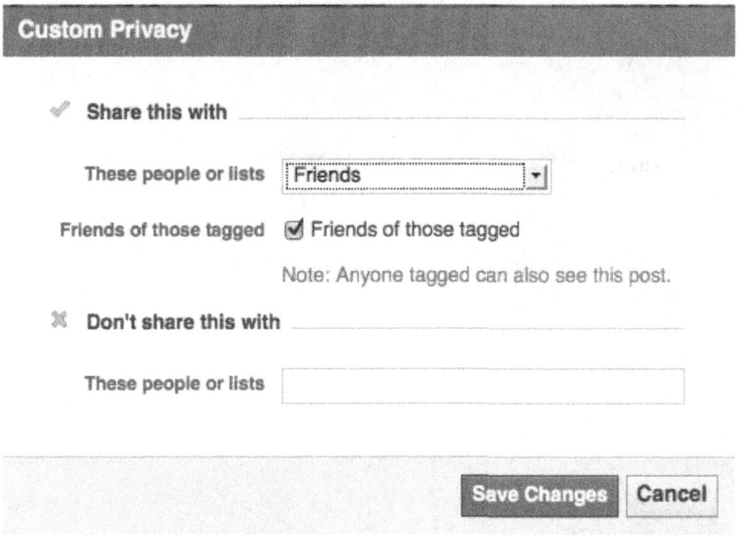

FIGURE 4.3

The Custom privacy setting options on Facebook.

access. For example, if someone rants about work, they may want to share it with all their friends except coworkers. In the options shown in Figure 4.3, they could add their list of coworkers to the "Don't share this with" list. Users can also create a custom list of people who can see a specific post in the "Share this with" section by selecting each person who gets permission to see the post.

Google+ has similar privacy features. They have made friend lists (like the co-workers, high school friends, and fellow Chicago Cubs fans lists mentioned above) even more central to the design of their site. They encourage users to create "circles," which are essentially lists of friends. When sharing a post, users have to explicitly choose which people or circles to share with. This is a bit different than most sites that tend to have a default setting that users can override if they choose (Figure 4.4).

DEFAULT PRIVACY

While these advanced settings are available to users, the fact is that they often are not used. Most users of social media sites have a default setting. They may change that for certain posts on Facebook, for example, but advanced customized privacy levels remain relatively rare.

CASE STUDY: RANDI ZUCKERBERG

Even using the relatively simple privacy settings can be confusing. This was illustrated, perhaps most ironically, in 2012.[1] Randi Zuckerberg, the older sister of Facebook founder and CEO Mark, took a photo of her family all using the then-new Facebook app called "Poke" at the same time. Mark stood in the corner with a slightly

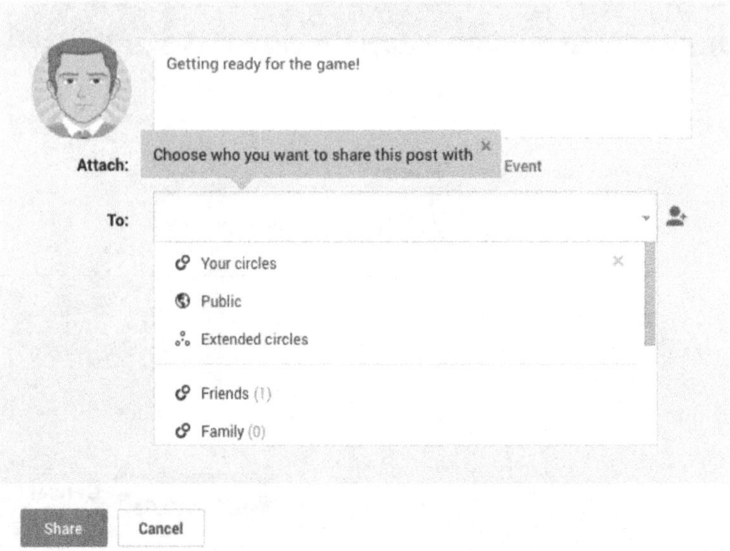

FIGURE 4.4

The Google+ posting interface. If a user tries to post without typing in a setting, they are reminded to choose whom the post will be shared with.

confused look on his face. Randi shared the photo on her Facebook page, with the privacy set to Friends Only.

A short time later, Callie Schweitzer (of Vox Media) tweeted the photo. Randi Zuckerberg sent her a public and angry message saying, "Not sure where you got this photo. I posted it to friends only on FB. You reposting it to Twitter is way uncool."

Schweitzer took the post with the photo down, but not before many other media outlets grabbed a copy. However, Callie got a copy of the photo in a completely legitimate way that Randi Zuckerberg did not expect. Randi had tagged her family members in the photo. Callie was a friend with another of the Zuckerberg sisters. Although Randi had set the privacy level so only friends could see the photo, Facebook's system still allows friends of anyone tagged to see the photo as well, essentially making the picture more public than the original poster intended.

That the complexities of Facebook's privacy controls caused a Facebook insider's post to be widely shared illustrates the difficulties faced by everyone trying to control access to their content. This story also illustrates something that privacy settings within a system can't control: people downloading a user's posts and sharing them somewhere else. Randi Zuckerberg posted her family photo on Facebook, but it was shared widely on Twitter after Callie Schweitzer downloaded a copy and reposted it.

Indeed, it is now commonplace to see media stories with photos pulled from Facebook, Twitter, Instagram, and other sources. If one person has access to the content within a site, that person can save a copy and share it elsewhere. No privacy setting can prevent this, which goes to support the adage that once something is posted online, control over who sees it and how it is used is lost.

PRIVACY AWARENESS

While nearly all social media sites have some privacy options and, as we have seen above, some have very powerful privacy settings, the average user's understanding of privacy controls can be limited. Statistics vary widely about how many users have interacted with privacy controls and how often, but a few demonstrative projects have illustrated—to users and others—how people are often unaware of how much information they are sharing.

CASE STUDY: PLEASE ROB ME

One of the first examples of this was Please Rob Me. As background, the location-sharing social media service Foursquare allows users to "check in" at places, recording their presence there. Foursquare has strong privacy protections, never sharing these check-ins publicly; they are always restricted to a group of approved friends due to the sensitivity of the information. However, Foursquare allows its users to share their check-ins on Twitter. Since Twitter defaults to be publicly visible to everyone on the internet, and the vast majority of users maintain public accounts, the result was people's locations being widely shared. Not only did this allow a user's movements to be tracked, but also it revealed when they left home. A simple white pages lookup (using their Twitter name, which is often a real name, and the name of their current city) would yield an address.

To highlight the insecurity of this oversharing, the Please Rob Me site was launched. It looked for Foursquare posts on the public Twitter feed. The list could be filtered by location (Figure 4.5).

There were a lot of negative reactions to Please Rob Me from people who felt unfairly targeted when their names appeared on it. However, the goal of the site was always to bring awareness to people who were oversharing. The site was not responsible for the privacy problem; the users were making poor choices.

CASE STUDY: TAKE THIS LOLLIPOP

A year later, Take This Lollipop was responsible for raising anxiety levels in millions of people. The interactive, personalized horror film was part art project and part privacy lesson. Facebook users could go to http://takethislollipop.com and log on with their Facebook account. The site then plays a short film where a mentally disturbed stalker becomes increasingly agitated while viewing the user's Facebook page. The movie integrates actual information from the user's account, including photos, friend lists, comments, and messages. Figure 4.6 shows a frame from that movie with the stalker's face reflected on the monitor that is displaying the user's page.

When the site launched, people reacted by believing their accounts had been hacked and suggesting the site had stolen their information. In fact, the users' had set up their accounts with privacy settings that allowed apps to access all this data freely. Even stringent privacy settings often could not prevent an app from accessing some of this information and illustrating how vulnerable their data was.

FIGURE 4.5

The Please Rob Me website, showing people who have just left home, based on their Foursquare check-ins shared through Twitter, with locations.

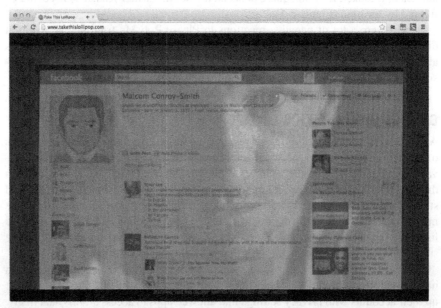

FIGURE 4.6

A frame from the Take This Lollipop movie, showing a stalker browsing the user's Facebook page.

PRIVACY AWARENESS IMPACTS

Research has also shown that these kinds of privacy warning sites can effectively increase people's awareness about privacy. In a scientific study, people took a test where they were asked to check off which pieces of data they believed Facebook apps could access. They were also asked about their level of concern regarding their data. Then, they watched the Take This Lollipop video. When they retook the test, they were significantly more aware of what data was shared and they showed higher levels of concern about their privacy.

There is a long way to go before average users can really understand the complexities of how their social media data is shared, but these two sites illustrate how unaware people often are about this sharing and their reactions when they find out that people can see a lot of what they post.

INVESTIGATING PRIVATE ACCOUNTS

If someone has made their account private, how can you investigate them? Each of the chapters that follow about specific social networks will have suggestions. However, there are a few general techniques. The most basic of these is to try to get approved access to the target's account. It could be that someone you know already has a social connection with the target. This might allow you to access the target's posts by logging on through your associate's account.

On some networks, friends of the target's friends can see some information. Thus, even if you cannot befriend the target, becoming connected to one of the target's associates on the social media site might increase the access you have.

If you want to keep your identity private, one option is to create a fresh account and use that to request a social connection. However, this option should be exercised with caution. It is a violation of the terms of service of *some* social media sites to create accounts with false personal information.

Even if creating a dummy account is not a violation, it may be transparent to the target. Accounts with very little history or few social connections may appear suspicious to the target. Ultimately, this depends on the target's personal preferences. Some people create as many social connections as possible on social media, while others are much more careful about curating their friend lists.

CONCLUSIONS

Privacy controls allow social media users to control who can see their content. These can be simple settings that toggle an account between public and restricted to an approved group, or they can be sophisticated that give users control over every person who can see each individual post.

While privacy controls are important for users, especially when they are sharing sensitive personal information, people often do not fully understand how public their data is nor how to use all the controls at their disposal.

Future chapters will discuss specific tactics for accessing information that is protected on the target's social media profiles. However, the most common and successful strategies generally involve creating closer social connections with the target.

NOTE

1 Hill, Kashmir. 2012. "Oops. Mark Zuckerberg's Sister Has A Private Facebook Photo Go Public." Forbes. December 26. http://www.forbes.com/sites/kashmirhill/2012/12/26/oops-mark-zuckerbergs-sister-has-a-private-facebook-photo-go-public/.

Finding people on social media

Each of the chapters in this book that is about a specific social media site (e.g., Facebook, Twitter, and LinkedIn) has sections that are specifically about finding people. If you're interested in finding someone on those sites, it's always a good idea to do a search for them there.

However, there are also more general techniques you can use to find people on any social media site. This chapter introduces some of those.

THE IMPORTANCE OF USERNAMES

Everyone needs a username to be on a social media site. This is the unique name they use to login and it often appears in the web address (URL) of their page on the site. For example, if a person's username is "**malcomcsmith**," his Facebook page is at http://facebook.com/malcomcsmith and his Twitter page is at http://twitter.com/malcomcsmith.

People frequently reuse their usernames across sites. Thus, if you know someone's username in one place, you can often use it to find other accounts. So how do you find someone's username?

The email address is a good place to start. If you only have an email address, you might try using the part before the @ in the address as a username. For example, if the target's email is malcomcsmith@gmail.com, you can use "malcomcsmith" as a first guess at a username.

Email is also an important clue, even if the first part is not the target's username on other services. Many sites allow you to search for the email address a person used to register and will then return a link to their page—including showing their username. Once you know someone's username on one site, you can use it to search for them on other sites as well. Thus, email addresses—even old ones that are not active anymore—and known usernames are good places to start finding people on social media.

FINDING PEOPLE
BY GOOGLE SEARCH TECHNIQUES

Google is a great source for finding social media pages about people, and sometimes, it returns better results than the social media sites' own internal search tools. To use it effectively, there are a few advanced Google search tools that will help you.

Searching Domains

First is the ability to search within a site or domain. A domain is the core part of a web address, usually the last two parts. For example, facebook.com, twitter.com, npr.org, and example.net are all domains. Google allows you to use the domain for a site to search on that site only. To do this, you use the prefix "site:," followed by the domain. For example, if we wanted to search for our example user Malcom Conroy-Smith on Twitter, we would search for his name and then add site:twitter.com (Figure 5.1).

This search will look for the words Malcom and Conroy-Smith *only* on twitter.com.

Searching for Exact Phrases

When you use multiple words in a Google search, Google searches for all of those words in any order and will also look for pages that have only one of the words. Google will sometimes even make best guesses at close matches. In this case, it may find people named Malcom Smith. That flexibility in search can be very helpful, but sometimes, it returns too many results. To search for the exact name you want, you can put it in quotes. In that case, Google will only return pages with an exact match for the phrase in quotes (see Figure 5.2).

Searching Images

If there are many search results returned, a Google image search for the same term may be effective. In Figure 5.2, under the search box, you can see a list of search types ("Web," "Videos," "News," "Images," etc.). If you click on Images, it will take you to a set of search results with photos only. If you include the "site:" part of the search, it will return images from that site only. Thus, you will often find profile pictures with this kind of image search.

If you happen to have a photograph of the target, especially if it is a profile picture from another site, Google has an image search functionality that can help there, too. Go to the Google Images search page, either as described above or by going to http://images.google.com. On the right side of the search box, there is a camera icon. This is their "Search by Image" feature. It allows you to upload a picture and it searches

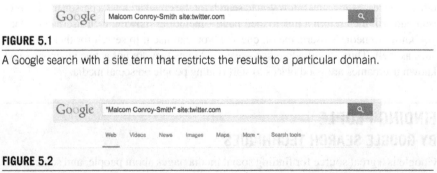

FIGURE 5.1

A Google search with a site term that restricts the results to a particular domain.

FIGURE 5.2

Using quotes around a term on a Google search forces Google to search for that exact phrase.

FIGURE 5.3

The Google Images search page. Note the camera icon on the right of the search box; click it to Search by Image.

FIGURE 5.4

The default Search by Image box where you can input the web address (URL) of an image.

for matching and near-matching images. Figure 5.3 shows the main Google image search page.

Click on the camera icon to bring up the dialog box to search for matching images. Figure 5.4 shows the page that comes up. If you have the web address of the image of interest, you can paste it in this search box.

If you do not have an online version of the image, click the "Upload an image" text next to the "Paste image URL" tab. That will bring up a dialog box, shown in Figure 5.5, where you can select the image from your computer. Then click the "Search by Image" button next to the search box. The results will include exact matches and visually similar images.

A matching image result could take you to the target's other social media sites, websites where they have profiles, or pages where they are mentioned.

BY CACHE OR ARCHIVE

Before we move on entirely from Google, there is one other Google search tool that may be of value: the "cache" option, which can show you old versions of a page. For example, if your target once had a public page on a social media site, but now

FIGURE 5.5

The "Upload an image" tab allows you to choose an image file from your computer to search.

it is protected, you can search for cache:[url] where you replace [url] with the web address of the page. That will show you an older version of the page.

If you want to see many previous versions of someone's social media page, try using the Internet Archive's Wayback Machine. This is, as the name suggests, an archive of the internet. Available at http://archive.org, you can put in the URL of any web page and see older copies that the service has saved. For example, Figure 5.6 shows the results for the author's personal Twitter page at http://twitter.com/golbeck.

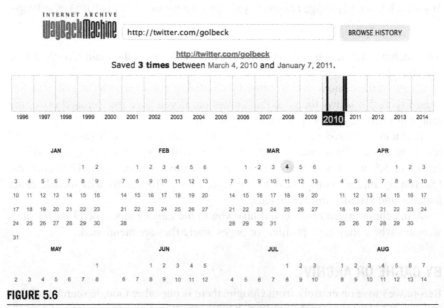

FIGURE 5.6

The Internet Archive results for the author's personal Twitter feed.

The time line at the top shows years across the bottom with markers indicating the dates the page was saved. Clicking on a year brings up a calendar underneath the time line. Dates with archived pages are highlighted in blue. Clicking on a date brings up the archived version of the page. The Internet Archive works for many pages besides social media, but this can be an effective way to locate old online data in some cases.

There are other ways beyond Google to find current social media pages, too. Social media search engines take names or possible usernames as input and then search across social media sites to find accounts. These services are constantly changing, and the companion website for the book has an updated list. A Google search for "social search engine" will likely bring up the latest results.

BY OTHER SERVICES

Finally, people finding/background check services on the web may be a good source of background information. While most of these search tools provide things like names, addresses, and phone numbers, instead of links to social media sites, some have email addresses that are useful for username tracking as described above. Furthermore, additional information about a target that these sites provide, like his current city, could be useful in narrowing down search results on specific social media sites to identify the correct person.

BY OTHER TECHNIQUES AND CONSIDERATIONS

There are other techniques you can use to find people online. One of the most effective is to search through the target's known associates. Even if your target is online, he may use a fake or abbreviated name that makes him hard to find. He may even have most of his profile private and protected. However, a target's friends are not always as careful, and this can make them a useful source of information to locate the target's account or find public information about him.

Each chapter of this book that deals with specific social media sites includes information on how to find associates' accounts and look for the target among their social contacts, but there are some general rules that are useful to know.

First, if you want to find a person's profile on a social media site, you can begin by finding his known associates. At least some friends and family members are likely to have accounts somewhere, since many social media tools have hundreds of millions of users. Once you have located associates (using some of the tips above, if simple searches on the social media site don't turn them up), you can look at their social connections. It is possible your target will be identifiable in that list, by either photo or name.

Even if you can't find a profile for your target in his associate's contact lists, you may be able to find information about him posted by the associate. Look through the associate's photos, posts, and other information. It is possible you will come across information about the target in this way.

Regardless of where you find information—from social media sites, web searches, or on other people's social media pages—it is important to remember that social media is not an authoritative information source.

CASE STUDY

One of my clients—let's call him "Fred"—was trying to track down someone for whom they had no contact information. We knew Fred had grown up in Johnston, Iowa, a suburb of Des Moines. He later attended the University of Michigan in Ann Arbor and then moved to Dearborn, just outside of Detroit. At the time of our search, we knew he was 35 years old.

Fred had a common last name, so there were many people with the same name. However, a few searches turned up a man with his name but with some inaccurate information. One page listed his previous residence as Urbandale, Iowa, the next town over from his hometown of Johnston. There was no mention of his actual hometown of Johnston. There was also no mention of Dexter, Michigan, where we knew Fred lived. However, the same person who appeared to be from Urbandale, Iowa, was listed as living in Detroit. His age appeared as 39 years old.

So was this the Fred we were searching for or not? My client was deeply worried that it was a different person, but the fact is that probabilities suggest it was indeed the right Fred. Location information can come from many places. While Fred may have never lived in Urbandale, Iowa, the fact that it shared a border with his hometown of Johnston means that he likely had connections to Urbandale. He may have worked there, attended high school there, or have used a friend's address in Urbandale at one point.

Similarly, it is very common to see people listed as living in the large city closest to them. It is not unusual to see the names of little-known suburbs dropped in favor of an identifiable city. And, as was the case with Fred's hometown, it would be likely that Fred worked, had a post-office box, or maintained some other connection to the neighboring large city of Detroit.

Finally, the age of the Fred we found was 4 years older than the Fred we were searching for. People lie about their birthdays and age all the time on social media. This may be to protect their privacy, to throw off potential investigators, or simply for amusement. Even ages that are pulled from external data sources instead of being supplied by the user can be wrong for a variety of reasons.

The important consideration is probability. What is the likelihood that there was another guy with the same first and last name as our Fred who grew up very near where our Fred grew up, who was close in age, and who moved to the same city several states away? While it is certainly possible, the probability of this is low, and it is reasonable to assume that the Fred we found is the Fred we were looking for. Indeed, in this case, the slightly off version of Fred was indeed the target, and using the profile we found, my client was able to make contact and resolve her issue.

CONCLUSIONS

As a starting point for finding people on social media, your best bet is to search for them on the specific sites you care about. Details for how to conduct those searches are contained in the relevant chapters in this book. However, there are useful higher-level tips.

People often reuse their usernames. Thus, if you can find someone on a particular site, the username there may be the same as the username on other sites. Similarly, if you have an email address for someone, you may be able to search for accounts by email or use the part of the address before the "@" sign as a best guess at a username.

Google and other services offer a number of search tools and operators that will help you find people on particular sites and more broadly on the web. Older versions of pages may be cached at Google or available in the Internet Archive, and these can be useful in learning if you have found the correct account for someone.

Finally, searching for people through their associates and allowing for flexibility and some incorrectness in search results will help you discover targets in ways that you might not have initially expected.

Location data

6

The use of the internet, and social media in particular, has increasingly moved from desktop computers to mobile devices. In 2013, a study by Adobe found that 71% of people use their mobile device to access social media.[1] But unlike desktop computers, mobile devices (such as smartphones) have nearly constant access to a person's location. (GPS is the best known method, but several others exist as well.) Consequently, everything people do on a mobile device, including their activities on social media, can be associated with a precise location.

Social media companies have taken advantage of this. Most offer users the ability to add a location to their status updates.

But why include location with updates? There are many reasons. In some cases, it can encourage face-to-face interaction. For example, on some platforms (like Foursquare), if a user indicates that he is at a particular place, he is automatically notified if any of his social media friends are there, too. Users may want to label their photos' locations to remember where they were taken.

Marketers are also interested. Some businesses offer discounts or other perks to people who post that they are there, since the posts serve as a type of advertising or publicity. They may also look for people who are nearby. An ice cream shop may offer a discount to someone who has posted from a nearby store, hoping to entice him to purchase a sundae.

This location information can be a valuable tool for investigation. This chapter shows how location information is connected to posts, how to find it, and what you can do with it once you collect it.

THE LEXICON OF LOCATIONS

Before delving into finding and using location data from social media, it's helpful to understand the associated terms and symbols used.

Most platforms have adopted a relatively standard location icon, based on location markers typically used in mapping programs:

> Update Status   Add Photos/Video
>
> What's on your mind?
>
> Where are you?
>
> Friends ▾   **Post**

FIGURE 6.1

The Facebook status update box. The location icon at the bottom left has been clicked, bringing up the small text area that says "Where are you?" Users can enter a location, like a city or a restaurant name, in that box.

Malcom Conroy–Smith at Reagan Washington National Airport
Flying out.

Like · Comment · Share · 8 minutes ago in Arlington, VA · ▾

FIGURE 6.2

A check-in at Reagan Washington National Airport.

On most platforms, moving the mouse over this icon or selecting it will reveal location information. Sometimes, this presents the option to add a location.

For example, on Facebook, users can add a location to a post, even if they are posting from their home computer that does not have a GPS location. The status update box has this location icon, and clicking on it adds a field prompting users to enter their location with the text "Where are you?" (Figure 6.1).

There's also a common vocabulary associated with adding location to posts. *Geotagging* refers to the process of adding a location (or "geolocation") to a post, photo, or status update. This is typically determined via GPS coordinates, indicating a precise location of the post. This is easy on mobile devices, which know the user's precise location. For status updates with a place-name or a street address, *geolocation* is what maps that name or address to a pair of latitude-longitude coordinates.

Another way people share their location is through a *check-in*. Unlike geotagging, which adds a location to a post, a check-in usually involves the user explicitly indicating that they are at a specific location. For example, Figure 6.2 shows our example user Malcom having checked in at Reagan Washington National Airport. The name of the location is a link in Malcom's status update, and the airport's location (Arlington, VA) is listed at the bottom of the update.

COLLECTING LOCATION INFORMATION

When searching for location information about an individual under investigation, there are two major categories of data: the individual's own posts and automatically encoded sources.

Future chapters on specific social media websites explain how to find location data on each site. In the meantime, here are general guidelines for finding this information on any site.

USER-PROVIDED LOCATION DATA

Look for the location icon. On Twitter, for example, posts will have the location icon at the bottom of the post. This is shown in Figure 6.3.

On Twitter, location names are usually shown, but these are geocoded. Clicking on the name of the place reveals a map with the GPS coordinates shown.

The place-name in Figure 6.3 is "Jaleo-Bethesda." If we were to click on that link, the following map would appear (Figure 6.4):

FIGURE 6.3

Note the location icon after the date in the bottom row of text. The location is listed after that, including a link to the specific place.

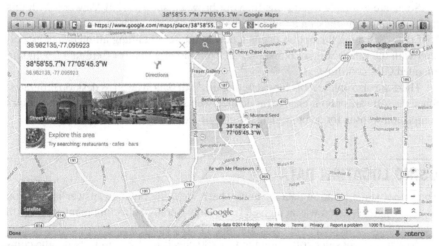

FIGURE 6.4

The map with the GPS coordinates of the location shown in Figure 6.3. Note the coordinates at the top of the window, along with the location on the map (shown with a pin).

Many sites follow this same pattern: using a location icon to indicate when a user has included a location in a post and linking the location's name to its GPS coordinates.

Check-ins also have locations. These may be addresses, place-names, or GPS coordinates. Facebook's check-in feature, shown in Figure 6.2, features both a place-name (Reagan Washington National Airport) and a city name (Arlington, VA). Some Facebook check-ins also have coordinates.

Other services are specifically designed around sharing locations. For example, Foursquare is a social game based on the premise of users sharing their location. Users are awarded points for each check-in, receive offers and coupons, and can track places their friends visit. In location-centric systems like this, every single post has an associated location. Sometimes, that location data propagates elsewhere—even sites that aren't built around locations. For example, some users may choose to share their Foursquare check-ins through other social media services, like Twitter.

AUTO-ENCODED LOCATION DATA

When users don't explicitly share their location, there are still ways to obtain it. Photos and videos have associated metadata, which can include information about the GPS coordinates where the image was taken. This data is called Exif ("Exchangeable Image file Format"). Not all photos' or videos' Exif data contains GPS coordinates—but many do, especially those created on mobile devices (like smartphones).

Exif data can be extracted from any image online. The data doesn't appear automatically; you will need some software to view it. There are many free tools to do this, requiring varying levels of expertise.

Some are available as add-ons for your browser, such as Exif Viewer.[2] With this tool, you can right click on an image, and the add-on provides an option to view the Exif data. Selecting the option opens a new window containing all metadata associated with the image. Figure 6.5 shows an example of a photo's Exif data (including encoded GPS coordinates).

There are also online tools for extracting this Exif data, as well as desktop programs. Since the software options change (as do their web addresses), please consult this book's companion website for an up-to-date list of Exif-extracting software options.

USING LOCATION DATA

You've got some location data … now what? Well, the obvious answer is that you can see where a person was at a given time. However, by collecting many posts with location data, there are possibilities for much richer analysis.

To start off, consider collecting the last 200 check-ins for a user. (Note: the companion website for this book has a program you can download that will do this when the data is available.) One quick option is to plot that data on a map. Google Maps

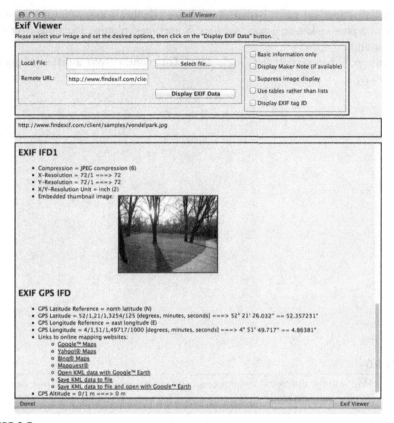

FIGURE 6.5

Exif data for a picture of a park. The "Exif GPS IFD" section includes the latitude-longitude coordinates of where the photo was taken. Other Exif data (not shown in this image) includes the date the photo was taken, allowing an investigator to know exactly when the photographer was at this location.

has many options for doing this. There are also a number of websites that let you easily copy and paste a list of coordinates and view the output on a map. Again, the companion website has a list of options with instructions.

Figure 6.6 shows the map of check-ins for a user who lives near Vancouver, British Columbia:

A number of interesting patterns emerge in this map. There are two clusters of check-ins to the right: one by the highway and one near Langley (south of the first). Then, there's a spread of check-ins to the west, near Burnaby and Vancouver.

This alone reveals a lot about the user's movements and habits. Cross-referencing these points with place-names and their types (e.g., restaurants, shopping locations, and offices) can reveal where a person works, lives, and goes out.

Another important point is that every post—whether it's a social media status update or a photo—has an associated *time*. Sometimes, plotting locations over time can be useful.

Figure 6.7 shows another Google Map. This comes from a different anonymous user.

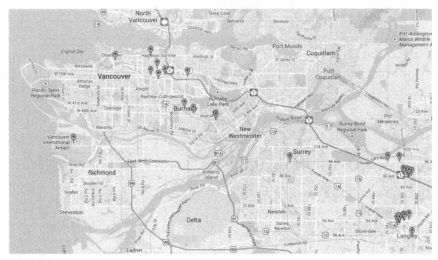

FIGURE 6.6

A Google Map with the check-in locations of an anonymous user near Vancouver. Note the two clusters near the right of the image: one on the highway and one just north of Langley.

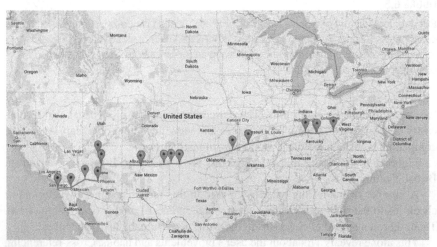

FIGURE 6.7

A series of locations gathered from one person's Twitter account, with a line connecting them based on the order they were posted. This clearly shows the person was headed west toward San Diego.

This user's last 200 posts were analyzed for location (when available), and the points were plotted on the map. A line connects the points based on the order in which they were posted.

In this case, we clearly see the person posting on Twitter as they move west toward San Diego. Reading the posts that contain these locations reveals that the user was in the process of moving from Washington, DC, to San Diego, and he posted as they drove cross-country.

CHALLENGES TO USING LOCATION DATA

There are a number of challenges associated with location data, centered around the fact that it can be hard to access.

A 2013 Pew study[3] showed that the frequency of check-ins is slowly declining. Meanwhile, users who include location data with their (noncheck-in) posts are increasing significantly. Nevertheless, only about 30% of adults report including location information. This means that, for most users, location information is not available with their social media posts.

As social media use increasingly moves to mobile devices, it's reasonable to expect that more location information will become available. However, including this is an opt-in process, not an automatic one—so it is unlikely to become something we will see by default.

Privacy concerns are also closely tied to location data. As a result, some systems (like Foursquare) keep users' check-ins restricted to their friend lists. Thus, it may be hard to actually access location information in certain environments, unless you already have an existing connection with the person being investigated.

CONCLUSIONS

As more and more users access social media from mobile devices, the availability of location information—both from their posts and embedded in their photos and videos—also increases. It can be found in geotagged posts, check-ins, and the embedded metadata of images and videos. Once it's collected, there are several ways to plot it, analyze it, and discover the patterns and movements of the person being investigated.

In later chapters, we will see how to find location information in a variety of websites and in what form the data can be found.

NOTES

1 http://www.socialmediafrontiers.com/2013/09/mobile-marketing-using-social-media-on.html.
2 https://addons.mozilla.org/en-US/firefox/addon/exif-viewer/.
3 http://www.pewinternet.org/2013/09/12/location-based-services/.

Legal issues

7

This chapter will come nowhere near laying out a clear and complete picture of what the law says about using social media for investigation. That's because the law is entirely unclear on these issues. There have been many court cases and lawsuits regarding a variety of investigative techniques, but the results are unclear and sometimes contradictory.

Guidelines often depend on who is doing the investigating. Law enforcement or parties in lawsuits have different rules and expectations compared to businesses doing background checks on job applicants or a private citizen undertaking a personal investigation.

That said, this chapter will lay out the current legal landscape. What is presented here is an overview of how current cases have been handled and an interpretation of them. However, this chapter should *not* be taken as legal advice! I, your author, am not a lawyer or a law expert. If you are considering undertaking an investigation but are worried about the legal risks, you should contact a lawyer from your company or organization or a personal attorney. This issue is currently unclear for the law so consulting an internet law expert is essential for your own protection.

There are two core legal issues that come up in this area: a person's right to privacy and the investigator violating a site's terms of service (TOS). We will look at those areas individually along with a list of common investigative techniques that have not seen any legal challenge.

RIGHT TO PRIVACY
MELVIN COLON

In 2011, Melvin Colon was one of eight gang members charged with murder, attempted murder, and a number of drug and gun charges. He had posted photos of himself on Facebook, which were accessible to anyone online, that showed him flashing gang signs and flashing cash (e.g., Figure 7.1). In posts that had privacy settings that restricted access to his friends, Colon posted more incriminating material, including threats of violence and photos of illegal activity.[1]

The police obtained a warrant to collect Colon's private Facebook information. In order to show probable cause to obtain the warrant, the police accessed some of this private information through the assistance of a corroborating witness. Colon's friend

FIGURE 7.1

An example of Melvin Colon's posts. His username and face are blurred here for privacy, though the original photo is still available on his Facebook profile to the general public.

list was public, and the police used this to find a friend who was willing to show them Colon's restricted posts. Colon's attorneys argued this was a violation of his Fourth Amendment rights, claiming he had a right to privacy for the posts he restricted to his friends.

A judge ruled against this, stating, "Colon's legitimate expectation of privacy ended when he disseminated posts to his 'friends' because those 'friends' were free to use the information however they wanted—including sharing it with the Government".[2]

OCCUPY WALL STREET

In another case, a protestor in the Occupy Wall Street protests challenged an attempt by the government to collect public tweets he had posted before his arrest during a demonstration. The subpoena went to Twitter, and the company argued that the user had a right to quash the subpoena. A judge ruled he did not because a user has "no propriety interest" in tweets—essentially, Twitter owned the data, not the user.

The user also argued that the Fourth Amendment should protect the privacy of his tweets. The New York City Criminal Court disagreed, stating that there can be no expectation of privacy for tweets shared with the general public.[3]

GEORGIA STUDENT

Another case that reinforces this argument is that of a minor student in Georgia. The student had posted a publicly visible photo of herself in a bikini on Facebook. This photo was found and used in a presentation by her school district on internet safety in a context that implied the student was promiscuous and abused alcohol. The student and her attorneys argued that this was a Fourth Amendment violation,[4] but a judge ruled against her stating that she had no expectation of privacy for a photo she had published publicly. (Note that there may be other arguments against the school using this photo, such as copyright violation, but that was not the privacy argument at issue here.)

Indeed, most websites' terms state something to this effect. Facebook, for example, says, "When you publish content or information using the Public setting, it means that you are allowing everyone, including people off of Facebook, to access and use that information, and to associate it with you (i.e. your name and profile picture)".[5]

While there are likely to be more challenges on this front, it appears that the courts are inclined to accept that once a person shares data with someone else, he loses his expectation of privacy. This precedent has held since the predigital age—including written and mailed letters—and is likely to continue.

TERMS OF SERVICE

The TOS of a website provide a set of rules that users agree to follow when they use a site. A site might also use them to offer disclaimers or deny legal responsibility for some actions.

Each social media site has its own TOS, and so, there is no single rule an investigator can follow in order to ensure he or she is within the bounds of allowable activity on every site—except that it is important to read the terms for each site.

FAKE ACCOUNTS

For investigations, the main issue that arises with respect to TOS is that of creating profiles with fake identities. If you are investigating someone, it is obvious that you would not want to use details from your personal account. You may not want to personally add someone as a friend or otherwise reveal your true identity as someone who is looking at what the target posted. Thus, creating a fake or anonymous account can be a solution.

However, not all sites allow fake accounts. Facebook does not, and, at the time of this writing in fall 2014, it was actively enforcing this requirement by shutting down accounts it believed to be fake. Facebook's Terms of Service page[6] makes this requirement very clear:

Registration and Account Security

Facebook users provide their real names and information, and we need your help to keep it that way. Here are some commitments you make to us relating to registering and maintaining the security of your account:

- *You will not provide any false personal information on Facebook, or create an account for anyone other than yourself without permission.*
- *You will not create more than one personal account.*
- *If we disable your account, you will not create another one without our permission.*
- *You will not use your personal timeline primarily for your own commercial gain, and will use a Facebook Page for such purposes.*
- *You will not use Facebook if you are under 13.*
- *You will not use Facebook if you are a convicted sex offender.*
- *You will keep your contact information accurate and up-to-date.*
- *You will not share your password (or in the case of developers, your secret key), let anyone else access your account, or do anything else that might jeopardize the security of your account.*
- *You will not transfer your account (including any Page or application you administer) to anyone without first getting our written permission.*
- *If you select a username or similar identifier for your account or Page, we reserve the right to remove or reclaim it if we believe it is appropriate (such as when a trademark owner complains about a username that does not closely relate to a user's actual name).*

You can see that a number of these items explicitly exclude fake accounts. Aside from the explicit requirements, the requirements of keeping contact information up-to-date, not sharing passwords, and not transferring accounts may prohibit many activities investigators may take with fake accounts.

The policy is out of sync with reality, where as many as 10% of accounts may be totally fake,[7] and many users report including some fake information to protect their privacy. For example, a Pew study showed that 26% of African-American teens had at least some fake data in their profile for privacy reasons.[8]

As a side note, this "real name" policy has come under sharp criticism because of the real danger it presents to a lot of users.

Not all social networks prohibit fake accounts, however. Twitter has no rules about using a true identity. Google, and its social media services including YouTube and Google+, used to have a real name policy, but they eliminated that policy in 2014. They published this statement on Google+ describing the removal of the policy.[9]

When we launched Google+ over three years ago, we had a lot of restrictions on what name you could use on your profile. This helped create a community made up of real people, but it also excluded a number of people who wanted to be part of it without using their real names.

Over the years, as Google+ grew and its community became established, we steadily opened up this policy, from allowing +Page owners to use any name of their choosing to letting YouTube users bring their usernames into Google+. Today, we are taking the last step: there are no more restrictions on what name you can use.

We know you've been calling for this change for a while. We know that our names policy has been unclear, and this has led to some unnecessarily difficult experiences for some of our users. For this we apologize, and we hope that today's change is a step toward making Google+ the welcoming and inclusive place that we want it to be. Thank you for expressing your opinions so passionately, and thanks for continuing to make Google+ the thoughtful community that it is.

LinkedIn does require the use of real names and accurate information[10]:

2.3. Service Eligibility

To be eligible to use the Services, you must meet the following criteria and represent and warrant that you: … (4) will only maintain one LinkedIn account (and/or one SlideShare or Pulse account, if applicable) at any given time; (5) will use your real name and only provide accurate information to LinkedIn.

So it depends on the service whether or not you are required to create an account with your true identity. Reviewing the TOS is important if you want to ensure that you are not violating an agreement in your investigation—especially if you plan to bring evidence gathered from the investigation to court.

FAKE ACCOUNTS IN COURT CASES

There are a few ways the creation of fake accounts has come up in the courts so far: using a fake account and impersonation.

Let's first look at simply creating a fake account. The TOS are presented as legal agreements. Would it count as a violation of law if a person were to violate the terms?

United States v. Drew

The main court case to look at this is *United States v. Drew*. Lori Drew, the defendant, is a Missouri woman and mother of a teen girl in 2006. Drew's daughter, Sarah, had been friends with another girl, Megan Meier, who was 13 years old at the time. When the two girls had a falling out, Lori Drew created a fake profile on Myspace claiming to be a 16-year-old boy named Josh. "Josh" friended Megan and the two became online friends, though the account was secretly being run by Sarah's mom and another 18-year-old girl.

In October 2006, "Josh" changed from his friendly tone and sent Megan a message that said, "I don't know if I want to be friends with you anymore because I've heard that you are not very nice to your friends." His account then started to publicly share private messages that Megan had sent. His last message read, "You are a bad person and everybody hates you. Have a shitty rest of your life. The world would be a better place without you." Twenty minutes after their last exchange, Megan hanged herself by a belt in her closet and died the next day.[11]

Lori Drew, the mother who had operated the "Josh" account, was arrested and charged with violating the Computer Fraud and Abuse Act (CFAA), a US federal law. The government argued that by creating the fake account on Myspace, Drew had gained "unauthorized access" to a computer in violation of the CFAA.

Drew was convicted of these charges, but a federal district court judge later overturned the conviction stating that violating the TOS does not constitute a crime under CFAA.[12]

Facebook v. Power Ventures

Another case, *Facebook v. Power Ventures*, established that it is not a crime to violate the TOS.

Power Ventures is a company that was collecting public information from people's Facebook profiles. Facebook's terms prohibit the automated collection of information from its pages. It blocked Power Ventures' IP addresses, and Power Ventures changed them to continue getting access. Facebook then sued Power Ventures, asserting their actions violated Section 502 of the California Penal Code, which deals with unauthorized access to computer systems.

The court ruled that simply violating the TOS was not a crime.[13] Other issues in that case are pending, but the courts made clear that a person was not committing a computer crime simply by violating the TOS on a social media site.

However, even if fake accounts are not crimes that can be prosecuted, there can certainly be consequences to using them. First, the social media site can shut down the fake accounts at any time and refuse to reinstate them. Occasionally, this has even been the case for people who use *real* identities that the social media sites simply don't believe.[14]

If a fake profile claims to be another real person (rather than an invented person), there are many potential consequences. Twitter is an excellent site to learn about this because they allow fake accounts and even parody accounts (as long as the accounts identify themselves as parodies).

Coventry First

In one case, insurer Coventry First sued an unidentified John Doe for his Twitter parody account. Coventry First is a secondary insurance company; they buy life insurance policies and collect when the insured person dies. This marketplace has been criticized for being morbid, since they essentially profit from the deaths of people. (And the more quickly the people die, the more money the company makes.) The market gained some infamy in the 1980s for buying up policies of AIDS patients, because secondary insurance companies expected them to die quickly.

The fake Twitter account posted messages essentially rooting for mass death in order to increase profits (Figure 7.2).

coventryfirst Coventry First
2 increase shareholder value, would it b wrong to root for mass
deaths in the world? preferably, 1st-world countries. LMK, kthxbai
6 Jun

 coventryfirst Coventry First
plane crashes r bad 4 the passengers and airline corp but those
crashes also increase shareholder value in the death industry.
coventryfirst
6 Jun

FIGURE 7.2

Examples of tweets from the Coventry First parody account.

The account did not properly identify itself as a parody account (though one could argue that the parody was quite clear from the contents of the tweets), and Coventry First sued for trademark infringement and unfair competition.[15] Fortunately for John Doe, Coventry First did not file the proper paperwork to obtain his real identity, and after they were challenged by Doe's lawyer, they dropped the case.[16]

Todd Levitt

Similar circumstances were at play when Todd Levitt, a Central Michigan University professor (and criminal defense lawyer), sued a student for parodying him on Twitter. The parody included tweets like "Buying me a drink at Cabin karaoke will get you extra credit, but it's not like that matters because you're guaranteed an A in the syllabus".[17] Levitt sued for defamation and intentional infliction of emotional distress. The student's lawyer argued that the parody tweets were protected by the First and Fourteenth Amendments, since they were caricatures and "rhetorical hyperbole".[18]

At the time of writing, the lawsuit is still under way.

Jim Ardis

One parodied man took things into his own hands. Peoria, Illinois, mayor Jim Ardis was so upset about a Twitter account (@peoriamayor) that parodied him that he sent a SWAT team to raid the home of Jon Daniel who operated the account on charges that he was impersonating a public official.[19] Police detained him and seized his computers. No charges were filed against Daniel, but with the backing of the American Civil Liberties Union (ACLU), he filed a lawsuit for wrongful arrest, claiming that his tweets were protected under the First Amendment. His case is also still pending.

These examples all show that it is currently unclear what is protected and what actions can be taken against someone who impersonates another person online. While we have looked at examples of parody accounts, law enforcement officials and other investigators face more complex challenges. For example, is it appropriate to impersonate someone a target knows in real life? That is a different type of impersonation than parody, but there are no clear legal guidelines to follow in cases like this.

CONCLUSIONS

Fortunately, we have not seen any legal issues arise from one person simply accessing the public information provided on a person's social media site. It appears that if a private citizen looks at someone's content for his own purposes, no one has decided to sue as a result. However, once a social media post is used for something, it has been challenged.

Courts seem to be in agreement that users do not have an expectation of privacy for content they share on social media, whether it is shared publicly or not. In terms of creating alternative accounts to help access information, the story is more mixed.

There appears to be agreement that it is not a crime to simply violate the TOS of a website, though investigators who hope to bring information to court should be wary of such practice, as it calls into question the validity of an investigation. There is no case law that firmly establishes how acceptable it is to create fake accounts that impersonate another person. We examined this in the case of parody accounts, but investigators might think about creating fake accounts that appear to be someone from a target's life. We do not know how courts would rule on such an activity, so it should be undertaken with caution.

The one issue that is very clear is that legal precedent around social media is still evolving. The current case law is likely to change, and new laws are popping up at all levels, from the federal government to small towns. Investigators will be well served to keep abreast of developments on this topic.

NOTES

1 Oremus, Will. 2012. "Melvin Colon Ruling: Facebook Friends Can Share Your Private Posts with the FBI." Slate. http://www.slate.com/blogs/future_tense/2012/08/17/melvin_colon_ruling_facebook_friends_can_share_your_private_posts_with_the_fbi.html.

2 Pauley III, William H. 2012. "United States of America v. Joshua Meregildo et al. (1:11-Cr-00576-WHP)." United States District Court: Southern District of New York. http://www.scribd.com/doc/102937713/Facebook-Privacy-Ruling.

3 Preziosi, Stephen N. 2014. "Twitter And Tweets: You Do Not Have A Proprietary Interest In The Material You Post To A Social Media Website." New York Appellate Lawyer. http://www.newyorkappellatelawyer.com/twitter-and-tweets-you-do-not-have-a-proprietary-interest-in-the-material-you-post-to-a-social-media-website/.

4 Batten Sr., Timothy C. 2013. "Chelsea Chaney v. Fayette County Public Scool District and Curtis R. Cearley (Case 3:13-Cv-00089-TCB)." http://www2.bloomberglaw.com/public/desktop/document/Chaney_v_Fayette_County_Public_School_District_et_al_Docket_No_31.

5 Facebook. 2013. "Statement of Rights and Responsibilities." Facebook. https://www.facebook.com/legal/terms.

6 Ibid.

7 Munson, Lee. 2014. "Facebook: At Least 67 Million Accounts Are Fake." Naked Security. http://nakedsecurity.sophos.com/2014/02/10/facebook-at-least-67-million-accounts-are-fake/.

8 Madden, Mary; Lenhart, Amanda; Cortesi, Sandra; Gasser, Urs; Duggan, Maeve; Smith, Aaron; Beaton, Meredith. 2013. "Teens, Social Media, and Privacy." Pew Research Center. http://www.pewinternet.org/files/2013/05/PIP_TeensSocialMediaandPrivacy_PDF.pdf.

9 Google+. 2014. "[Untitled.] Google+". https://plus.google.com/+googleplus/posts/V5XkYQYYJqy.

10 LinkedIn. 2014. "User Agreement." LinkedIn. https://www.linkedin.com/legal/user-agreement.

11 United States District Court for the Central District of California (10 November 2008), *Government's Trial Memorandum (Case 2:08-cr-00582-GW Document 64).*O'Brien, Thomas P.; Ewell, Christine C.; Krause, Mark C. 2008. "United States of America v. Lori Drew (Case 2:08-Cr-00582-GW)." United States District Court for the Central District of California. http://www.scribd.com/doc/23406419/Governments-Trial-Memo.

12 Zimmerman, Matt. 2009. "Judge Overturns Lori Drew Misdemeanor Convictions." Electronic Frontier Foundation. https://www.eff.org/deeplinks/2009/07/judge-overturns-lori.

13 Hofmann, Marcia. 2010. "Court: Violating Terms of Service Is Not a Crime, But Bypassing Technical Barriers Might Be." Electronic Frontier Foundation. https://www.eff.org/deeplinks/2010/07/court-violating-terms-service-not-crime-bypassing.

14 Jordan, Yitz. 2014. "Facebook's 'real Name' Policy Isn't Just Discriminatory, It's Dangerous." Quartz. http://qz.com/267375/facebooks-real-name-policy-isnt-just-discriminatory-its-dangerous/.

15 Roberts, Jeff. 2011. "Insurer Sues Twitter Imposter Who Cheers Death, Mayhem." Reuters. http://www.reuters.com/article/2011/06/09/us-coventry-idUSTRE7586ST20110609.

16 Balasubramani, Venkat. 2011. "Coventry First Withdraws Twittersquatting Lawsuit Against @Coventryfirst — Coventry First, LLC v. Does." Technology & Marketing Law Blog. http://blog.ericgoldman.org/archives/2011/07/coventry_first_1.htm.

17 Staumsheim, Carl. 2014. "Former Central Michigan U. Adjunct Instructor Sues Student over Fake Twitter Account @insidehighered." Inside Higher Ed. https://www.insidehighered.com/news/2014/07/03/former-central-michigan-u-adjunct-instructor-sues-student-over-fake-twitter-account.

18 Aleck II, Ghazey H.; Bloem, Gordon M. 2014. "Defendant's Answer to Plaintiff's Complaint and Affirmative Defenses." Todd L. Levitt and Levitt Law Firm, P.C., v. Zachary Felton (File No. 14-11644-NZ). https://www.insidehighered.com/sites/default/server_files/files/LevittFeltonAnswer.pdf.

19 Press, The Associated. 2014. "Fake Peoria Mayor Tweets Stir Debate about Parody." The Chicago Sun Times. http://politics.suntimes.com/article/springfield/fake-peoria-mayor-tweets-stir-debate-about-parody/fri-09192014-933am.

Facebook

8

In my own work, I was approached by a woman who wanted help finding someone online. Her niece, "Carol," had lived several states away in the Midwest. Carol had died a few years earlier in a highway accident. She had had a rocky relationship with her husband, "Mike," and they had been separated at the time of her death. Carol was cremated, and after the funeral, Mike was given possession of a family heirloom that had been given to Carol when she left home. It had little monetary value but a lot of sentimental value for the family. My client's sister, Carol's mother, had requested the heirloom be returned, and Mike had offered to hand it over for a price. Carol's mother balked at the idea of paying for this kind of transfer, so Mike left town and brought Carol's heirloom with him.

Not having the family heirloom had become an emotional hardship for Carol's mother. My client saw this and decided to make a deal with Mike on her own to get the object back. The only problem was that my client did not have any information about how to reach Mike. No email address, no phone, and no idea exactly where he was living.

We started by searching Carol's Facebook profile. It was still active several years after her death, but she had deleted all of her connections with Mike when they had separated shortly before her death. This ruled out finding him through a known associate. Furthermore, Mike had a common last name, so there were thousands of people on Facebook who had his name. It was impractical to search for them all. A search using an old email address for him also turned up nothing.

Finally, we turned to Facebook's graph search. This allows you to search for a name and then use filters to narrow down the search results. We searched for Mike using his full name and then filtered the search to only people living near the medium-sized city where he had last lived. This returned only four people. We ruled out one by the picture (a man shown with his wife and three children who was clearly not our Mike), one was excluded because he attended a high school in a different state than where our Mike was from, and one was excluded because he graduated from a university that we knew Mike had not attended.

This left one option, but it was not necessarily the Mike we were looking for. Our Mike might have used a fake name or location or simply not have been on Facebook at all. Examining the profile, however, showed conclusively that this was our target Mike. He listed Carol's father on his profile page as "father-in-law" and mentioned Carol in several posts.

Using a fake Facebook account created just for this purpose, my client sent a friend request to Mike. After he approved it, she reached out to him with a Facebook message and offered to make arrangements with him to transfer the heirloom. Mike responded within a few hours and named a price. My client agreed, and within a few days, she flew to the Midwest airport closest to Mike, met him at a prearranged time, and made the exchange.

Carol's heirloom is now home with her mother, all as a result of a Facebook investigation that allowed my client to reach out to her husband.

FACEBOOK OVERVIEW

Facebook is a social networking site and jockeys for position with Google as the most used website in the world. They report 1.4 billion monthly users, which constitute over half the worldwide population of internet users (currently estimated at ≈ 2.4 billion).

Reflecting back on the categories of sites listed earlier in the book, Facebook can fairly be called the social networking site, since there is a heavy emphasis on creating connections with friends. The information users post is shared with their friends, and when users log in, they see a list of posts that their friends have made. However, Facebook is not just a social networking site; in many ways, it can be considered a one-stop destination for everything a person might want online.

We will discuss the different types of available data in detail below, but Facebook is a place where people come to share links, play games with friends, post photos and videos, share their location, and find trending news. Its usefulness goes far beyond the ability to post a simple update or maintain a profile.

BASIC FACEBOOK ACTIVITIES

Users can do many things on Facebook, but this chapter will focus on a core set of activities.

Adding Friends

Having social connections is a prerequisite for any social network. It's therefore no surprise that one of the main features of Facebook is the ability to create lists of friends. When a user finds someone on Facebook they want to be friends with, they can send a *friend request*. If the recipient of the request approves it, the two users become friends. The main result of this is that each person will be able to see updates that the other has created. We discussed how this information is displayed later on in this chapter.

Status Updates

The main way that users share information with their friends is through a *status update*. Updates are usually text but may also contain links, photos, videos, and location information. Users can also "call out" friends by name in their updates.

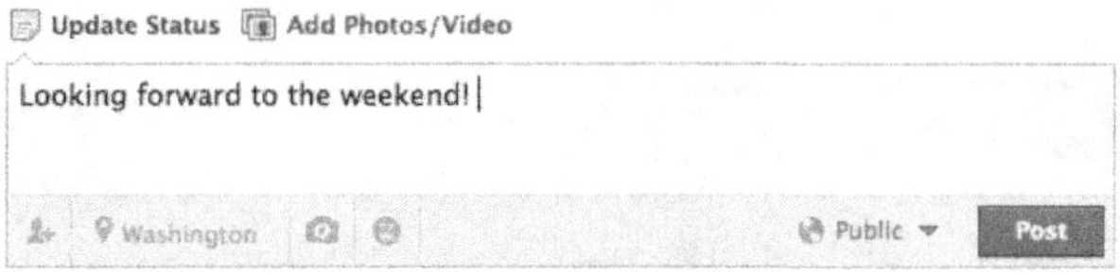

FIGURE 8.1

A basic status update in the making. Note the row of icons along the bottom. The location icon indicates the status is taking place in Washington. To its right is a photo icon, allowing the option to include a picture with this update.

Figure 8.1 shows the basic interface for creating a status update. This appears on the top of most pages that users see on Facebook. They can type their update into the box and add other data if they choose. Note that in Figure 8.1, the location icon at the bottom left of the window says "Washington." This is Facebook automatically including the users' location with the update. To the right of that is a camera icon that gives the user the option to choose a photo to include with the update.

Another important icon to note in Figure 8.1 is just to the left of the "Post" button in the bottom right. This has a globe with the word "Public" next to it. That indicates the privacy level of the post. This post is visible to anyone online. The small triangle to the right allows the user to select different privacy levels from a pull-down menu. They can choose to make the post visible to their friends only, to themselves only (making it practically invisible), or to a custom-defined group of people.

Likes, Comments, and Shares

Users can also interact with status update made by others. Figure 8.2 shows a post made by the grocery chain Whole Foods Market. At the bottom of this post in a gray box under the image are the options "Like," "Comment," and "Share."

Liking something on Facebook is one of the most common ways users interact. It indicates exactly what the name suggests; the user clicks "Like" when they like a post.

User can also *comment*. In Figure 8.2, you can see the user has started typing a comment: "Yum!" The comment feature is a way that people can have a discussion about a link, photo, or other updates.

The option to *share* is the way people can repost something so that their friends can see it.

Liking "Pages"

Liking on Facebook isn't only available for posts. A user can also like a "page."

These pages are maintained by companies, celebrities, and other public entities. Figure 8.3 shows the top of the page for Whole Foods Market. You can see a "Like" button in the lower right. Clicking that is similar to creating a friend relationship on Facebook. If the user likes the page, he or she will see this brand's updates posted on his or her newsfeed page.

FIGURE 8.2

An update by the grocery chain Whole Foods Market with options to like, comments, and share the post.

FIGURE 8.3

The page for Whole Foods Market is shown here. The option to "like" the page is made available through the button in the lower right.

Third-Party Integration

Facebook has even extended the ability to like and share content to other websites. Figure 8.4 shows a screen from the retailer REI website. REI is unaffiliated with Facebook, but they have integrated a Facebook icon (visible at the top right of the page). When a user clicks this, it allows them to automatically share a link to the current page with their friends on Facebook.

Tens of thousands of websites have this capability integrated. This has made it very easy for people to share interesting information on Facebook even when they are using other websites.

COMPONENTS OF THE FACEBOOK SITE

Facebook is broken down into two major sections: the *News Feed* and the *Timeline*.

The News Feed

The first is for all the *News Feed*. This is the first page people see when they come on to the Facebook website. It's a collection of all the status updates and activity announcements that their friends have made as well as updates from brands or celebrities whose pages the user has liked. (Facebook also mixes ads in with this content to make money.)

The News Feed can be sorted in reverse chronological order, so the user sees his or her friends' most recent posts first. By default, though, Facebook tries to highlight the post they think are most relevant to the user. Facebook does not explain exactly how they determine relevance, but it combines how recent post is, how many likes and comments have been received from people, and other factors that are in a constant state of change.

FIGURE 8.4

The REI website includes a link to share product info on Facebook. This is done by clicking the Facebook icon above the product name (on the right of the page).

FIGURE 8.5

The News Feed of, for example, user Malcom.

Figure 8.5 shows the News Feed for our example user Malcom. If you were to scroll down, you would see more posts from his friends and the pages he has liked.

The News Feed aggregates posts from all of a user's friends.

The Timeline

All the posts a user has made are contained in that user's *Timeline*. To access a user's Timeline, click on their name anywhere within Facebook. Clicking on the name brings you to their Timeline by default. Figure 8.6 shows the top of example user Malcom's Timeline.

In addition to the user's updates, all other personal data about a user is aggregated and accessible to users from the Timeline. In Figure 8.6, you can see "About," "Photos," "Friends," and "More" in the navigation bar beside Malcom's profile picture, toward the top of the page. Rather than explore all of these items here, we'll cover each in more depth later in the chapter, when discussing how to obtain information about people.

FACEBOOK DEMOGRAPHICS

Because Facebook is so popular (1.4 billion users), it can be hard to distinguish their demographics from the demographics of the population at large. Close to 70% of the US internet-using population has Facebook profiles; similar numbers are seen in

FIGURE 8.6

Our example user Malcom's Timeline on Facebook.

Europe. Penetration is higher in many countries abroad. Over 70% of India's online population is on Facebook, and penetration is close to 90% in Indonesia, Turkey, and the Philippines.

Facebook users tend to be a bit overrepresented in the middle-age bracket, and the male-to-female ratio is slightly skewed toward female when compared to the overall population. Rates of adoption tend to be a bit higher among educated, wealthier adults; but there is a good chance of finding any adult on Facebook, regardless of his or her demographic characteristics.

FINDING PEOPLE

When you want to find a person on Facebook, there are a number of interesting ways to find them.

BY NAME

The most straightforward way to find someone is to search by name. The search bar at the top of the Facebook window can be used for all the searches discussed in this chapter. When you type in someone's name, you get a preview list of the results, as shown in Figure 8.7.

If the person you are searching for does not appear in this list, you can also try to search for them through Google. This requires an advanced search technique. You can limit the search results to a Facebook by including `site:facebook` in the query. To search for Alice Smith's Facebook page on Google, the search would be as follows:

```
site:facebook.com "Alice Smith".
```

This will return only public pages on Facebook that contain the name "Alice Smith" and results for profiles with that name will be prioritized.

BY EMAIL ADDRESS

If this still doesn't get you to the person you are looking for, you can also search by email address. Depending on a user's settings, this may bring up their profile page even when the name does not.

FIGURE 8.7

A search for someone named "Alice Smith."

It is possible that both of these techniques fail. There are privacy settings in Facebook that allow people to prevent themselves from being found in the search. Fortunately, for the investigator, there are a number of other strategies although this may not be so fortunate for unaware users.

BY KNOWN ASSOCIATIONS

One technique is to look for someone through their associates. If you know who your target's friends are, try to find those friends by name or email address. From there, you can navigate to the associate's friend page. Your target may be listed there. (More details on the "Friends" page are in the next section.)

BY LIKES

Another option is to find the target through their likes. When someone likes a page on Facebook, they usually appear on the list of people who have liked the page.

Using Graph Search

Facebook has recently added new support for this kind of search through a tool they call *graph search*. These searches can be entered into the same search bar at the top of the page that you would use to search for someone by name. However, the searches can be more complex.

For example, you can enter the search "People who like Georgetown University." This brings up a list of everyone who has liked that page and some additional information about those people. Figure 8.8 shows a result page with the identities of the people blurred out to protect their privacy.

You can filter the results by someone's gender, employer, etc., in your search. Using these filters can help narrow down the number of results dramatically.

For example, if you started with the search above and then added filters to select only men who graduated from Georgetown (in addition to liking it) in the class of 2000, there are only two people in the results, shown in Figure 8.9. Note that the query in the search bar updated is updated to "Male graduates of Georgetown University in 2000 who like Georgetown University."

OBTAINING DATA

Once you have found your target, you can begin looking for information on their Facebook page. Facebook does not inform a user when someone has looked at their profile, posts, photos, and so on. Thus, a user will not know that you have browsed what they've posted. The only way for a user to know that you had looked at their page is if you comment, like, or otherwise send a message indicating you were there.

FIGURE 8.8

Results of the graph search for people who like Georgetown University. Note the information on the right that shows over 1000 people like this. A list of attributes for filtering also appears there.

USER TIMELINES

Users' Timelines have collections of the status updates they have made. Figure 8.6 shows Malcom's Timeline.

Each status update has the text a user has entered, but there is more information embedded in it. If you click the date or time listed on a status update, it will bring up only that post in the browser.

Figure 8.10 shows one of Malcom's updates that has been opened in this fashion. Next to his name, it says "at Elephant & Castle." This is location information indicating exactly where the user was when he posted this update. Location data is discussed more below.

Under Malcom's name is the exact date and time of the update, along with the city where it was posted. The globe icon to the right of this indicates that the privacy setting for this post makes it available to the general public. Different icons will appear based on the privacy setting the user has applied. Privacy levels are discussed in depth later in this chapter.

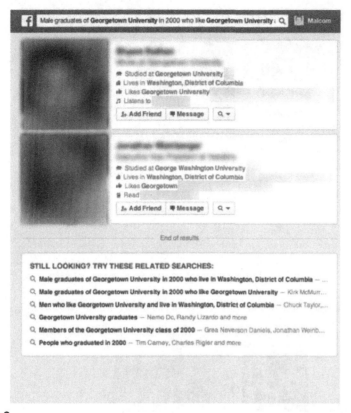

FIGURE 8.9

A filtered graph search for men who like Georgetown University and who went to school there, graduating in 2000. Unlike the many results in Figure 8.8, these results have only two people.

FIGURE 8.10

A post with all the associated information.

Personal Profile

Users maintain extensive personal profiles, which are relatively static and contain background and demographic data. Once you have found a person, you will be taken to their Timeline, which mostly contains their status updates. The majority of profiles' attributes are on the user's "About" page. You can access this by clicking "About" in the navigation bar next to the user's profile picture at the top of the page (see Figure 8.11).

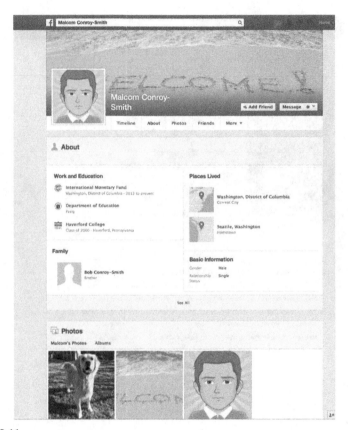

FIGURE 8.11

The "About" page for Malcom. It includes information like work and education, family, places Malcom has lived, background information, and photos.

This section is where you will find background information, including users' employment and education history, personal traits, their relationship status, lists of relatives, organizations they belong to, and things (books, music, movies, sports teams, ideas, and celebrities) they like. Figure 8.11 shows example user Malcom's About page.

At the bottom of the first large section, titled "About," there is a link that says "See more." Clicking this will bring up more extensive personal information, including contact information if the user has made it available.

Readers are encouraged to visit Malcom's "About" page to see all the information available there.

Social Connections

Each user also has a "Friends" page with a list of his or her friends. This is accessible on another tab toward the top of a user's page. Figure 8.12 shows Malcom's friend list.

From this page, you can click on a friend's name to visit their Timeline and find more information about them.

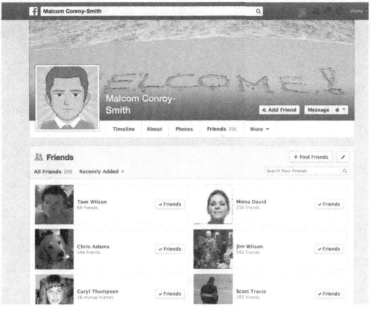

FIGURE 8.12

The "Friends" page for the example user Malcom.

Note that someone's friends can be valuable sources of information as well. For example, *Forbes* magazine describes how Facebook friends can share damaging evidence during divorce cases:

> *Married couples often have dozens of mutual friends and connections. If the marriage breaks up, obviously some of these people will be more loyal to one spouse than the other. I've had more than one client report a steady stream of information about her estranged husband's financial activities, as relayed by mutual friends who were still following his Facebook updates. So, even if he's blocked you from seeing his posts directly, your mutual friends can still tell you all about the ski trip he took to Switzerland with his girlfriend a week after claiming he couldn't afford to pay spousal support.*

> **—Jeff Landers, Forbes.com**[1]

Activities

Users may post updates about their activities in their status updates that are visible on their Timeline. But for some events, there is a more formal log. In the same row of options with the Timeline, About, and Friends pages, there is an option that says "More ▼" Clicking this opens a menu that lists additional information about the user. This menu is highlighted in Figure 8.13.

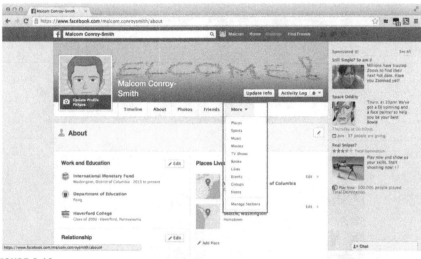

FIGURE 8.13

The "More" menu on a user's Facebook page.

Most options on the More menu are simply sections of the "About" page, but there is some additional information. One such option is "Events." Clicking that will bring up a list of events the user has attended. These "events" are created by other Facebook users and allow people to RSVP (or choose not to). The events might be parties, sporting events, concerts, special events that businesses put on, or pretty much anything else.

Figure 8.14 shows two upcoming events that Malcom is planning to attend. The events screen was accessed by clicking on the "Events" button. Past events will also be listed on this page.

Location Information

There are a few ways to find out where a target has been. Using the events page mentioned above is one option. It shows when people have been to an event, and patterns in those events may reveal a club, bar, or sports venue that the target visits frequently.

Status updates may also contain location information. Not every update will have a location, but users can choose to include that. If a location is included, it usually appears with "- at «location name»" at the end of the status update. Figure 8.15 shows a status update from Malcom that includes the location "Elephant & Castle," a bar in Washington, DC. The status update automatically gets a map that shows the location when the user lists one. You can click on the place name or the map to see more precise information about the location.

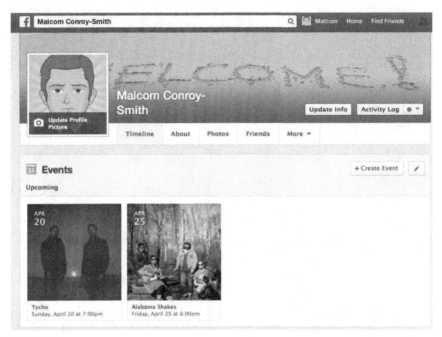

FIGURE 8.14

The events page from Malcom's profile. This includes two upcoming events he is planning to attend.

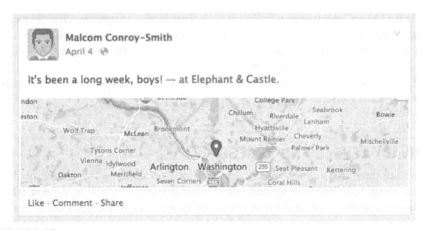

FIGURE 8.15

A status update with a location "Elephant & Castle."

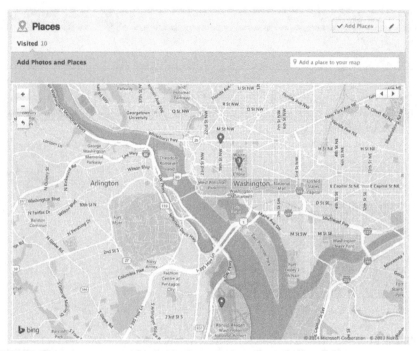

FIGURE 8.16

The map from Malcom's Places page showing places he has mentioned in his status updates or listed in his profile.

In the "More" menu shown in Figure 8.13, there is also an option called "Places." This has map pins for every place users list in their status updates and all the places they have worked, lived, or attended school. Figure 8.16 shows Malcom's Places page zoomed in on Washington, DC.

Clicking on a pin in this map will show all the status updates or profile information associated with that location.

PRIVACY LEVELS AND ACCESS

There are three major levels of privacy on Facebook. Information can be public, which means it is visible to anyone online, even without a Facebook account. This is indicated with a small globe icon next to the post. You can see this icon in all the figures in this chapter that show a post by Malcom.

Users can restrict their information to be visible to their friends only. This requires someone to have a friendship that the user has approved. They can also limit access to be visible to no one or to a customized list of people.

All the different types of information described above—including status updates, likes, and personal information—can be shared at different privacy levels. A user may make one status update public and restrict another to be visible only to friends. Thus, if you are looking at a person's profile without a friend relationship with that person, you are not necessarily seeing all the information they have posted; you can see what is public, but not content restricted to a smaller audience.

Exact numbers on how openly people share are hard to come by and change quickly. A 2012 study suggested 28% of US Facebook users were sharing most of their posts with an audience bigger than just their friends. This means there is a decent chance you will be able to find some information about a person on Facebook, even if you are not friends with them.

Obviously, becoming friends opens up a much wider set of information. In most cases, you will have access to the vast majority of a target's content if your target has accepted your account as a friend.

EXAMPLE: MALCOM CONROY-SMITH

Malcom's Facebook account is located here:

```
https://www.facebook.com/malcom.conroysmith
```

Browsing through his profile reveals many interesting things. He has posted background information, including where he grew up, where he went to school, and his job history. His contact information is also available.

But beyond the information he has explicitly shared, you can learn many things about his habits. Under the "Places" tab, you can see that Malcom posts a message almost every Friday evening from Elephant & Castle, a bar just a block from the International Monetary Fund where he works. That makes it a good place to look for him on Friday evenings. It's also somewhere you might find other people who know him.

He also posts photos of his dog Barley and talks about taking her to the dog park. While no dog park is listed in Malcom's Places, it is reasonable to make a first guess that the dog park is near Malcom's house. Other places indicate that he goes grocery shopping (at Whole Foods Market Georgetown), to the CVS pharmacy, and to get his dry cleaning in the Georgetown neighborhood of Washington, DC.

A Google search for "dog park georgetown washington dc" pulls up several pages for Montrose Park, a leash-free park very close to Malcom's residence. This would be another good location to look for people who know him or to spot Malcom himself.

CASE STUDIES

Because of Facebook's popularity, there are many cases where it has been used in investigations. We will look at the results of both criminal and civil investigations that leveraged Facebook.

CRIMINAL CASES

Arrests that come from Facebook usually happen because the target was unable to keep his or her mouth shut about their crimes. Sometimes, posts are picked up and spread widely across social media that brings them to the attention of authorities. These cases are interesting; but in this chapter, as with this book as a whole, I focus on investigations of specific targets where information turned up online.

The beating of an 11-year-old. In April 2014, police arrested three people in Flint, Michigan, after they posted a video of themselves beating an 11-year-old boy with a belt as punishment.[2] The video went viral and was eventually brought to the attention of police.

Colleen Cudney, a 22-year-old Michigan woman, was on probation for a drunk driving conviction.[3] Part of the conditions of her release was that she will not drink.

On St. Patrick's Day of 2014, she went out and drank anyway. The following day, she had to take a breathalyzer test, which she passed. She was so pleased that she decided to post about it on Facebook: "Buzz killer for me, I had to breathalyze [sic] this morning and I drank yesterday but I passed thank god lol my dumba@@."

A local police officer saw the post and alerted her probation officer, ultimately leading to her arrest for violating her probation.

Jeremy Thompson, an Indiana man, was arrested for illegal manufacture and sale of liquor.[4] After receiving a tip about the man, officers began monitoring his Facebook account. The target then posted a photo of himself with an illegal still on Facebook (Figure 8.17). Investigators found other photos of him illegally making

FIGURE 8.17

Lesson: Don't post photos of yourself with illegal stills on Facebook. This man was arrested as a direct result of posting this picture.

Photo provided by Indiana State Excise Police.

and selling moonshine. Ultimately, this provided cause for a search warrant. He was arrested and charged with five misdemeanors.

Danny Gough. On the other side of the world, criminals have used Facebook to obtain information about subjects as well. One of the more dramatic cases is that of Danny Gough. Following a feud that took place in the summer of 2010, authorities alleged that three men plotted a revenge killing. Gough had left town on vacation, but his alleged killers tracked his movements on Facebook and determined when he would be returning home. Gough was confronted outside his home by three masked men who brutally killed him. The alleged perpetrators were shown to have accessed Gough's Facebook page just hours before the crime.[5]

CIVIL CASES

There are countless cases of people being sued, fired, or otherwise punished because of the things they posted on Facebook. These are not necessarily the case of targeted investigation of an individual, but rather the case where information was posted on Facebook. The posting was then brought to the attention of people who used it to make their argument. One of the most recent and dramatic stories comes from Florida.

Patrick Snay, a school administrator, had sued the school he worked for. The two parties settled and the school agreed to pay Snay $80,000. As part of the settlement, he signed a confidentiality clause, agreeing not to reveal any details of the settlement to anyone besides his attorneys and his spouse.

However, Snay told his teenage daughter about the settlement. She went on Facebook and posted the following status update:

```
Mama and Papa Snay won the case against Gulliver…Gulliver is now
officially paying for my vacation to Europe this summer. SUCK IT.
```

The school found the post and used it as grounds to refuse to pay the settlement. Snay appealed and lost—making his daughter's status update a very costly Facebook post.[6]

CONCLUSION

Facebook, as the most popular social networking site in the world, is the most likely place to find a target. There is a wide range of information, from personal history, to social connections, to location. Within their posts, people often reveal a lot about their preferences and patterns of activity.

Facebook users do have a lot of control over the privacy of their information, and they often allow only friends to see it. However, a lot of people make their posts more public, which means an investigator may be able to access them without having an account that the target has friended. Because of the vast amount of accessible data, Facebook is widely used in investigations of all types.

NOTES

1 Add cite to http://www.forbes.com/sites/jefflanders/2013/08/20/how-social-media-can-affect-your-divorce/.
2 "Mother, 2 Others Arrested in Boy's Beating Posted as Facebook Video" by Stephen A. Crocker, Jr. *The Root*. April 20, 2014.
3 "'I drank yesterday but I passed': Michigan woman arrested after bragging on Facebook that she passed Breathalyzer" by Joe Kemp *New York Daily News,* Tuesday, April 1, 2014.
4 Officers: Ind. man arrested after posting photo of illegal still on Facebook. By Brad Evans WLWT.com, April 4, 2014.
5 Cite to http://www.mirror.co.uk/news/uk-news/danny-gough-hacked-death-in-2997482.
6 Girl costs father $80,000 with "SUCK IT" Facebook post. By Matthew Stucker, CNN, March 4, 2014. http://www.cnn.com/2014/03/02/us/facebook-post-costs-father/.

Twitter

CASE STUDY PARAGON: *ANTHONY WEINER*

Perhaps, the most famous case of someone's Twitter activities revealing far too much is that of Congressman Anthony Weiner (D-NY). On May 27, 2011, Weiner, a member of the US Congress representing New York, sent a public tweet directed at a 12-year-old woman who followed him on Twitter. The tweet contained a link to a picture that was a close-up of an erect penis concealed by a pair of boxer briefs.[1]

Because the post was publicly accessible for a time—until it was deleted—many people saw and archived it. Weiner was not explicitly being investigated by most of these people; politicians' accounts are regularly followed by people who are interested in all their activities, including those who are interested in any content that could be potentially damaging.

However, it turns out Weiner's Twitter activity was also being explicitly investigated by a group of conservatives.[2] For months before the tweet described above was posted, a group calling themselves the #bornfreecrew monitored Weiner's posts. They sent public messages to the women who followed him, warning them to "stay away" from him. The New York Times reports that there is even evidence that this group or others created fake Twitter accounts to try to entice Weiner into making inappropriate statements.[3]

It was one of these #bornfreecrew members, Dan Wolfe, who retweeted Weiner's inappropriate photo to his followers and eventually shared it with conservative publisher Andrew Breitbart. Breitbart then published the picture on his website.

As the news broke, Weiner responded by claiming that he had not posted the picture and that, instead, his account had been "hacked".[4] On June 6, 10 days after the original photo was tweeted, Breitbart published another photo of Weiner, this time shirtless, that was obtained from a woman who said Weiner had emailed to her.[5]

Weiner called a press conference the same day and confessed to posting the original tweet, sending other pictures to women, and conducting "inappropriate" conversations on Twitter, Facebook, and other platforms. Ten days later, on June 16, Weiner announced he would resign from Congress.

When you are being monitored on Twitter, a single post can have dramatic consequences.

TWITTER OVERVIEW

Twitter is a "microblogging" website. Recall that blogs emerged in the late 1990s and resembled online diaries. People could write anything they wanted and post it for people to read or comment on. While blogs could take any form, the posts were often essay length. Microblogging allows users to make posts, but they tend to be very short. Twitter limits posts to 140 characters. This creates an environment that is fundamentally different from blogging, since it is easy for someone to read hundreds of posts in a short amount of time.

Twitter is the largest microblogging website. It launched in 2006, and studies estimate there are close to one billion Twitter accounts. Twitter reports approximately 250 million active users (where "active" is defined as someone who accesses the site at least once a month).

BASIC TWITTER ACTIVITIES

On Twitter, all activities center around two things: posting and reading.

Posting ("Tweeting")

On Twitter, posts are called *tweets,* and the act of posting is called *tweeting.* Figure 9.1 shows a tweet by our example user, Malcom. Roughly half of the 250 million active users will have tweeted in the last month, while the rest spend their time reading posts others have made.

Tweets are public by default. Anyone can read someone else's tweets by going to their Twitter account page. Figure 9.2 shows Malcom's Twitter profile with all of his tweets.

@mentions

Users can have public conversations on Twitter. This is done by using something called "@mentions" (pronounced "at mentions"). A user types an at sign, immediately followed by someone's username (sometimes called a "handle"). For example, if someone wanted to send a tweet directed at Malcom, then he or she would begin the tweet with "@malcomCsmith."

FIGURE 9.1

A tweet posted by Malcom.

FIGURE 9.2

Malcom's Twitter profile with all of his tweets.

Like all tweets, these are publicly visible. However, the user who is mentioned will have the tweet highlighted in a section of their profile. Some users receive a notification that they have been @mentioned.

Direct Messages

There is also an option to have private conversations, using a feature called *direct messages*. However, we won't focus on them here, since they're hidden and inaccessible to an investigation.

Hashtags

Finally, an online convention seen more and more across the web—but which began on Twitter—is the *hashtag*.

As discussed earlier in the book, a *tag* is a label applied to something in order to make finding it easier. On Twitter, tags are prepended with a "#" character (hence the name "hashtag").

Some hashtags are obvious in meaning. For example, people often use a hashtag to indicate a sports team they are discussing, like #redsox or #chicago-cubs. Other hashtags evolve by convention. The #ff hashtag stands for "follow Friday," indicating a tweet where people list other users that they think are worth following.

Hashtags are also links. Thus, if a hashtag doesn't make sense to you by itself, you can click on it to see other tweets with the same hashtag. The context of the other tweets may reveal the hashtag's meaning.

Reading

If a user likes a tweet someone has posted, they can choose to show it by one of two actions: *favoriting* and *retweeting*.

Favoriting Tweets

Under Malcom's tweet in Figure 9.1, there is a small *Favorite* link beside a star icon. Sometimes, only the star icon is shown (see Figure 9.2). Clicking this will mark the tweet as a favorite.

User can go back and revisit their favorites. The tweet's original poster is notified when the tweet is favorited.

Retweeting Tweets

A user can also *retweet,* which reposts the original tweet onto the user's profile. In each of the figures mentioned above, the "retweet" option with a double arrow icon is shown to the right of the Favorite link. When a tweet is retweeted this way, it appears as though it came from the original poster.

Alternatively, some people retweet manually. This was commonly done in the early days of Twitter. A manual retweet is simply the copy-pasted text of another tweet, preceded by "RT" (meaning "ReTweet") or "MT" (meaning "Modified Tweet," if the user changed the original text). Manual retweets are still used when someone is adding a comment to the original. In Figure 9.3, Malcom has retweeted a post from NASA with commentary.

Following Users

If a user finds that someone often has interesting tweets, they can *follow* that person. By doing so, the followed user's tweets are aggregated and displayed in reverse chronological order on the home page when a user logs in (see Figure 9.4).

There's an important difference between following and the "Add Friend" feature common among other social networks: following is a *one-way* relationship.

On sites like Facebook, friendships are mutual. If you add someone as a friend, they must approve the friendship, and it establishes a two-way relationship.

On Twitter, there is no requirement that a relationship goes both ways. For example, in Figure 9.4, we can see that Malcom follows the official accounts for the NFL team Baltimore Ravens, the Discovery Channel show *MythBusters*, and Netflix's show *House of Cards*. By following them, Malcom is able to see their updates, but those accounts do not need to follow Malcom back (and probably won't).

Malcom Conroy-Smith
@MalcomCSmith

AWESOME! RT @nasa Liftoff of the @SpaceX
Falcon 9 rocket carrying #Dragon to #ISS !
pic.twitter.com/G8KslUTHgB

↩ Reply   🗑 Delete   ★ Favorite   ••• More

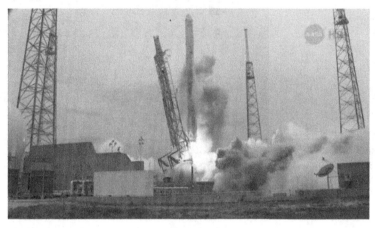

12:55 PM - 18 Apr 2014   Flag media

FIGURE 9.3

Malcom has retweeted a post by NASA. Malcom's text ("AWESOME!") appears at the
beginning of the tweet. Then, the "RT" characters indicate the subsequent text is a
retweet. The "@nasa" indicates that NASA's account posted the text, and finally, the
original text from NASA's tweet appears.

To follow someone, simply find someone's Twitter profile (more on this later),
and click the Follow button (see Figure 9.5). The user will receive a notification that
they have a new follower.

TWITTER DEMOGRAPHICS

Twitter skews slightly toward women, who make up 53% of users. Twitter users tend
to be under 30 and it is much less popular among older Americans. Urban dwellers
are also more active on Twitter.

One standout point about Twitter users comes in race. Twitter is much more popular among African-American users. Among all African-Americans online, 22% use

FIGURE 9.4

Malcom's home screen with tweets from the accounts he is following (and an ad from Amazon listed as "Promoted").

FIGURE 9.5

The profile summary for NASA. Notice the "Follow" button in the lower right. Clicking this instantly makes the user follow the tweets posted to NASA's account.

Twitter compared with 16% of Caucasian internet users.[6] Among younger people, the rate is even higher with 40% of African-Americans under 30 using Twitter.

FINDING PEOPLE
BY SEARCH

There are two major methods for finding people on Twitter. First is through search. At the top of every Twitter page is a search box. You can see an example of this in Figure 9.4 at the far upper right. You can enter a person's name in that box, and you will get a set of results that are different than what you would find on many other services.

The Twitter search returns a mix of tweets and people that match the search term. Figure 9.6 shows example results if we searched for "Malcom Smith." You can see the three top users who match the search term at the top of the screen, followed by a list of tweets that match.

You can narrow this using the sections on the left. Note the check mark next to "Everything" at the top of the column on the left. If you click on "People," you will see a list of people who have names, usernames, or personal descriptions that match your search term; the results will not include tweets. This is shown in Figure 9.7.

FIGURE 9.6

The results page on Twitter after searching for "Malcom Smith." Notice both people and tweets are listed.

FIGURE 9.7

The "People" section of the Twitter search results page, showing a list of users who match the search term.

As with Facebook, people can be found using their name *or* their email address. Searching for an email address is often an effective way to find people who have chosen not to use their real name on Twitter. Even with a fake name, if you know the email addresses a target uses, you may be able to find them.

BY FOLLOW LISTS

Another way to find people is to look for them in the "Following" and "Follower" lists of their known associates. This is essentially doing a search of the target's social network, even though the network is not explicitly a friend network on Twitter like it is on sites like Facebook.

For example, if we want to find our target Malcom Conroy-Smith and can't find him using search, we may search the lists of his associates. Say we know he associates with the person who runs the account for Hopper Dog, a golden retriever.[7] If we go directly to Hopper Dog's profile page, we can see several relevant links toward the top of the page. Figure 9.8 shows the number of "Following" (people Hopper Dog is following) and "Followers" toward the top of the page.

FIGURE 9.8

The top of Hopper Dog's profile shows the number of people she is following and the number of her followers. Clicking on one of those numbers will link to a list of those people.

FIGURE 9.9

A list of people following Hopper Dog.

Clicking on the number of Following or Followers will take us to a list of those people. For example, if we click on "Following," we see all the people who are following Hopper Dog (see Figure 9.9). We can then browse through this list to see if Malcom Conroy-Smith appears there.

OBTAINING DATA

You can get to a target's page by going to http://twitter.com/«SCREEN-NAME» (where "«SCREEN-NAME»" is replaced with the screen name the person uses on Twitter). Our example target uses @MalcomCsmith as his Twitter screen name, so his profile would be at http://twitter.com/MalcomCsmith.

USER PROFILES

A target's profile contains some basic information about them. (Note that Twitter doesn't have "full" profile pages, like Facebook.) At the top of a person's page, you'll see their name, a short description of themselves, and—if they've chosen to share it—their location.

The location on a user's profile is manually entered; it's not detected from their tweets. So, it could be specific (like a city name), generic (like "Earth"), or even something made up (e.g., "The Hanging Gardens of Babylon 5").

Figure 9.10 shows Malcom's profile.

Malcom Conroy-Smith
@MalcomCSmith

Living the dream in Washington DC with my dog Barley. Fan of beer, hockey, and the two together.

Washington, DC

FIGURE 9.10

Malcom's biographical information from his Twitter profile.

TWEETS

Much more information can be found in the tweets themselves. On a user's profile is a list of their tweets in reverse chronological order. Figure 9.2 above shows a list of Malcom's most recent tweets. The content of the tweets themselves often reveals a lot of information. However, you can find metadata about the tweets that are also very helpful.

TWEET'S TIME

Each tweet has an associated date and time it was posted. At the top of each tweet, you will see the user's real name, followed by their screen name, followed by a date or time.

The specific date and time is not always shown on the user's main page. For example, in Figure 9.2, we can see his top tweet has a date of "Apr 16" but no time. The two tweets below that are also dated "Apr 16" followed by one on "Mar 11."

Clicking on the date (e.g., "Apr 16") takes you to a page for that specific tweet. This page has more extensive data—not only the date and time but also other data. Figure 9.11 shows the detail for Malcom's first tweet from Figure 9.2.

TWEET'S LOCATION

On a specific tweet's page, its location may also be available. Not all tweets will have location information, since users can choose not to share it.

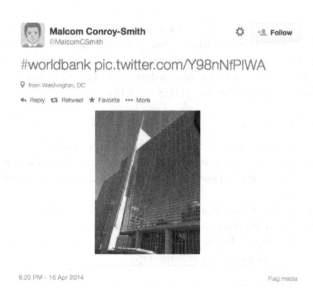

FIGURE 9.11

The details of one of Malcom's tweets. Note the additional date and time information at the bottom of the page. Under the image is a more specific date and time.

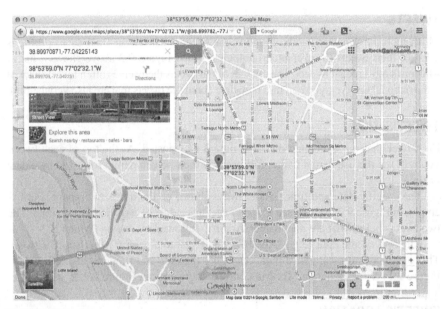

FIGURE 9.12

The map that we are taken to when clicking on the location of Malcom's tweet shown in Figure 9.11. Note that the precise GPS coordinates are given in the location box, and the pin shows the precise location along with the coordinates.

However, when location information is there, it is extremely specific. In Figure 9.11, Malcom's tweet is listed as being in "Washington, DC." This is under the text of the tweet but above the photo next to the pin icon. The name of the city is itself a link. Clicking the link takes you to a detailed Google Map, with a pin marking the exact GPS coordinates of the tweet (Figure 9.12).

FOLLOW LISTS

Finally, friends and followers are available through a person's profile. These social connections are different than what we find in many social networks, since they do not reflect any relationship between the two users. Followers are simply interested in someone's tweets.

This isn't to say that social relationships don't exist on Twitter but rather that they can't be assumed from the presence of a follow relationship.

In this case, looking at the tweets people exchange (especially through @mentions) can reveal the nature of their relationship.

PRIVACY LEVELS AND ACCESS

Privacy is very straightforward on Twitter. Users either can make all of their tweets totally public or can restrict access to their accounts. This is called a "protected" account. In this case, only a user's followers can read the user's tweets, and those followers need to be approved by the user. Estimates put the percentage of protected accounts under 12%, so the vast majority of people have totally public accounts.

There is no mechanism for limiting access to some tweets and not others. Thus, if you find someone's page and it is not marked as protected, you know you are seeing all of the target's tweets.

As mentioned above, direct messages between users are not public. These are similar to email messages sent within Twitter. They are restricted to 140 characters, but access to these direct messages is always limited to the two people participating in the conversation.

EXAMPLE

When users have location information turned on in their Twitter accounts, it can reveal a lot about their lives. Consider our example target Malcom. He has location tagging turned on for almost all of his tweets. We could collect the GPS location of each tweet manually and then plot these on Google Maps or some other mapping tool.

In fact, interest in this kind of analysis is so common that there is a tool to do it called GeoSocial Footprint: http://geosocialfootprint.com.

At that website, you can put in a target's Twitter screen name and it will pull location from the target's last 200 tweets and plot them on a map. As an example, if we put Malcom's screen name into this website, it produces the following map (Figure 9.13).

Each pin marks a location from which Malcom has tweeted. Clicking on the pins pulls up the tweet associated with that location. Thus, not only can we see where Malcom goes, but also we can find out what he is doing in those locations. We can see many tweets centered around his place of work in the center of the screen and in the place he lives (toward the left on the map).

FIGURE 9.13

A heat map from geosocialfootprint.com of Malcom's tweets.

CASE STUDIES

Twitter is a very popular social media site, and it is particularly useful for investigation since almost all tweets are totally public. Thus, it is an easy platform to find out a lot about targets if they have accounts.

FAMILY LAW

Rackham Karlsson, a Boston-area attorney, shared a story with me of a family law case he worked. An unmarried couple with two children had separated and were fighting for custody and child support arrangements. The father claimed he had very little income. The mother knew he had worked as a nightclub promoter, but the father insisted he was not making any money from that job.

Using the father's known email addresses, attorneys were able to find a Twitter account for him under a different name, which he was actively using as part of job as a promoter. This allowed the opposing side to offer evidence both of his deception and of his income that was used to calculate child support.

HIRING AND FIRING

I spoke with many people who were in charge of hiring and firing who reported using Twitter. To my surprise, the majority of their responses were positive; many people emailed me reports of looking up applicants online and being so impressed with their online presence that they made them a job offer. However, as you might expect, some of the more interesting stories were negative.

Mitch Donaberger is the social media manager for Saladworks, a nationwide chain of salad-oriented restaurants with over 100 locations. As part of his job, he monitors employees and the company's reputation online.

One example he gave of how he used Twitter was in investigating a person who posted this photo (Figure 9.14).

The employee tweeted that she had worn flip-flops into an active kitchen—a violation of company policy and health safety laws. To comply, she put bags over the flip-flops and, as we can see, took a photo and posted it. Though she did not reveal her name or location on Twitter, Mr. Donaberger was able to cross-reference it against her other social media accounts and identify her name and general location and ultimately the store she worked in. Within a day, she was fired for damaging the brand through her post.

CRIME

Bad guys use Twitter, too—sometimes to investigate their targets. A dramatic case of this occurred in the United Kingdom.[8]

James Charters, known publicly as DJ Ironik, is a rapper and musician based in the United Kingdom. He has had notable musical success, including his song "Tiny Dancer," which featured Elton John and reached number three on the charts.

FIGURE 9.14

A photo posted by a former Saladworks employee of plastic bags worn over flip-flops in the kitchen.

On November 6, 2010, he was returning home after a performance at the Element Nightclub in Southend-on-Sea in the United Kingdom. As he approached his home, two hooded men attacked him in an apparent robbery. Ironik tried to throw his diamond necklace toward the men and flee, but the attackers managed to stab him in the leg. The wound was severe enough that he spent the weekend in the hospital receiving treatment.

The attackers apparently knew of his location by monitoring his Twitter account. After Ironik had boasted on TV about the value of his jewelry, the muggers monitored his Twitter account to track his location. On the night before the attack, Ironik had tweeted about his performance at the Element Nightclub. The attackers used this to learn when he would be returning home and to wait there to ambush him.

Fortunately, Ironik fully recovered from his attack.

CONCLUSIONS

Twitter is a social media platform where people often post frequent updates. Photos and location information are quite common relative to what you might see on other sites. Also, the privacy issues are relatively simple since a person's tweets are either totally public or completely restricted to approved followers.

While profile information on Twitter is limited, people who post tend to do so frequently, sharing a lot of information about their daily activities.

NOTES

1 Martel, Frances. 2011. "A Twitter Whodunit: Big Government Posts Lewd Photo Suggesting It's From Rep. Weiner". Mediaite.com. http://www.mediaite.com/online/a-twitter-whodunit-big-government-posts-lewd-photo-claiming-it-to-be-of-rep-anthony-weiner/.

2 Preston, Jennifer. 2011. "Conservative Group Scanned Weiner's Twitter Posts, Warned Women". The New York Times. http://www.nytimes.com/2011/06/08/nyregion/conservative-group-scanned-weiners-posts-warned-women.html.

3 Preston, Jennifer. 2011. "Fake Identities Were Used on Twitter to Get Information on Weiner". The New York Times. http://www.nytimes.com/2011/06/18/nyregion/fake-identities-were-used-on-twitter-to-get-information-on-weiner.html.

4 "Rep. Weiner: I Did Not Send Twitter Crotch Pic". 2011. CBS News. http://www.cbsnews.com/news/rep-weiner-i-did-not-send-twitter-crotch-pic/.

5 Memoli, Michael A.; Oliphant, James. 2011. "New Half-Naked Photos: Rep. Weiner Calls a News Conference". The Los Angeles Times. http://articles.latimes.com/2011/jun/06/news/la-pn-anthony-weiner-photos-20110606.

6 Smith, Aaron. 2014. "African Americans and Technology Use". PewResearch Internet Project. http://www.pewinternet.org/2014/01/06/african-americans-and-technology-use/.

7 "Hopper Dog (hopper_dog) on Twitter". 2010. https://twitter.com/hopper_dog.

8 Sheridan, Emily. 2010. "DJ Ironik Stabbed by Muggers Who 'Tracked Him on Twitter'". Mail Online. http://www.dailymail.co.uk/tvshowbiz/article-1327466/DJ-Ironik-stabbed-muggers-tracked-Twitter.html?ito=feeds-newsxml#ixzz14m65t0HC.

Foursquare

10

DESCRIPTION

Foursquare is a location-based social media service. It works primarily on mobile devices, like iPhones and Android phones. Users check in at places like stores, restaurants, sporting arenas, and other venues. Their friends can see where they checked in. There is also a game element of Foursquare. Users receive points for each check-in, and they can see a leaderboard that lists all their friends ranked by the number of points they have.

Foursquare is the most popular location-based social media service behind only Facebook, which offers location-tagging abilities to all of its 1.4 billion users. Foursquare has around 45 million users, with around 6 million check-ins per day.

When a user launches the Foursquare app, they see a list of places near them where they can check in. If a place is not on Foursquare already—for example, if a new restaurant opened—the user can add it. Figure 10.1 shows an example list of nearby places.

When a user chooses a place, they see information about the venue, including the address and hours, business details when appropriate (like if they accept credit cards), tips provided by other users, a map, and the name of the mayor.

Figure 10.2 shows the venue page for the Smithsonian Air and Space Museum. The "mayor" of a venue is the person who has checked in there the most, with higher weight given to more recent check-ins.

On that page at the top is a "**Check In Here**" button. A user may press it to check-in at the venue. At this point, they are shown information that gives them details about their personal experience with the venue. Figure 10.3 shows an example.

After dismissing the check-in info, the user now sees additional information about the venue, including other people currently checked in there. Figure 10.4 shows the additional information that appears on the venue page. Profile pictures for other users are blurred to protect their privacy.

A user receives points for each check-in. The game component of Foursquare allows them to see how many points they have relative to their friends. Through their profile page, a person can see his or her leaderboard, which ranks the user and his or her friends according to points (see Figure 10.5).

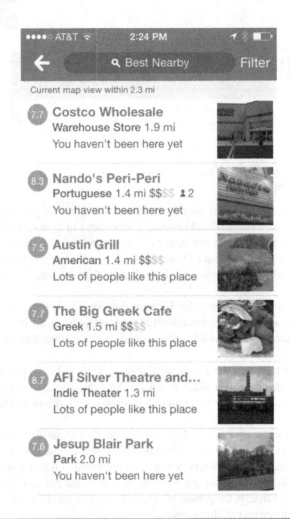

FIGURE 10.1

A list of nearby venues for a user.

FOURSQUARE DEMOGRAPHICS

Foursquare users tend to be male (60% male vs. 40% female) and college-educated (60% have a college degree). It is roughly as popular with younger users (ages 18-29) and slightly older users (ages 30-42), with both comprising about 40% of the user base. The average income is around $50,000 per year. Hispanics also tend to be more frequent users of Foursquare, using check-in services at twice the rate of the overall population.

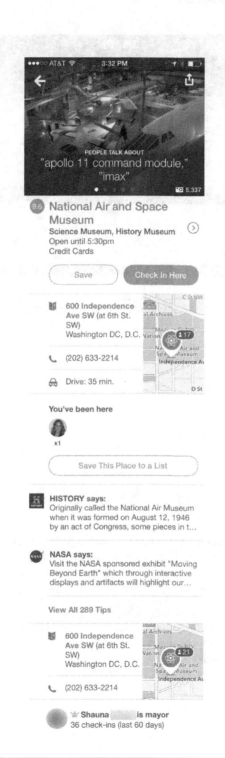

FIGURE 10.2

The Foursquare venue page for the Smithsonian's National Air and Space Museum.

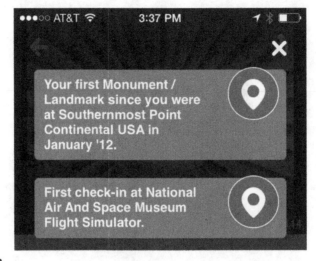

FIGURE 10.3

Example information shown to a user when he or she checks in at a venue.

FIGURE 10.4

Additional information appears on a venue page after a person checks in. In particular, a list of other people checked in is available. Their profiles are blurred here to protect their privacy.

FIGURE 10.5

A leaderboard for a user. Friends and points for each user are shown in this screen.

FINDING PEOPLE
BY FACEBOOK, TWITTER, OR CONTACT INFO

If you are connected to a person on Facebook or Twitter, you can link your accounts and add them that way. If you know the person's email address or mobile phone number, you can put them in your contact list on your mobile phone and then add people that way. These options are shown in Figure 10.6.

BY NAME

Figure 10.6 shows that you can also search for a person by name. If you choose this option, you can search by first or last name. Users' full names and profile pictures will appear in the search results, but the results are usually limited to roughly 100 results (even for searches with common names like "Smith"). Figure 10.7 shows a search results page.

BY FRIENDS' PROFILES

You can also locate people through social contacts. When you look at the public profile of a person, you can see a list of that person's friends. That means even if you are not friends with a target, or if you want to avoid connecting with a target, you can still get to their profile if you can find an associate.

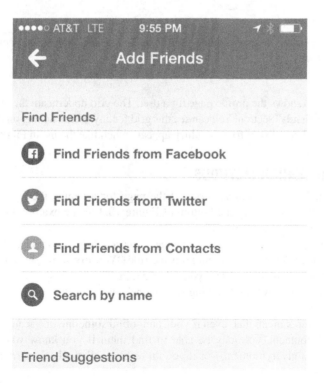

FIGURE 10.6

The screen for adding friends on the iPhone Foursquare app.

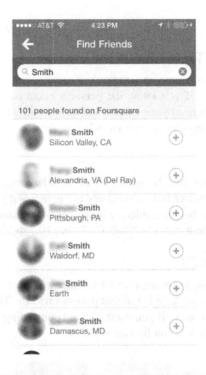

FIGURE 10.7

The result of a search for users named "Smith" on Foursquare. Names and faces are blurred for privacy.

Figure 10.8 shows the profile page for a user. The grid underneath the profile photo includes a "**Friends**" section. You can see this grid for any user. Clicking on that Friends section will link to a list of friends, which appears much like the list in Figure 10.7.

BY OTHER SEARCH METHODS

As mentioned above, when you look at the page for a venue, the mayor is listed. Clicking on the mayorship (the bottom of Figure 10.2 is one example) takes you to the public page for the mayor.

Similarly, when you check in to a venue, you see a list of others checked in there (shown in Figure 10.4). If you click on the title "**You are here**" in that section of the page, it brings up a list of everyone checked in. This list is shown in Figure 10.9 (with blurring for privacy). Clicking on anyone's name in this list will take you to their public page.

These features mean that, even if you cannot find someone in a search or through other social contacts, you may be able to find them if you know where they are checked in at a given moment—or if you know places they check in frequently and may be listed as mayor.

FIGURE 10.8

The home page for a user. The grid in the middle of the page includes a box that links to a list of friends.

OBTAINING DATA

Once you have found a person, you can find out information from their profile. Depending on whether or not you are friends with them on Foursquare, different data is available.

FROM NONFRIENDS

Figure 10.10 shows a profile page for Malcom as it appears to a nonfriend. This is the view you will have if you locate someone through a mayorship, check-in, or someone else's friend list.

This has a grid of icons. The "**Friends**" square in the upper left links to a list of Malcom's friends. The "**Stats**" square in the top center links to a list of *mayorships* that the user holds. This can be extremely informative. A user becomes *mayor* of a place when they check in there very frequently. If a person has many mayorships, it can paint a detailed picture of the places they frequent.

Figure 10.11 shows the mayorships for Malcom on the "**Stats**" page. You can see he is listed as mayor of the IMF, where he works. He is also mayor of a Chipotle restaurant.

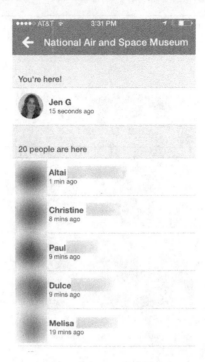

FIGURE 10.9

A list of other people checked in at the same venue as the user. Clicking their name will take you to their public profile page.

FIGURE 10.10

The view of a user's profile when you are not friends with them.

FIGURE 10.11

Malcom's "Stats" page showing his mayorships.

There are many of these restaurants, but clicking on the item in the mayorship list will take you to the venue page for that specific restaurant and show you its address. This could let you know which restaurants Malcom frequents.

Other items on the grid include "**Photos**," which links to pictures the person has taken at different check-ins; "**Tips**," which are tips associated with specific venues; "**Badges**," which list accomplishments in the game component of Foursquare; and "**Lists**," which may include lists of favorite venues or places the person wants to visit.

FROM FRIENDS

Much more information is available to friends. Figure 10.12 shows Malcom's profile page when we are friends with him. Beneath the grid in Figure 10.10, there is a list of the user's check-ins. The list can be scrolled to reveal more check-ins the person has made. Once you hit the bottom of the list, it loads the next batch of check-ins, allowing you to scroll continually back in time.

Each check-in has a date, time, and the location of the check-in. When a user has many check-ins, this list can help you build a profile of their activities, including the places they frequent, the neighborhoods they often visit, and when they tend to be in each area.

Friends may also have access to one another's email address and phone number. In the top right of the profile page (as shown in Figure 10.12), there is a contact link. That will take you to the contact information that a user has made available to friends.

FROM OTHER SOCIAL NETWORKS

Finally, some users connect their Foursquare accounts to other social media, especially Twitter. If you know someone's Twitter account, you may find links to their Foursquare check-ins there. This can give you access to individual check-ins, even if you are not friends with the person on Foursquare. Figure 10.13 shows what a Foursquare check-in looks like on Twitter.

FIGURE 10.12

The view of a profile when you are friends, including a list of the person's check-ins.

If you click on the 4sq.com link in the tweet (or other social media post), it will reveal a Foursquare page for the check-in itself, which includes the specific location, date, and time of the check-in. Figure 10.14 shows the page for the check-in from Figure 10.13.

PRIVACY

Because location information is quite sensitive—especially a very comprehensive list of all the places a person goes, which is available for active Foursquare users—there are many privacy protections available on the service. As seen above, check-in

FIGURE 10.13

A Foursquare check-in on Twitter.

FIGURE 10.14

The Foursquare page for an individual check-in linked from Twitter.

data is only available for a person's friends to see. A user may also control which, if any, of their contact information is visible to friends.

Users can also control how publicly they can be seen. They can prevent them-selves from being seen on the list of people checked in at a venue (as shown in

Figure 10.9). They can also opt out of being eligible for mayorships, since that "office" is always public.

Users cannot opt out of appearing in search results, but they are not required to use their full name. Some only identify by a username, while others (like the author, whose account "**Jen G**" appears in some Figures) use a shortened version of their name.

CASE STUDIES

Despite its privacy controls, Foursquare has been used to investigate people and catch them misbehaving.

ALI ESLAMI

In Middletown, Connecticut, the Community Health Center, a nonprofit medical clinic, used Foursquare check-in data in a complaint against its former information technology director.[1] Ali Eslami, the IT director and "director of innovation," was involved in a complex disagreement with the clinic. He claimed he was fired for revealing information about security weaknesses in the clinic's information systems. The clinic claimed he stole emails and posted them online, illegally obtained patient records, and threatened his superiors online.

The latter claim is where Foursquare entered the picture. After his firing, Eslami posted a message on Twitter, directed at the clinic, that read "**911 dispatch, how can we assist. We need a swat team here**" with a picture of the CEO's house attached. He then used Foursquare to check in at the children's museum founded by the CEO's wife. He also repeatedly checked in at the clinic on Foursquare as he drove past.

The clinic used this information as evidence of "threats" in a complaint filed against Eslami.

CREDIT CARD COMPANIES

Credit card companies are also using Foursquare to analyze people's habits and in particular to predict whether someone is likely to get divorced.[2] The idea is simple: married people tend to patronize different types of businesses than single people. Credit card companies already have insights into this from people's purchases on their cards. However, Foursquare can provide those insights even when people mix cards or pay cash. This lets a card company use a person's behavior to predict credit risk and make decisions about extending credit and managing accounts. It's a large-scale way that Foursquare is used to investigate individuals.

AVOIDR

And in one amusing way to use Foursquare to investigate people, an app called Avoidr connects to Foursquare and helps people avoid their exes.[3] It will track your ex's (or other enemy's) check-ins and let you know where they are, so you never have to run into them.

CONCLUSIONS

Foursquare, a popular location-sharing social media site, allows people to check in at different venues, track where they visit, and earn points in an in-app game with their friends. You can find users by name or social connection or through venues they are visiting or frequently visit.

Without being friends, you can still discover the places a user frequents through mayorships and possibly through their external social media sites, like Twitter, where they may post check-in information. If you *are* friends with a person on Foursquare, you can see the full list of all their check-ins, which allows you to develop a detailed understanding of where they go, when they go there, and what patterns appear in their behavior.

Although Foursquare has conservative privacy policies that allow users to protect a lot of their information, there are many traces that can be picked up about a person and where they go.

NOTES

1 Gecan, Alex. 2014. "Community Health Center Suing a Former IT Director." The Middletown Press. Accessed 2014 July 22. http://www.middletownpress.com/general-news/20140624/community-health-center-suing-a-former-it-director.
2 Dash, Raj. 2010. "Foursquare Becomes Great Predictor Of Divorce." SocialTimes. Accessed 2014 July 22. http://socialtimes.com/foursquare-becomes-great-predictor-of-divorce:b10007.
3 "Foursquare App Helps to Avoid Your Divorced Spouse". 2011. The Law Firm of Charles D. Jamieson, P.A. Accessed 2014 July 22. http://divorcewpb.com/foursquare-app-avoid-ex-spouse/.

Pinterest

11

DESCRIPTION OF THE SITE

Pinterest is a relative newcomer to the social media scene, but it is quickly becoming one of the most prominent sites in terms of driving traffic and holding users' attention.

PINS

The site's premise is simple: it's a visual bookmarking tool. It replicates a more old-fashioned concept; people would cut out pictures or articles from magazines and pin them onto a bulletin board (hence the name *pin*terest) or organize them in folders. Pinterest does the same thing for the web. Users can create a post, called a *pin*, from any site. The pin must be an image. Users can add a caption and the image will have a link back to the original site. Pins are organized on thematic boards.

Figure 11.1 shows an example of an image pinned on Pinterest. It includes information about the top with a button that allows the user currently looking at it to add the image to one of his own boards, a number showing how many other people have pinned the image, and options to like the image, visit the link, or share it.

BOARDS

A Pinterest board is a collection of pins. Figure 11.2 shows a board with images from the Hubble Space Telescope. Clicking on an image will bring up a larger version, such as what is seen in Figure 11.1.

Users can create as many boards as they like on Pinterest. Boards do not need to follow any organizational structure, but they tend to each have a specific theme. Figure 11.3 shows what a user's list of boards might look like. This is the main view of a user's page on Pinterest as well. Clicking on a board will bring you to a page of photos, like in Figure 11.2.

ADDING PINS

People generally add pins to their boards in one of two ways: They repin posts from other users that they find within Pinterest; or they pin content from external sites.

FIGURE 11.1

An example of a single pinned image on the Pinterest site.

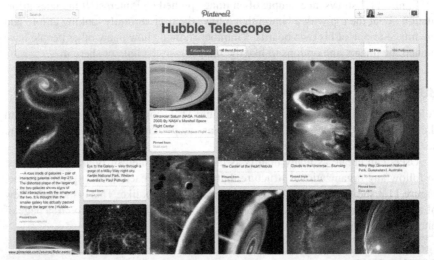

FIGURE 11.2

The first images on a Pinterest board dedicated to the Hubble telescope. Scrolling down will reveal all the other images on the board.

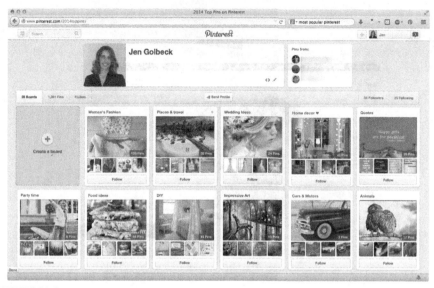

FIGURE 11.3

A list of boards on a user's main page on Pinterest.

Via Repinning

Figure 11.1 shows the red "Pin" button at the top of a post, which allows anyone to repin that photo (with its accompanying link) to their own board.

Pictures and links to external sites can be added in a couple major ways. First, many sites now have built-in functionality to share an item on Pinterest within their own sites. Figure 11.4 shows an example from the *J.Crew* website. Note the Pinterest icon in the lower right (found in the red box, which is added for emphasis).

Clicking the Pinterest icon there brings up a window to create the pin, shown in Figure 11.5. This window is actually part of Pinterest (you can see pinterest.com in the address bar at the top of the page). Once the user clicks the red "Pin it" button, the image is added to the board they have selected.

Via New Pins

The second way people can add images from external sites is by using a Pinterest "bookmarklet" or browser extension. Users can add this extension from the Pinterest site or through their browser's extension marketplace.

Figure 11.6 shows this browser extension at work. It appears as a Pinterest icon to the right of the address bar (a red circle with a curly "P" in it). If users click that, they see a list of all the images on the page. They can choose the one they want and pin it much in the same way as is shown in Figure 11.5.

Users can also upload their own photos from their computer, but this is a much less common way of adding content to the site.

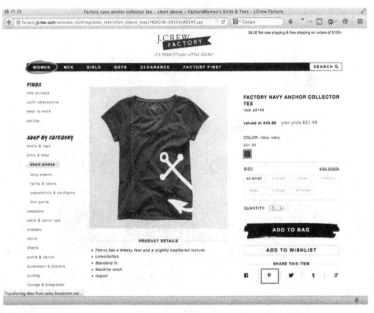

FIGURE 11.4

A T-shirt on the J.Crew website with a Pinterest icon at the bottom (boxed in red) to allow users to easily add it to Pinterest.

FIGURE 11.5

The pin window that appears when a user clicks the Pinterest icon shown in Figure 11.4.

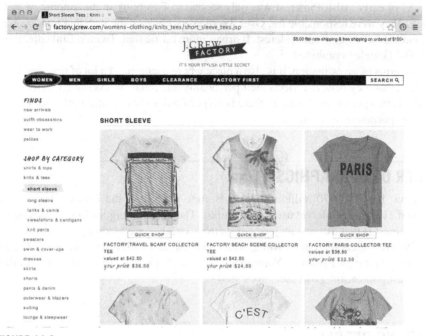

FIGURE 11.6

The Pinterest browser extension appears as a button to the right of the address bar. When clicked, all the pinnable images on the page appear so the user can select which he or she wants to add to a board.

FOLLOWING USERS

The social aspect of Pinterest is in following others. Following on Pinterest works in much the same way as it does on Twitter; users can follow one another, and it is a one-way relationship (i.e., it doesn't require approval or "following back"). When this occurs, any pins from the followed person are displayed on the home page. A person can follow all of another user's boards or select particular boards.

INFLUENCE ON TRAFFIC

The power Pinterest is assuming in the social media space is because of its ability to drive traffic to other sites. Because it is based on the idea of sharing images that link to other places, every pin is a link. Sites have started creating interesting, beautiful, or attention grabbing images specifically to be attractive for sharing on Pinterest. This sharing gets links to their content in front of a large audience.

As of early 2014, Pinterest was only second to Facebook in the amount of web traffic they were responsible for. Over 3% of every click on the web that took people to another site came from Pinterest. It drives more traffic than Twitter, LinkedIn, reddit, and Google+ combined.

In terms of investigation, it is also a place where users spend a lot of time curating content that they believe reflects their personality and interests. As such, it can reveal a lot about a person even though there is no personal text or location information, as is so important on other sites.

USER DEMOGRAPHICS

Pinterest has about 70 million users. It is quite popular in the United States, with around 21% of US internet users on Pinterest. The most distinguishing characteristic of Pinterest is that the vast majority of its users ($\approx$80%) are women.

Pinterest users tend to be white, well educated, and with higher incomes. Age is not a big factor on Pinterest. Younger users ages 18-29 make up around 20% of the Pinterest population as do users ages 30-49.

FINDING PEOPLE

As with many of the social networking sites we have seen, there are two major ways to find people on Pinterest: a direct search for their name and through social connections.

VIA SEARCH

At the top left of each Pinterest page, as you can see in Figures 11.2 and 11.3, is a search box. This is a universal search for pins, boards, and people. You can search for a person by their actual name or by their username. When you search, you will see three tabs toward the top of the window on the left: *Pins*, *Boards*, and *Pinners*. This is shown in Figure 11.7. Clicking the Pinners tab will take you to a list of users who match your search term. While full names and usernames will work here, email addresses will not.

VIA USER PROFILES

If you cannot find someone through a direct search for their real name or username, you might try looking at their profile. For any individual user, you can see the full list of people whom they follow and who follow them. On a person's page, there are tabs for both of these groups, shown in Figure 11.8. If you know or can find the Pinterest page for an associate of your target, you may find the target's profile in one of these lists.

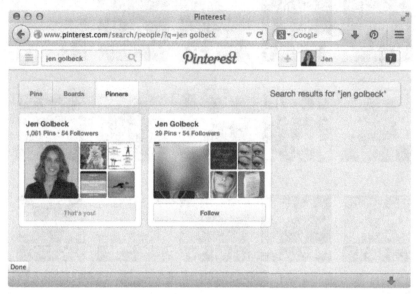

FIGURE 11.7

A search results page on Pinterest.

FIGURE 11.8

The lower right of this image shows the tabs that link to lists of people who follow the user and who the user is following.

OBTAINING DATA

To investigate a target on Pinterest, his main page will be the primary source of information. The boards they have will reveal their interests and tastes, as will the individual pins on them.

For example, consider Figures 11.9-11.12. These show the first fifteen boards of four randomly selected Pinterest users. You should be able to develop a profile for each user with very little additional information; all four users have quite distinct interests.

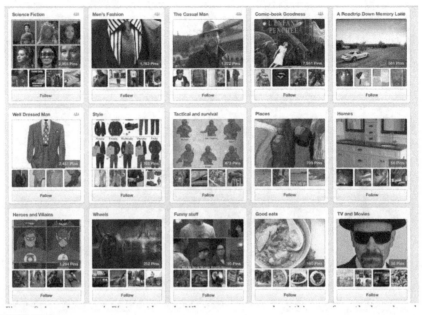

FIGURE 11.9

A random user's Pinterest boards. What can you guess about this user from the boards and pins?

FIGURE 11.10

Another random user's Pinterest boards. This reveals a very different profile of user from Figure 11.9.

FIGURE 11.11

A third random user's Pinterest boards, again showing a different set of interests.

FIGURE 11.12

A final random Pinterest user's boards, showing someone with a particular focus of content on the site.

In fact, the ability of Pinterest to reveal private insights into users' life events is actually something that has been documented in the media on occasion.[1] Because Pinterest allows users to easily collect ideas for planning life events—the two of the most popular search terms on Pinterest are "wedding" and "baby shower"—the creation of boards on a topic has signaled events to friends who follow a person on the site. *Good Morning America* reports many stories of women who started boards on Pinterest to plan their wedding or pregnancy and who received messages in response from friends or family who found out about the upcoming event through the board.

PRIVACY LEVELS AND ACCESS

Privacy on Pinterest is quite straightforward. By default, all boards and pins are public. The only way to change that is to create a "secret" board. These boards can be shared with individual users. Many people can be part of a secret board, but they need to be invited individually. There is no way to create boards visible only to "friends," for example. Secret boards do not show up for anyone other than the user and those invited to the board, so their existence can't be discovered by anyone not authorized to see them.

Since most content is posted from external sites, rather than being personal information uploaded directly, there tends to be less sensitive information shared on Pinterest. As a result, the vast majority of content is public.

CASE STUDIES

Aside from the examples of pregnancy and marriage described above, there are examples of where Pinterest has revealed insights into targets' state of mind or criminal interests.

SHANNON CONLEY

A 19-year-old American girl, Shannon Conley, was arrested on terrorism charges after a six-month dramatic transformation[2]. The girl had met her 32-year-old Tunisian "boyfriend" online at that point and quickly turned to extremist Islam. Her social media interests went from pretty typical teen postings to violent Islamist posts. Her parents had contacted authorities a number of times over the 6 months of her change. She was eventually arrested as she boarded a flight to Turkey, where said she planned to join ISIS (Islamic State of Iraq and Syria), sponsored by her boyfriend.

While her Facebook and Pinterest pages were not used to discover her terrorist activities, they did illustrate the shift in her interests. She posted pictures of herself in a burka and quotes and images promoting violent jihad and that were anti-Christian and Jewish.

REBECCA SHAW

Contact through Pinterest has also led to legal problems for some people. In 2013, Rebecca Shaw was arrested for violating a restraining order because she followed her estranged daughter on Pinterest.[3] Whether or not this was an actual violation of the order is a tricky question. When the mother followed the daughter, Pinterest automatically sent a message informing the daughter of the new follower. The mother did not intentionally contact her daughter. However, the action of following could send a message of "I am watching you," which can be considered threatening. This kind of issue is one that will have to work its way through the courts.

PAUL WEISER

Pinterest revealed similar things about Paul Weiser.[4] He had written to advice-columnist Dear Abby in 2012 about his sexual interest in children. She reported him and he spent several years in prison for possession of child pornography. After his release, he was listed in the Wisconsin Sex Offender Registry.

He fell under suspicion again when he tried to order dolls designed for little girls. Investigators looked at his Pinterest page that included one board called "Things I Love." That board was a collection of photos of open-mouthed preadolescent girls. The Department of Justice eventually discovered he had been recording and photographing children in his neighborhood, and he was rearrested and sent to jail. While the Pinterest pictures themselves were not illegal, they indicated to police that Weiser was still pursuing his sexual interest in children.

CONCLUSIONS

Pinterest is a fast-growing social media site dedicated to visual bookmarking. Users post *pins*, individual photos that link back to their source website. Pins are collected on boards that generally have a common theme. Users can follow other people's boards to keep up to date on what they are pinning.

The vast majority of Pinterest users are women, and they use the site for many purposes, including planning life events. This is one insight you may be able to obtain through a Pinterest investigation. Overall, it is also an excellent reflection of a person's interests and aspirations, allowing you to develop a good understanding of a target's personality and hobbies.

NOTES

1 Effron, Lauren. 2013. "Is Pinterest Revealing Your Secrets, Future Plans Before You Do?." ABC News. http://abcnews.go.com/Technology/pinterest-revealing-secrets-future-plans/story?id=18602589.

2 Parrish, Robin. 2014. "Colorado Nurse Arrested After Plotting Terrorism with Fiancé on Social Networks." Tech Times. http://www.techtimes.com/articles/9685/20140703/colorado-nurse-arrested-plotting-terrorism-fianc%C3%A9-social-networks.htm.

3 http://www.salemnews.com/local/x1196441346/Woman-charged-with-using-Pinterest-to-violate-restraining-order/print.

4 Sanchick, Myra. 2014. "Back in Jail: Years Ago, a Sex Offender Wrote 'Dear Abby' about His Fantasies, so What Now? | FOX6Now.com." Fox 6 Now. http://fox6now.com/2014/07/11/back-in-jail-years-ago-a-sex-offender-wrote-dear-abby-about-his-fantasies-so-what-now/.

LinkedIn

12

INTRODUCTION

One of the best stories of using LinkedIn for investigation comes from Michael Lewis's book *Flash Boys*. The book is about a group of guys who work on Wall Street and realize that a type of computerized trading, high-frequency trading (HFT), has biased the equity market in favor of the big investment banks. The group, the eponymous flash boys, set out to investigate the big banks and expose how they are using HFT.

As part of their search, one of the men, John Schwall, begins searching for people involved in HFT on LinkedIn. However, many banks did not want to appear as though they were involved in HFT. Thus, they did not advertise their HFT groups, and their employees did not have titles that reflected this.

Schwall was determined to identify the people involved in HFT. He began with one person, Josh Stampfli, who had joined the electronic trading group at Credit Suisse after working for now-disgraced investor Bernie Madoff. After identifying Stampfli as being involved with HFT at Credit Suisse, Schwall looked him up on LinkedIn and, from there, found a list of his contacts. From there, he followed to a list of their contacts, and so on. Among the people he came across were dozens of programmers who openly listed their responsibilities as including programming for HFT. At the end of his search, Schwall was able to construct the entire organizational chart for the group at Credit Suisse undertaking HFT.

DESCRIPTION OF THE SITE

LinkedIn is a social networking website where people maintain profiles and create connections with associates. It is explicitly designed for professional interactions. The site has roughly 200 million members, with roughly one-third of its traffic coming from the United States. Profiles are extensive and focus on education, work experience, projects a person has worked on, and a list of skills that others endorse.

Since LinkedIn is very professional, instead of creating a fake account for our example user Malcom, we will look at the author's profile in this chapter. Pictures and names of other users are blurred out in the images to protect their privacy.

The main activities on LinkedIn are profile maintenance and adding contacts.

USER PROFILES

A user's profile consists of a number of sections, set up to approximate what you might find on a resume. They include work experience, education, projects, publications, skills, and organizations. Figure 12.1 shows the author's profile with summary information and the beginning of the experience section.

VIEWING PROFILES

Because professional networking is the core of LinkedIn's model, there are some important things to note about accessing information on the site:

- If you are not logged in, you see a different version of a person's profile than if you are logged in.
- If you have an account and are logged in, when you visit a person's profile, your visit is logged and information about your visit is shared with the target. (You can browse "anonymously" while logged in, but you need to change specific settings to make it happen.)

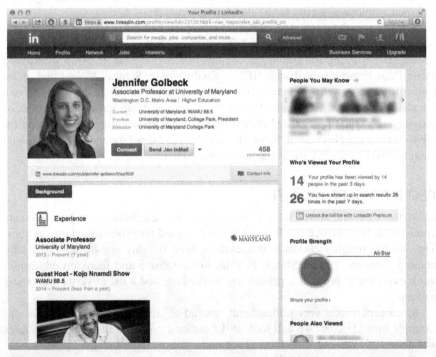

FIGURE 12.1

A LinkedIn profile page including summary information and some background.

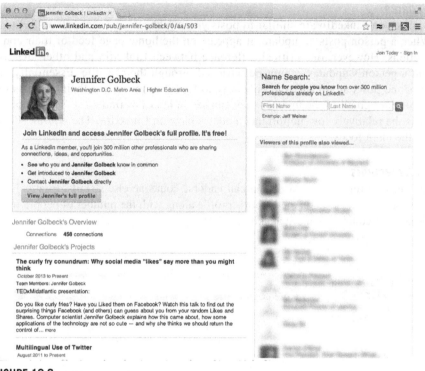

FIGURE 12.2

A profile view when the viewer is not logged in to LinkedIn.

This makes LinkedIn a significant exception to the general rule that your social media browsing will not be tracked.

Figure 12.1 shows a profile's appearance when the viewer is logged in. If the viewer is not logged in, a more résumé-like profile is shown. Figure 12.2 depicts the author's profile in the logged-out view.

ADDING CONTACTS

To create a social connection on LinkedIn, the "Connect" button next to the person's photo on their profile page (also shown in Figure 12.1) will launch a dialogue. The person initiating the connection must indicate he knows the person he is connecting to, either through their work at the same organization, through a shared educational institution, or by providing an email address. This is designed to limit spam and anonymous connections, since the site wants to encourage real-life connections. All relationships on LinkedIn are reciprocal; when one person requests a connection, the other must approve it.

Once people have made connections, there are two main activities: updates and endorsements.

Updates

Updates on LinkedIn are similar to posts you might see on Facebook or Twitter. When a person posts an update, it appears on the home page feed of their connections. However, one critical difference between LinkedIn and other sites is that a person's updates cannot be retrieved through their profile. Essentially, if someone posts an update, the only way to find it is for one of their contacts to scroll through all of the updates they can see in hopes of finding it. This emphasizes the relatively low-importance updates have on LinkedIn. The relationships are the main focus.

Endorsements

As part of a relationship, a person can endorse someone else's skills. Figure 12.3 shows the list of skills on the author's profile along with the number of people who have endorsed that she has that skill.

FIGURE 12.3

A list of endorsements for the author's LinkedIn page.

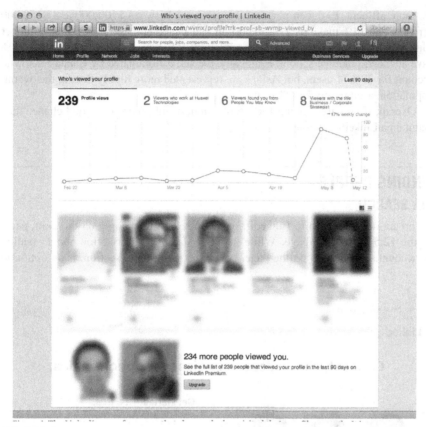

FIGURE 12.4

The LinkedIn page for a user that shows who has visited their profile recently. It is rare among social media websites that a user can see who has been viewing their information.

Viewing the Viewers

Finally, because social connections are so important on LinkedIn, it has a very unique feature: a user can see who has been looking at his profile. Figure 12.4 shows the author's page of views. Faces and names of people who viewed the profile are blurred for anonymity.

The view in Figure 12.4 is what someone with a free LinkedIn profile can see. People who pay to upgrade their accounts can see additional information and longer lists of people who have visited their page.

USER DEMOGRAPHICS

Because LinkedIn is a professional site, it has demographics that are quite different from most social media sites. It tends to have more men than women, about 62% to 38%. The population of users is older than many other sites. The 25-34, 35-44, and 45-54-year-old age groups each make up about 20% of the users on the site. Users are more affluent. Eighteen percent of users make between $100,000 and $150,000 per year, and 14% make over $150,000. In that same vein, users tend to have higher education levels than the overall US population; 78% have a college degree, and 27% have attended graduate school. Ethnically, the site is dominated by Caucasians, who account for 79% of users, but Asians are represented more highly than in the overall population, accounting for 6% of the users.

Overall, if you are looking for a professional adult, there is a good chance they maintain a LinkedIn profile.

FINDING PEOPLE
VIA SEARCH

If you are not logged in to LinkedIn, you can search for people on the main page. Figure 12.5 shows this page. While it largely features information about creating an account, lower down on the page, below the main white section, is an option to

FIGURE 12.5

If you are not logged in to LinkedIn, you can search for people with the "Find a colleague" section that appears under the main white part of the page. In this example, "Jennifer" and "Golbeck" are filled in the first and last name sections.

"Find a colleague." This includes first and last name boxes. The results of this search will be similar to what is shown in Figure 12.2. If multiple people match the search, you will see short summaries for each, similar to what appears in the top section of Figure 12.2 next to the photo.

You cannot access any more information about people from this point unless you log in to LinkedIn.

When you are logged in, you get a denser set of search result as shown in Figure 12.6. From here, you can click on a person's name to see their full profile as it appears in Figure 12.1. (Remember: visiting someone's LinkedIn page while you are logged in leaves a trace that the person can see.) Either a link to your profile or a slightly anonymized version of your profile without a link will be shown to the user on the page shown in Figure 12.4. This means you should carefully consider how you browse someone's LinkedIn profile.

VIA KNOWN ASSOCIATES

On other sites, it is possible to find someone through their known associates, but this ability is much more limited on LinkedIn. You cannot see someone's social connections if you are not logged in to LinkedIn. If you are logged in, you can see how many connections a target has (this is in the lower right corner of the top box in Figure 12.1). However, you can only see a full list of who those connections are when you have a LinkedIn relationship with the target. If you are exploring the target's profile and you are not connected to the target, you can only see people who are your mutual connections. If you have no mutual connections, you cannot see anyone on the target's connection list.

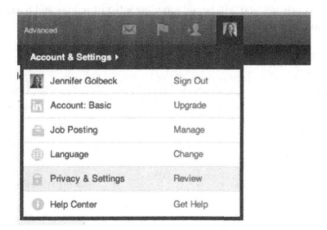

FIGURE 12.6

To change your privacy settings, including the ability to browse anonymously, click "Review" next to "Privacy & Settings."

Thus, if you do not know where the target's account is, you may be able to find him by connecting with his known associates. This allows you to browse the associate's connections. Without connections to people close to the target, this technique will not be effective on LinkedIn.

OBTAINING DATA

As mentioned above, LinkedIn records information about your visits to other people's profiles. This is an important factor to consider if you do not want targets to know that you have visited their profiles. If you want to browse anonymously, you must change a setting.

In the upper right corner, mouse over your profile picture and click "Review" next to "Privacy & Settings" (see Figure 12.6).

About halfway down the privacy settings page, find the section labeled Privacy Controls (see Figure 12.7). Click on "Select what others see when you've viewed their profile."

The pop-up will show three options. To browse anonymously, choose the bottom option, "You will be totally anonymous." The middle "anonymous" option will not truly anonymized your browsing. See Figure 12.8 for the options in this window.

There are two major types of data you can obtain on LinkedIn for a target:

- *Profile information* is accessible on a target's page, as shown in Figures 12.1 and 12.2. This includes work history, interests, projects they have worked on, and publications.
- *Contact information* (a list of the target's connections) is available for people with whom you have a LinkedIn relationship. In Figure 12.1, you can see a number of contacts in the lower right of the summary profile box toward the top of the page. This number appears in blue and is "458" in Figure 12.1. Clicking this number will take you to a list of the person's contacts. If he has not made the contacts private, you will be able to view a list of names and basic profile information, and then, click links to see the contacts' profile pages.

FIGURE 12.7

Click "Select what others see when you've viewed their profile" (highlighted here in blue (dark grey in print version)) to change the privacy settings for your browsing on LinkedIn.

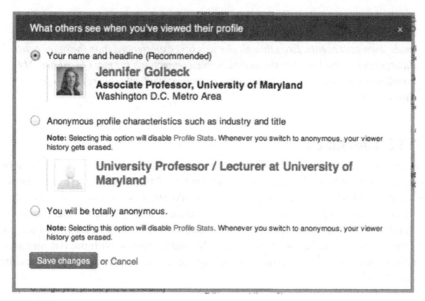

FIGURE 12.8

Choose the bottom option "You will be totally anonymous" to prevent people from seeing your information when you browse their profile.

PRIVACY LEVELS AND ACCESS

Users can limit the accessibility of some of their profile information. They can restrict who can see their profile photo, limiting it to only connections or only people within the user's network. They can also restrict the visibility of their connections (i.e., friends). Those are visible to the user's other connections by default, but they can be limited so only the user himself can view them.

CASE STUDIES

Because LinkedIn is business-oriented, most of the case studies for how it is used in investigation deal with hiring and firing decisions.

GETTING HIRED

Heidi Nazarudin, president of bloggerbabes.com, reports how she has used LinkedIn in her hiring decisions:

> *I was looking for a Content Manager and, there were about 6-7 shortlisted candidates but one candidate stood out considerably due to the fact that ...checking out her LinkedIn profile, had about 2000+ connections from the print and digital*

media industries. Upon asking her about this she told me she once worked as an event manager for a media association and those people were contacts she had made from past events. Even though she was less experienced than the other candidates, due to the fact that she had valuable connections for me, I hired her. My hunch proved right and until today, her contacts proved valuable regularly for me time and time again.

NOT GETTING HIRED

A poor LinkedIn profile can also prevent someone from getting a job. Michelle Campbell of the advertising agency Potratz explained to me that the HR director for their company had looked up an applicant on LinkedIn. For an advertising company, someone's ability to present themselves well online speaks directly to their ability to sell products. This particular candidate had an extensive list of past jobs on LinkedIn, but none of these matched with experience he had discussed with the HR manager. The disconnect made her question all the experience the candidate reported, and he was not hired.

LEGAL MATTERS

Family lawyers have also reported to me that they use LinkedIn. For them, it serves more as background information. In particular, they describe using it to determine someone's employment status (which they may be hiding to reduce alimony or child support obligations).

CONCLUSIONS

LinkedIn is a business-oriented professional network. As such, the information there is mainly relevant to someone's work experience and employment information. The major consideration for an investigator using LinkedIn is that it is hard to access information without having an account and being logged in *and* that your visits to a person's page are logged and visible to them. You can adjust this, but if you want to browse anonymously, it is important to change this setting first.

Google+

13

INTRODUCTION: BEFORE GOOGLE+

Google+ (pronounced, and sometimes written, as "Google Plus") is Google's online social networking platform. It is similar to Facebook in many ways.

Before we get into the details of Google+, it is interesting to look at Google's history of social networking platforms.

ORKUT

One of Google's earliest ventures into social networking was with a platform called Orkut. Launched in 2004, it was similar to many social networks at the time, including Myspace. It became quite popular, especially in India and Brazil. However, it failed to keep up with Facebook in the US market.

GOOGLE BUZZ

To compete in the growing social networking space, Google launched Google Buzz in 2010. The launch is almost universally agreed to have been a disaster because of major privacy issues. Google automatically created a Google Buzz account for everyone who used Gmail, Google's email system. They opted all these users in, turned on their accounts, and publicly listed the names of the people each person corresponded with most frequently in Gmail. Thus, without any action by a user, Google shared all this information with the world. The privacy implications of this became clear quickly.

Business Insider lists a few troubling possible scenarios.[1] A husband's profile shows that he has had a lot of contact with an ex. A boss sees that a competitor is a top contact of his employee. What about the case where journalists are emailing confidential, anonymous sources? Those sources could be revealed. Physicians and therapists who used Gmail to correspond with their patients would have their patients' identities revealed as well—a legal violation and a privacy violation.

One case where this had implications was from a woman who had a serious need to keep her information private. She wrote the following about her problems[2]:

> I use my private Gmail account to email my boyfriend and my mother. There's a BIG drop-off between them and my other "most frequent" contacts.

You know who my third most frequent contact is? My abusive ex-husband.

Which is why it's SO EXCITING, Google, that you AUTOMATICALLY allowed all my most frequent contacts access to my Reader, including all the comments I've made on Reader items, usually shared with my boyfriend, who I had NO REASON to hide my current location or workplace from, and never did.

My other most frequent contacts? Other friends of [boyfriend] Flint's.

Oh, also, people who email my ANONYMOUS blog account, which gets forwarded to my personal account. They are frequent contacts as well. Most of them, they are nice people. Some of them are probably nice but a little unbalanced and scary. A minority of them—but the minority that emails me the most, thus becoming FREQUENT—are psychotic men who think I deserve to be raped because I keep a blog about how I do not deserve to be raped, and this apparently causes the Hulk rage.

Google eventually corrected many of these issues, but in a sense, the damage was done. The public outcry at the launch of the site and discussion of major privacy flaws led to users having low trust in the site. It was shut down after less than two years.

DESCRIPTION OF THE SITE
THE RELEASE OF GOOGLE+

Google+ came next and has been Google's most successful rival to Facebook. It focused on the importance of privacy from the start, important both because of the history with Buzz and because Facebook was actively criticized for its privacy issues at the time. Google+ was, in part, promoted as a privacy-respecting alternative.

Google+ has roughly 550 million active users, which makes it extremely popular, but with less than half of Facebook's usage. Many more people *could* use Google+, since anyone with a Google account—used for Gmail, Search, and even YouTube—can instantly set up an account on Google+. Indeed, Google is working to make Google+ a more engrained part of their other experiences, linking Google+ accounts to YouTube, for example.

Aside from its role in other Google products, there are many features of the Google+ site itself. Its functionality is similar to Facebook's in many ways.

Posts

Users can post status updates. They can be text-only or they can have pictures, videos, links, or events created within Google+. Figure 13.1 shows a sample status update being created.

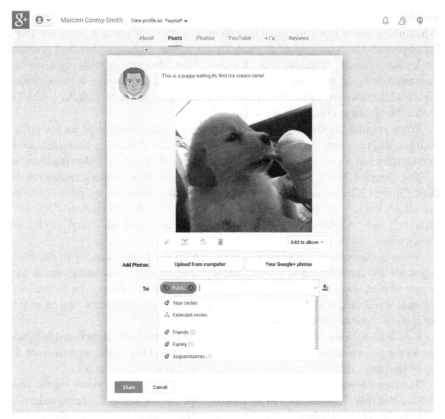

FIGURE 13.1

Posting a status update on Google+.

Also shown in Figure 13.1 is the "To:" feature of the Google+ status update. This is essentially the privacy level for a post; it indicates who can view the post within Google+. Users may also share photos and links from external sites through a Google "g+" button. Clicking this brings up a post window, like that shown in Figure 13.1, so users don't have to worry about saving or copying information to upload it through the Google interface.

The current setting shown in Figure 13.1 is for a public post, visible to anyone. However, the pull-down menu shows a number of other options. These are based on the idea of "circles," which is part of the core of Google+.

Before getting into the details of circles, it is important to note one major difference between Google+ and Facebook. On Facebook, friendships are mutual. If a person adds "Bob" as a friend, Bob must approve that friendship to create the relationship. On Google+, this is not the case. Google+ uses more of a Twitter model where users follow one another. Those relationships do not have to be mutual nor approved. Thus, users can follow anyone they like. Those people may follow back but they do not have to.

Circles

When users follow someone, they add them to a circle. A circle is basically just a list of people. Users can create as many circles as they like. Google offers premade circles for "Friends," "Family," and "Acquaintances," but a circle with any name can be created. When a user follows someone, they can add them to one or more circles. Figure 13.2 shows the menu that appears for adding someone to a circle, which includes the option to create a new circle.

When posting, as shown in Figure 13.1, a user can choose to share his update with people in any single circle or from multiple circles. When they share, anyone in those circles has permission see the content—even if they are not following the user.

The Google+ home page shows updates from all of a person's circles by default. Figure 13.3 shows Malcom's home page. Across the top of the page is a menu that allows the user to choose different circles. The three default circles—"Friends," "Family," and "Acquaintances"—have their own tabs, and additional circles are shown under "More."

When a user makes a post, it will show up on the home page, or in the circle pages, for anyone who has followed him. If a user creates a post and shares it with people who have *not* followed him (e.g., a celebrity that he follows), the person with whom it was shared will not see the post on her own home page but would be able to see it if she came to the user's profile page.

Figure 13.4 shows Malcom's profile page. The default view, shown in this figure, has all the posts by a user. Notice that "Posts" is highlighted on the menu toward the top of the page. This view also includes the people in the user's circles.

The menu toward the top of the page includes several other views for the user. Photos, YouTube, and Reviews show specific types of content as the name indicates. Note that YouTube and Reviews are actually pulling content from these other Google services that the user would have accessed with his Google account.

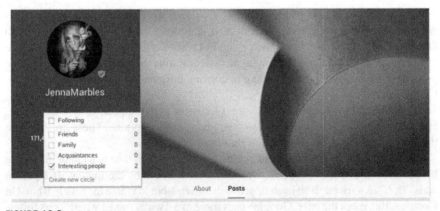

FIGURE 13.2

The menu for adding someone to a circle.

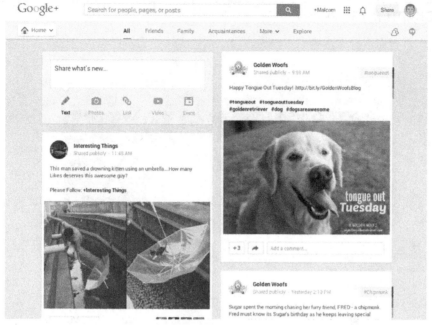

FIGURE 13.3

Malcom's Google+ home page. Note the menu across the top with different circles listed.

FIGURE 13.4

Malcom's posts on Google+, the default view for his profile page.

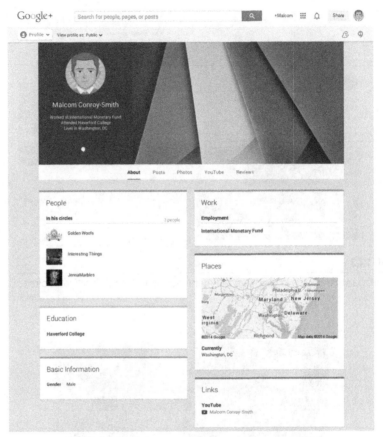

FIGURE 13.5

Malcom's "About" section in his profile page, which includes personal and background information.

The About section contains profile information, similar to what you would find in the About section for a user on Facebook. Figure 13.5 shows Malcom's About section. This includes another list of people in Malcom's circles as well as demographic and personal information.

It is difficult to see where to draw the line on what counts as a Google+ feature versus what counts as a different Google service. For example, Google advertises Hangouts (their group video chat service) as part of Google+, even though it can be used otherwise. For the purposes of this book and in the interest of investigation, we have limited our view to the core social networking features.

USER DEMOGRAPHICS

Google+ is sometimes touted as the world's largest social network, with 1.5 billion users, though this is misleading. This counts everyone who has a Google account as a user, though the majority of those people are not actively using Google+ in any real way. Google has pushed adoption of Google+. For example, anyone who wants to comment on a YouTube video (YouTube is owned by Google) needs to have a Google+ account. Thus, many people may technically have Google+ accounts and use them to comment on YouTube, but they may otherwise ignore the site entirely.

Because Google account holders are such a large percentage of the population, it is hard to gauge exactly what demographics are unique to Google+. However, the consensus of online demographic studies is that Google+ trends dramatically male, with men comprising over ⅔ of active users on the site.[3] Users also tend to be more technically oriented and younger than their Facebook counterparts.[4]

FINDING PEOPLE

Google+ has a number of ways to search for people. The most straightforward is to type a name into the search box at the top of every page. You can see examples of this in Figures 13.3–13.5, above. All people with matching names will be returned as results of the search.

Their "Find People" interface[5] offers a number of search options. Figure 13.6 shows the main page for finding people. In the center is a list of options to connect email accounts to search for contacts on Google+. Beneath that, Google+ has looked at the employer Malcom listed on his account—the International Monetary Fund— and found a list of other Google+ users who have also listed it. On the left, there is a menu that allows Malcom to see others who have listed his employer or alma mater (Haverford College). Clicking on those links will bring up a list of people that share the trait.

Beneath that are options to search for coworkers or classmates. Figure 13.7 shows the window that pops up when searching for a coworker (the classmate interface is basically the same). The user can type in an organization's name, and Google will help complete the name to help find the right match. Note that beneath that is a box that is checked that adds this place of business to the user's profile as somewhere they worked. That box needs to be unchecked in order to search any organization without adding it to the profile. The results of this search will be anyone who has the organization listed as a place they worked. The same logic applies to searches for classmates; people who have listed a school in their profile will appear in those search results.

Searching through social connections is also a viable option on Google+. If you cannot find a target, but you know who his or her associates are, you might be able to

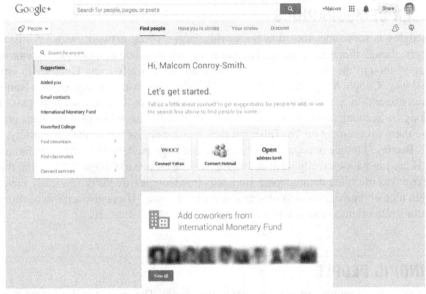

FIGURE 13.6

The main Find People interface on Google+.

FIGURE 13.7

The coworker search box in Google+.

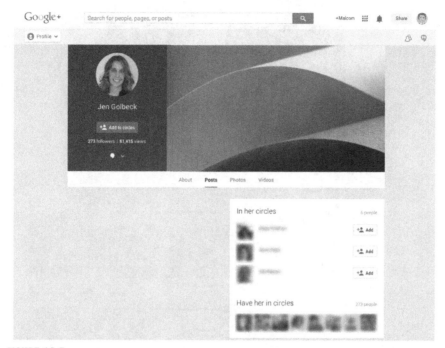

FIGURE 13.8

When looking at a user's profile, you can see people they follow ("In her circles") and people that follow the user ("Have her in circles"). This can aid a social search for a target.

find the target through them. Figure 13.8 shows the profile page for a user. Even though Malcom is not friends with the user, we can see two social sections: "In her circles," which lists people the user follows, and "Have her in circles," which lists people who follow this user. Next to each section is a list of the number of people. Clicking that number will bring up a browsable list of associates that you can look through to find a target.

At the time of writing, Google+ does not support search directly for a person's email account. However, if you link your email account (as shown in Figure 13.6) and you have the target in your contact list, you may be able to locate them that way.

OBTAINING DATA

Once you have located a target on Google+, there are a few types of information you can obtain about him. First, on his Google+ page, there is an "About" link under his profile picture at the top of the page. That will take you to his profile, which includes information like where the person works, where they went to school, descriptive personal text, and demographics like gender, age, and relationship status. Figure 13.9 shows Malcom's profile page.

FIGURE 13.9

Malcom's Google+ profile.

Figure 13.9 also shows links to other sections of a user's page under his profile photo and next to the "About" link. These include pages with posts and photos, along with links to videos the person posted on YouTube and reviews he has written within Google. These all can be valuable sources of information about what a user is doing. Each post has an associated date and time. Figure 13.4 shows examples of dates and times shown next to a post.

PRIVACY LEVELS AND ACCESS

As mentioned above, posts, including pictures and links, are shared according to "circles" of people the user has set up. Similarly, profile information can be shared with different groups of people. Figure 13.10 shows the window the user sees when editing his profile. For each box, he can choose a privacy level. The menu for the "Occupation" section is shown open. The user can share with different levels of people, including "Your Circles" (essentially, everyone the user follows), and a custom level. This latter option lets the user choose specific circles or even specific individuals who can see the information. These same settings are available for all profile information, including lists of circles. Thus, it is possible you will be able to see

FIGURE 13.10

The privacy options for profile sections are shown. Users can control who is able to view each piece of profile data.

profile information and posts for a target if you can find him on Google+, but it is not assured since privacy levels could prevent you from accessing this data. Of course, if the user adds you to one of his or her circles, you are more likely to gain access.

CASE STUDIES
AN UNWANTED INVITATION

A recent and high profile story of someone getting himself into trouble with Google+ is that of a man who was arrested for an automatic invitation sent to his ex-girlfriend.

When users sign up for Google+, Google prompts them to invite people to be their friends or to join. That can include inviting all of the user's contacts through a variety of email services. Google also invites people in ways users may not understand. *Fast Company* explains:

> *Some users have even complained that Google is mining Gmail contacts to send out Google+ notifications. For example, when users register for Gmail, they're automatically welcomed to Google+, too. And by default, when someone joins Google+ and that person is in your Gmail contacts, Google will automatically send you a notification, along with an invitation suggesting that you "add him [or her] to your circles to stay connected." The same occurs if someone adds you to a Google+ circle. (Users have the option of adjusting these settings.)[6]*

In this case, it is unclear what the arrested man did to send the invitation. What is clear is that his ex-girlfriend had a restraining order against him. When she received the Google+ invitation, she took it to the police who arrested him a couple hours later for violating the restraining order.

Initially, the man protested that he had no idea how the invitation was sent. For an average user, that would make sense. However, in his profile, he describes himself as an "IT Pro/Software Dev[eloper]"—someone who should understand when they take an action that would send a social media invitation. The man later admitted that the prosecution would have been able to prove that he did indeed send the invitation.[7]

STEINMETZ

Google+ was used as part of another investigation, when scientist Peter Steinmetz was arrested for bringing a riffle into Phoenix Sky Harbor International Airport.[8] Police and journalists turned to his social media accounts, including Google+, to understand his motivations. On his account, he had posted links and comments indicating he was a gun-rights advocate. Figure 13.11 shows an example of one such post.

At the time of writing, his case is still in progress.

FIGURE 13.11

A public post from Peter Steinmetz indicating an interest in gun rights.

CONCLUSIONS

Google+ is a comprehensive social networking website with many features similar to Facebook. Users can post updates, maintain profiles, and connect with friends. The social relationships on Google+ are more like those on Twitter. Users do not need to have mutual friendships and do not need to approve relationships created by other people.

Through profile information and posts, it is possible to gain a lot of insights into a target. And many people are using Google+, either explicitly for its social networking features or because they have accounts established through their use of other Google services.

NOTES

1 Carlson, Nicholas. 2010. "WARNING: Google Buzz Has A Huge Privacy Flaw." Business Insider. http://www.businessinsider.com/warning-google-buzz-has-a-huge-privacy-flaw-2010-2.

2 Arthur, Charles. 2010. "Google Buzz's Open Approach Leads to Stalking Threat." The Guardian. http://www.theguardian.com/technology/blog/2010/feb/12/google-buzz-stalker-privacy-problems.

3 Heino, Hilary. 2014. "Social Media Demographics—LinkedIn and Google+." Agile Impact. http://agileimpact.org/social-media-demographics-linkedin-google/.

4 Frasco, Stephanie. 2013. "A Google+ Overview: Breaking Through Misconceptions." Social Media Today. http://www.socialmediatoday.com/content/google-overview-breaking-through-misconceptions.

5 http://plus.google.com/people/find.

6 Carr, Austin. 2014. "Google+ Invite Lands Man In Jail." Fast Company. http://www.fastcompany.com/3024452/google-invite-lands-man-in-jail.

7 Manganis, Julie. 2014. "Man Admits to Evidence He Contacted Ex." The Salem News. http://www.salemnews.com/local/x2117391343/Man-admits-to-evidence-he-contacted-ex.

8 Stern, Ray. 2014. "Barrow Neurological Institute Puts Peter Steinmetz, AR-15-Toting Doctor, On Leave." The Phoenix New Times. http://blogs.phoenixnewtimes.com/valley-fever/2014/07/barrow_neurological_institute_puts_peter_steinmetz_ar-15-toting_doctor_on_leave.php.

Tumblr

14

DESCRIPTION OF THE SITE

Tumblr is a microblogging website. Users can post photos, videos, and text blog entries. There is no character limit (as on Twitter), but the site is organized and presented in a way that favors shorter content.

POSTING

The top of the Tumblr page has options for users to create posts. There are seven post types (see Figure 14.1): Text, Photo, Quote (a stylized text post), Link, Chat (another stylized type of text), Audio, and Video.

Selecting any post type brings up a simple interface for either entering text or uploading a file. Figure 14.2 shows the interface for creating a text post.

Posts are published to a Tumblr blog created by the user. Figure 14.3 shows part of Malcom's Tumblr blog.

HASHTAGS

Hashtags are used very frequently within Tumblr. Figure 14.3 shows a couple on the photo Malcom has posted. Since photos are a very common type of media to share on Tumblr, hashtags improve the searchability of content.

SHARING

In addition to creating their own content, users have the option to share posts by others through *reblogging*. At the bottom of each post is a double arrow icon. (See Figure 14.3, in the lower right corner of Malcom's first photo post.) Clicking that brings up a window where users can add comments and repost the original item to their own blogs. These appear in the list of posts, similar to how retweets on Twitter will appear on a user's page.

Users can also like posts by clicking the small heart next to the reblog post.

FOLLOWING

Users can also follow others. When they do, posts from other users appear on their dashboard. Figure 14.4 shows Malcom's dashboard. It includes his most recent posts along with those from other people. The dashboard is visible only to the user who controls it.

FIGURE 14.1

The post types on Tumblr.

FIGURE 14.2

The interface to create a text post on Tumblr.

Tumblr users can control the appearance of their blogs. Malcom's blog in Figure 14.3 is the simple, default appearance, or *theme*. Users can choose alternate themes. Some of these may show additional information, such as who the user follows or which posts they have liked.

USER DEMOGRAPHICS

Tumblr is smaller than some of the sites we have covered in this book. Estimates suggest it has 30-50 million active users. But Tumblr's parent company, Yahoo!, claimed they receive 300 million unique visitors each month. This difference can be accounted for by people who visit the site to look at content without having accounts.

Tumblr has a very young audience, with nearly half its members aged between 16 and 24. It also has a higher population of Hispanic users than might be expected. They make up roughly 20% of Tumblr users—twice the representation of Hispanic users online. The male-female split is pretty even, with women accounting for a few percentage points more of the population than men.

FIGURE 14.3

Malcom's Tumblr blog.

FINDING PEOPLE

Tumblr has a search option, but it's designed mainly to find content, not individual users. For example, consider a search for "Robert Smith" as a common example name. Tumblr's search results are shown in Figure 14.5. The results consist of blogs that mention Robert Smith in the title (generally about the lead singer for The Cure).

VIA AUTOCOMPLETE

The autocompleted suggestions under the search bar (in the upper right) show blogs that have similar names to the search term. The results on the page include blogs that mention the name, followed by posts that mention it. You may be able to find a user this way.

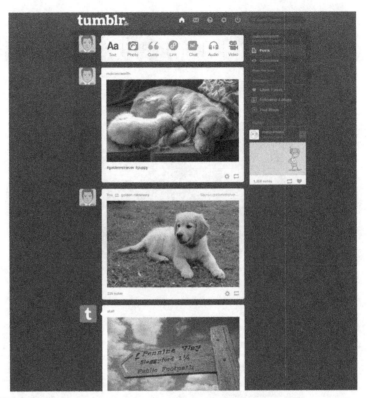

FIGURE 14.4

Malcom's Tumblr dashboard. It shows his posts and posts from people he follows.

FIGURE 14.5

Search results on Tumblr.

FIGURE 14.6

An example of a grid of icons that show who a user is following.

VIA KNOWN USERNAMES

If you know a common username used by the target, another option is to directly test it as a Tumblr blog name. Simply go to `http://«username».tumblr.com`, where «username» is replaced with the target's username.

VIA "FOLLOWING" LISTS

Most people do not share a list of people they follow on their blogs. However, some users choose to add this. It generally appears as a grid of icons, each representing the main picture of the blog being followed. Figure 14.6 shows an example (with the icons blurred to protect users' privacy).

When this is available, you may be able to perform a social search for a target. If you can find an associate of the target and if that associate has a list of people he or she follows, searching that list may turn up the target's account.

OBTAINING DATA

It is possible to browse Tumblr without having an account. After you have found a target, the main source of data you will find about him is in the posts he has made on his blog.

If you want a quick overview of those posts, particularly if you are looking at a lot of photos, you can append "/archive" to the end of the address for his page. For example, for Malcom's archive, you can go to http://malcomcsmith.tumblr.com/archive.

PRIVACY LEVELS AND ACCESS

Tumblr posts are all visible to the public, even if the viewer does not have a Tumblr account. But there's one exception: users can create private Tumblr blogs. Private blogs are password-protected. So, unless you know a password commonly used by a target, it will not be possible to access private blogs.

CASE STUDIES

Tumblr has been a source in a number of investigations.

JOANIE FAIRCLOTH

In 2013, a woman used her Tumblr account to accuse singer Conor Oberst of raping her nearly a decade earlier. Her original post read in part:

> I became a huge fan of Conor's music, and for my 16th birthday, Bright Eyes was playing a local show and my old English teacher (Conor's brother) arranged for me to go and meet Conor after the show as a birthday present of sorts. Conor definitely took advantage of my teenage crush on him. At first, I was flattered when he was playing with my hair and had his hand on my leg. It was like my dream come true at that point. But then he clearly wanted to go further and I made it very clear and told him I was a virgin and wasn't prepared to change that right then but he didn't stop.[1]

The singer denied the allegations and sued the poster, Joanie Faircloth, for libel. After her identity was revealed and she was sued, she retracted her post, saying:

> The statements I made and repeated online and elsewhere over the past six months accusing Conor Oberst of raping me are 100% false. I publicly retract my statements about Conor Oberst and sincerely apologize to him, his family, and his fans for writing such awful things about him.[2]

SHOPLIFTING COMMUNITY

On Tumblr, some people even create problems for themselves with the truth. A community of users formed on Tumblr around shoplifting. Posters would blog photos of the things they had shoplifted, including tallies of the value. They also posted lists of tips and tricks for successfully shoplifting.[3]

After one Tumblr user discovered the group, their posts were commented on and reblogged extensively. There are no reports of anyone being arrested as a result of these posts, but the public outing and shaming of this group of users illustrates what can be discovered when people think their posts are quiet and anonymous.

CHILD PORNOGRAPHY

As one might suspect on a photo-heavy site like Tumblr, pornography is popular. Unfortunately, cases of child pornography are being shared as well. In the summer of 2014, a Baton Rouge man was arrested for posting two pornographic images of children to his Tumblr blog, including one photo of a boy who was only 5-years-old.[4] A later search found additional images on his hard drive at home. He was subsequently arrested and charged with distribution of child pornography.

THREATS OF VIOLENCE

Another user who got himself arrested and jailed because of Tumblr posts is Caleb Jamaal Clemmons. The 20-year-old student created a Tumblr post that read: "Hello, my name is irenigg and i plan on shooting up georgia southern [university]. Pass this around to see the affect it has to see if i get arrested.[5]" Only hours later, he was arrested and charged with making terrorist threats. The man claimed his posts were merely a joke, but a judge disagreed. Not only was he sentenced to 6 months in jail and 5 years of probation, but also he was banned from four Georgia counties and banned from using any social media.

CONCLUSIONS

Tumblr is a microblogging platform where users share text, photos, and videos. It has a primarily young audience, with half their users under 25-years-old. Users can follow one another, reblog posts, and favorite each other's posts. There is basically no profile information on Tumblr, so the main source of information about a target comes from the content of his or her posts. These, however, can be quite revealing, so Tumblr is a worthwhile source to use if a target has an account.

NOTES

1 Testa, Jessica. 2014. "Conor Oberst Accused Of Raping Teenager 10 Years Ago, Denies Allegations." BuzzFeed. http://www.buzzfeed.com/jtes/conor-oberst-responds-to-rape-allegations-left-by-anonymous.

2 Testa, Jessica. 2014. "Woman Who Accused Conor Oberst Of Rape: 'I Made Up Those Lies About Him.'" BuzzFeed. http://www.buzzfeed.com/jtes/woman-who-accused-conor-oberst-of-rape-i-made-up-those-lies.

3 Dries, Kate. 2014. "'Bling Ring' Tumblr Shoplifting Community Gets Rocked By Outsiders." Jezebel.com. http://jezebel.com/bling-ring-tumblr-shoplifting-community-gets-rocked-by-1567744623.

4 Staff. 2014. "EBR Police and Fire Briefs for July 28, 2014." The Advocate. http://theadvocate.com/home/9832483-125/ebr-police-and-fire-briefs.

5 Jeffries, Adrianne. 2013. "Judge Says Tumblr 'Joke' Was Terrorist Threat, Levies Five-Year Social Media Ban." The Verge. http://www.theverge.com/2013/8/20/4641606/college-student-who-spent-six-months-in-jail-for-tumblr-post-caleb-clemmons-sentenced.

Instagram

15

CASE STUDY PARAGON: SALADWORKS

Earlier, we met Mitch Donaberger, social media manager for Saladworks. Instagram is a platform where Mr. Donaberger finds a lot of information. This is especially true because Saladworks employees are in the core demographic for Instagram and use it frequently.

Figure 15.1 is but one example of how Mr. Donaberger used Instagram to investigate the employee who posted the photo.

The employee tweeted that she had worn flip-flops into the Saladworks kitchen: a violation of company policy and health safety laws. To comply, she put bags over the flip-flops, took a photo, and posted it to Instagram. Although she never revealed her name or location on Instagram, Mr. Donaberger was able to cross-reference it against her other social media accounts, identify her name and general location, and ultimately the store she worked in. Within a day, she was fired for damaging the brand through her post.

INSTAGRAM OVERVIEW

At its core, Instagram is just a photo-sharing application. Users take photos with their mobile devices, possibly apply some artistic filters to the photos, and then upload them.

POSTING PHOTOS

Figure 15.2 shows two photos (left) and their Instagram-ed counterparts (right). Note that the Instagram photos are always square, which crops the original images; but the photos on the right have been modified further by filters. Filters can change colors, contrast, focus, add borders, or any number of other visual features.

When a user posts a photo to Instagram, they can add a caption and any number of hashtags. Other users can Like and Comment on the photo. One of the above photos is shown below in Figure 15.3, as it appears to our example user, Malcom.

Instagram photos can also attach location information. In Figure 15.3, under Malcom's username is the time "1 hour ago," followed by a pin icon, and the location "Georgetown University."

Instagram tends to be a real-time sharing platform. People take photos during the course of their daily activities and post them immediately, rather than sharing them

FIGURE 15.1

A photo posted by a former Saladworks employee of plastic bags worn over flip-flops in the kitchen.

FIGURE 15.2

The photos on the left are original and the photos on the right are versions with Instagram filters and cropping, and on the lower right, a border.

FIGURE 15.3

Example user Malcom's Instagram post.

later. This makes Instagram a relatively reliable source of information about what a person was doing at a specific time.

INSTAGRAM RELATIONSHIPS

Relationships on Instagram are similar to those on Twitter. Users can follow people who they think are interesting, but the relationship does not need to be approved or reciprocal. One exception is that people with private accounts (discussed below, under "*Privacy Levels and Access*") have to approve followers since that status grants them access to the user's posts.

INSTAGRAM DEMOGRAPHICS

Instagram is popular among a younger demographic. Over 35% of people aged 18-29 years use Instagram. The entire user population skews young; Instagram has about 150 million users, and over 90% of them are under 35.

Users also tend to be extremely engaged with the platform, with 70% of users accessing it daily. This is just slightly lower than the percentage of people who check their Facebook accounts everyday and, indeed, for younger users, Instagram is often the primary social media platform they interact with.

Women dominate Instagram, accounting for over ⅔ of users.

FINDING PEOPLE

One of the most important aspects of Instagram is that its primary use is via mobile devices. There is a web interface (seen in Figure 15.3), which displays photos and provides some limited functionality; but most features are exclusive to the app on a mobile device.

Searching for people is one feature that's *not* available on the Instagram website. There are a few other options to search for a person.

BY THE MOBILE APP

First, acquire the smartphone app on either an iPhone or Android device. In order to search, you need to have an account. (Your searches and browsing behavior are not shown to anyone.)

Figure 15.4 shows the Instagram interface on an iPhone. At the bottom of the window is a set of icons. The second icon, a compass rose, takes you to the "Explore" screen. It shows thumbnails of photos and includes a search feature at the top.

Tap the search box at the top. From here, you can enter a person's name or username to find them. In Figure 15.5, we searched for "Malcom," and our example user Malcom Conroy-Smith appears in the search results.

BY SEARCH SERVICES

If you do not want to use the Instagram app, there are a number of websites that allow you to search. A web search for "search Instagram" yields a list of Instagram-searching services, all of which work similarly with app search described above.

These sites also have the convenience of *not* requiring you to create an Instagram account to use them. One excellent website in this category is http://pinsta.me.

BY USERNAME

If you think you know someone's username—for example, if you know their Twitter handle and are testing if their Instagram handle is the same—you can simply enter the web address `http://.instagram.com/«USERNAME»`, where «USERNAME» is replaced with the username you are search for. Thus, our example user Malcom can be found at http://instagram.com/malcomcsmith.

BY SOCIAL CONNECTIONS

Another method for finding someone is to search through their social connections.

One way to do this is to find a known associate of the target (using the search techniques described above). On Instagram, the total numbers that a user is following and those who are following the user are public—but unlike many other sites, the actual list of people isn't available.

FIGURE 15.4

The Explore screen in the Instagram app (iPhone). To access it, tap the compass rose icon (second from the left, at the bottom of the screen). Note the search box at the top of the page.

However, you *can* select a photo and see the people who have liked or commented on the photo. Figure 15.6 shows an example from the author's Instagram page. Our example user Malcom has liked the image, and another user, "rescueacls," has both liked it and commented.

In Figure 15.6, note that the usernames are links. Click on a username to go to his or her Instagram page. Thus, even without a username or a successful search, you may be able to find someone by investigating interactions on their friends' photos.

The Instagram mobile app *does* let you browse a person's followers and the people they follow. Figure 15.7 shows the author's Instagram account. In the upper

FIGURE 15.5

The search results for our "malcom" search in the Instagram Explore interface.

right above the "Following" button are three numbers indicating posts, followers, and people the user is following. Tapping on one of those numbers will take you to a list of the corresponding information. When looking at followers, for example, you can then tap on one of the follower names to see their account information.

On the web, there are third-party services that will also let you view this information. For example, on pinsta.me, you can enter an Instagram username or search by name. When you find a person, you can browse photos, followers, and people followed in a similar way.

Figure 15.8 shows a search result from a search on pinsta.me. Note the box on the left shows profile information for the user hopper_dog. Clicking on the numbers above "Follower" or "Following" will display a list of users that can, in turn, be clicked to view their profile.

FIGURE 15.6

A photo on the author's Instagram page that was liked by "malcomcsmith," our example user, and another user "rescueacls."

FIGURE 15.7

A mobile app view of an Instagram account. Clicking on one of the numbers above "followers" or "following" toward the upper right will take you to a list of people in the corresponding category.

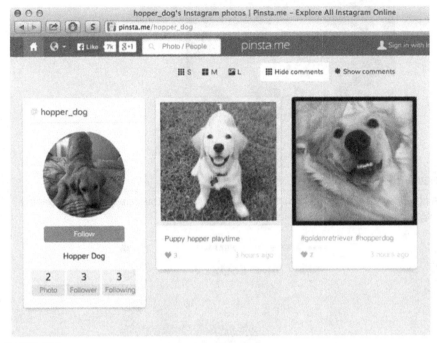

FIGURE 15.8

The pinsta.me website results for user hopper_dog. The large box on the left shows profile information for this user, including clickable numbers for lists of followers and people followed.

OBTAINING DATA
USER PROFILES

Once you have located a target, the username will be a point of access. As mentioned above, going to `http://.instagram.com/«USERNAME»`, where `«USERNAME»` is replaced with the target's actual username, will take you to the target's page.

On a user's profile page, you can see some basic biographical information about them. Figure 15.9 shows example user Malcom's page. There is a short description of himself next to his profile photo (Living in DC with my dog Barley). Users can also include a link to their website. In this case, Malcom has linked to his Facebook page.

The real information about a target is in photos and captions. Instagram photos tend to depict moments from everyday life as they happen, so they can say a lot about where a person spends time, what they like to eat, who they go out with, and how they like to present themselves.

Each photo has an associated time, although it's not as precise as on some social media sites. In Figure 15.3, the time of posting is "1 hour ago." In Figure 15.6, it is "17 months ago." In Figure 15.7, both photos have a time of "3 hours ago." This is as precise as time gets for Instagram posts. Thus, while photos are organized in reverse chronological order on a user's page, it's not always possible to have an accurate

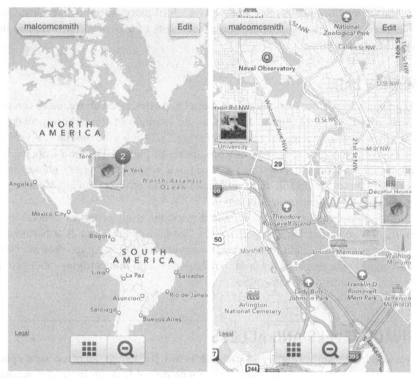

FIGURE 15.9

The default, zoomed out map view (left) shows that (2) pictures are geotagged near the same location. Zooming in (right) shows the photos on a map in their geotagged locations.

estimate of the exact time the photo was taken, especially for older pictures. The same is true for comments on photos, which follow the same time scheme.

Hashtags

Hashtags are common on Instagram. As with Twitter and other sites, hashtags can be clicked on to view other images with the same hashtag. Since Instagram photos are generally public—and the community usually views them as publicly shared images (rather than, say, communications with their friends)—hashtags are a way for someone's images to reach a greater audience than their own followers. It is not uncommon to have a dozen or more hashtags on an image. This will not always tell you a lot about the person posting the image, but it will tell you which communities of people on Instagram that they like to interact with.

Social Connections

Social connections can also reveal a lot of information about someone's community, though it is important to remember that relationships are not necessarily reciprocal on Instagram. Just because someone follows another person does not mean they have any kind of relationship. As described above, third-party websites like pinsta.me, or the mobile Instagram app, allow you to view lists of a target's followers and the people he or she follows.

LOCATION DATA

Instagram also has a number of location features. As described above, users can add a location to their posts. Figure 15.3 shows an example of this. Those geotagged photos then appear on a map for the user. Figure 15.7 shows the mobile app view of a user's profile page. Note the row of icons above the photos. The third from the left is a location pin icon. Clicking this takes you to a map with the user's photos on it. Figure 15.9 shows the default view of the map for Malcom, zoomed out. Zooming in pinpoints photos at their tagged location.

Instagram does not tag with GPS coordinates, but users can enter general locations (e.g., Washington, DC) or specific ones, like names of restaurants or businesses.

Clicking on the location for a given photo will take you to a page showing other photos tagged with that same location. This can be useful in identifying other people who have posted from the same place.

PRIVACY LEVELS AND ACCESS

Privacy on Instagram is simple and straightforward. By default, all of a person's photos are shared with the public. Even people who do not have an Instagram account can view them. Similarly, people's profiles are public.

Users have the option to make their Instagram account private. In that case, their photos and information is visible only to a list of approved followers. At the time of writing, Instagram has not released public numbers about what percentage of accounts are private, but rough estimates from independent sources put it at 3-5%.

People can also send direct messages to one another on Instagram. These messages are always private and are only accessible by the sender and recipient.

CASE STUDIES
CIVIL CASES
Family Law
Family law, as we are seeing in many chapters, is a place where information from social media is frequently used to investigate parties. Lisa Helfend Meyer, a Los Angeles-based family law firm *Meyer, Olson, Lowy & Meyers*, shared a story of how pictures from Instagram were used in one of her cases.

She represented the father in a case where the mother had a history of substance abuse. The mother claimed to be off drugs and was testing negative for them. Indeed, the mother portrayed herself in court as someone who stayed home every night and led a relatively simple, kid-centric life.

However, the mother also had an Instagram account where she posted frequently.

She shared pictures there of herself partying with people who were using drugs and alcohol. After surveying her Instagram friends, attorneys also discovered that she was friends with someone who worked the facility administering her drug tests.

One technique people use to confuse drug tests is to drink a lot of water. This dilutes urine and can lead to inconclusive tests. In this case, when the mother took a drug test that showed diluted urine, attorneys were able to use her Instagram feed to show that she had recently been out partying with friends—including the one who administered the drug test. They constructed a timeline and presented it to the judge to consider for his custody decision.

Firing

Haley Cousins of Naviga Business Services, a recruitment agency, told me the story of "**Jim**," whom she had helped get hired for a job. After starting at his new position, Jim called in sick on a Monday. Later that day, someone in Jim's company who was following his Instagram feed found a picture Jim had just posted, with the caption "Great day at the beach with friends!" Later that day, Jim posted photos that showed him with a drink and playing volleyball with friends.

Jim's boss quickly became aware of the situation. When Jim arrived at work the next day, his boss confronted him with the Instagram photos. Jim was fired shortly thereafter.

Hiring

Instagram does not always lead to doom and gloom, however. David Bitton of PayPanther.com says that his company seeks out nontraditional candidates for their work and almost exclusively hires based on social media presence.

David said his company found a candidate because of this online following, and David explicitly cited his 2500 Instagram photos, as well as his audience of over 1000 followers. This kind of attention to Instagram and other platforms showed that the candidate was influential and that he knew how to productively interact with people online.

Nine months later, David reports their Instagram-hire is the best employee in the office. Finding new candidates through social media is now the company's standard practice.

CRIMINAL CASES

Ephebophile

In May 2014, a 29-year-old man who played **Captain America** (and, for the purposes of this anecdote, that's what we'll call him) at Universal Studios in Orlando was arrested for sending sexually explicit photos to a 16-year-old girl he met at the theme park.

When the girl visited the park, she took a photo with Captain America and posted it to her Instagram account. Captain America found the photo and commented. That started a friendly relationship between the two, in which Captain America eventually escalated, sending pictures of himself naked, sometimes masturbating, and with sexually explicit text.

An investigation on Instagram established a pattern of behavior. Captain America had posted creepy comments on other girls' photos with him, including "Definitely my fav of the day!!" and "You're a sweetie."[1]

Fortunately, Captain America has been forced to retire his shield and uniform; after his arrest, he was fired from his position in Universal Studios.

Smash and Grab Robbery

In a slightly less scandalous story of Instagram arrest, police were able to identify a man who robbed a store, based on his Instagram connection with the business.[2] In April 2014, a man robbed an e-cigarette store in Boca Raton, Florida. He threw a brick through a window and made off with a backpack full of merchandise.

While reviewing the surveillance footage, the store's staff recognized the burglar as a frequent customer. Police went through the shop's Instagram account where they found photos of the man, including a picture of his driver's license.[3] He was later arrested in connection with this robbery—and the robbery of a gas station down the street.

This case is particularly interesting as an investigation example, because it shows how the followers of an account can be searched to reveal information.

CONCLUSIONS

Instagram is an extremely popular photo-based social media site, used primarily by a younger audience. The photos people post are almost always publicly available. Since most photos are taken, filtered, and posted all at once from mobile devices, someone's Instagram feed provides a unique view into people's daily activities. Geotagging on images can add an additional layer of insight to the photos themselves.

NOTES

1 Hathaway, Jay. 2014. "Captain America Arrested for Sending Dick Pics to a Teenage Girl." Gawker. http://gawker.com/captain-america-arrested-for-sending-dick-pics-to-a-tee-1572125529.
2 Gyllenhaal, Randy. 2014. "Instagram Leads to Arrest in Connection with Vape Shop Burglary." WPBF News. http://www.wpbf.com/news/instagram-leads-to-arrest-in-connection-with-vape-shop-burglary/25506496#!O1kdu.
3 Sacasa, Adam. 2014. "Tanner Bradshaw: The Boca Raton Man Was Arrested Monday, Accused of Burglarizing a Business." Sun Sentinel. http://articles.sun-sentinel.com/2014-04-15/news/fl-boca-instagram-burglar-20140415_1_boca-raton-police-instagram-boca-man.

YouTube

16

CASE STUDY PARAGON: *ELLIOT RODGER*

On May 23, 2014, 22-year-old *Elliot Rodger* began a mass killing in the college town of Isla Vista, California.[1]

After stabbing his three roommates to death, he left in his BMW. He stopped at the Alpha Phi sorority house at the University of California, Santa Barbara, and shot three young women who were outside, killing two of them.

He then continued driving, shooting at people on the sidewalk from his car window, running down cyclists, and eventually shooting at sheriff's deputies. When the spree finally ended, Rodger was dead from a gunshot wound to the head, six victims were dead, and twelve others were injured.

In the aftermath of the shooting, Rodger's 141-page manifesto, "My Twisted World," was made public, in which he ranted about his anger at the world. However, the most accessed of Rodger's public material was a series of YouTube videos (still available online at the time of writing: https://www.youtube.com/ElliotRodger). Their titles revealed his anger, including "Elliot Rodger, Lonely Vlog, Life is so unfair," "Life is so unfair because girls dont want me," and "Why do girls hate me so much?"

In his final video, "Retribution," Rodger detailed his plan for the massacre[2]

Well, this is my last video. It has all had to come to this. Tomorrow is the day of retribution, the day in which I will have my revenge against humanity, against all of you. For the last 8 years of my life, ever since I hit puberty, I've been forced to endure an existence of loneliness, rejection, and unfulfilled desires all because girls have never been attracted to me. Girls gave their affection and sex and love to other men but never to me.

He went on to detail his hatred of women for rejecting him, of his peers with whom he could not connect socially, and of humanity. He concluded with a detailed description of his plans:

You will finally see that I am in truth the superior one. The true alpha male. (laughs) Yes. After I've annihilated every single girl in the sorority house, I will take to the streets of Isla Vista and slay every single person I see there. All those popular kids who live such lives of hedonistic pleasures while I've had to rot in loneliness for all these years. Well now, I will be a god compared to you. You will all be animals. You are animals and I will slaughter you like animals. And I will be a god. Exacting my retribution on all those who deserve it. You do deserve it. Just for the crime of living a better life than me. All you popular kids, you've never accepted me, and now, you will all pay for it. And girls, all I ever wanted was to love you and to be loved by you. I've wanted a girlfriend, I've wanted sex, I've wanted love, affection, adoration. You think I'm unworthy of it. That's a crime that can never be forgiven.

Police knew about these videos in the weeks leading up to the shootings but determined that Rodger was not a threat to himself or others. The police reportedly saw his final video where he detailed his plans for the killings about an hour after they took place.[3]

While the YouTube videos were not enough to stop Rodger's massacre, they provided deep insights into the deranged thought process of an angry young man. They were used in investigations of Rodger before the killings and to investigate and better understand his motives afterward. The tragedy of this incident puts a spotlight on how much can be learned about a person from their YouTube content (Figure 16.1).

YOUTUBE OVERVIEW

YouTube is a video-sharing website. It's one of the most popular sites on the web, with over one billion unique visitors each month.

People can upload videos from their computers or mobile devices. They can then be viewed by anyone online or by a restricted group depending on the privacy settings. Viewers can comment on videos and rate them.

POPULARITY

The most popular videos are *wildly* popular. The most viewed video of all time is the music video for Psy's "Gangnam Style," which has over 2 billion views. To its credit

FIGURE 16.1

A screen capture from Elliot Rodger's final YouTube video.

(or discredit), YouTube is also responsible for Justin Bieber's music career. His amateur videos were accidentally discovered in 2007 when he was just 13.

Video sharing is dramatically increasing in popularity. This can be largely attributed to the ease with which smartphones can be used to capture, edit, and upload videos. And while people can easily email a few photos to their friends, video files are often too large for emailing. Thus, sites like YouTube become an obvious platform for sharing videos with friends.

VIDEO PAGES

Figure 16.2 shows a typical page for a video on YouTube. The video is shown at the top. Immediately beneath the video are the number of views (to the right) and the title and

FIGURE 16.2

A video page on YouTube.

name of the person who posted it (to the left). Beneath that is a list of options to share the video on a variety of platforms, and finally, beneath that is a space for comments.

Clicking on the name of the poster (in this case, "Malcom Conroy-Smith") will take you to a profile page for that user. This is sometimes called the user's "channel."

USER PAGES

Figure 16.3 shows Malcom's YouTube home page. It has a profile picture and background image at the top, beneath which are tabs with different sections of his profile information. The home page has all of the user's recent activity, including uploaded videos. A more organized and complete list of the videos appears in the "Videos" tab. The "Discussion" section allows people to make comments on the user's channel. Finally, the "About" section has a profile written by the poster. These tend to be short blocks of text.

Users do form social connections on YouTube. They can subscribe to one another, which means one person wants to see the videos posted by the person to subscribe to. However, these subscribers are kept private, so they aren't useful for investigation.

YouTube is owned by Google but operates relatively independently. Users' accounts on YouTube can be linked to other Google accounts—such as Gmail and the Google+ social network, discussed in another chapter—but they can also remain separate.

YOUTUBE DEMOGRAPHICS

There are two major demographics on YouTube: people who watch videos and people who post them.

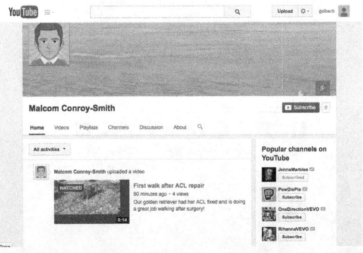

FIGURE 16.3

Malcom's home page on YouTube.

Statistics about viewers are relatively easy to come by—and they are impressive. Over 1 billion unique people visit YouTube each month. However, not all these people are sharing videos. *Pew* reports that 27% of adults have uploaded a video online. The percentage is much higher for younger users (ages 18-29): 41%.[4]

While YouTube is not the only place these people could have uploaded videos, it is the dominant site for sharing videos.

FINDING PEOPLE
BY SEARCH

To find someone on YouTube, you can use the search function at the top of the page. You can search for a person here by their name or their username. If the target has an account with that name, they are likely to appear in the results. The search box is shown in Figure 16.4.

You may also know, or have a good guess about, the target's username. This may be the first part of their email address (before the "@" symbol) or a username or screen name they use on other sites.

If that doesn't work, you can actually try going directly to the user's YouTube page. Simply append the screen name to https://www.youtube.com. For example, Malcom's username is "malcomcsmith," so his YouTube page is https://www.youtube.com/malcomcsmith.

BY ADVANCED SEARCH

If you want to search for someone by name, but can't find them in the YouTube results, you can use the advanced Google technique (discussed earlier in the book). Put the target's name in quotes and restrict the search to the youtube.com domain. For example, searching for our target Malcom would use the query "malcom conroy-smith" site:youtube.com. If you leave the quotes off the name, you'll get more search results, but they may be less relevant. For example, in this case, you might find people named Conroy Smith, without the "Malcom."

BY KNOWN ASSOCIATES

If the target doesn't post videos, you may still be able to find videos of them. You can follow the same search advice to see if any of the target's known associates have accounts and then scan the associates' videos to see if the target appears in them.

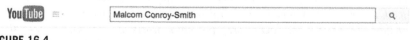

FIGURE 16.4

The search box at the top of the page with Malcom's name entered as the search term.

Similarly, searching for the target's name may not reveal videos *posted by* the target, but there may be videos *of* the target. If the target's name is included in the caption, the video will appear in the search results.

OBTAINING DATA

YouTube is somewhat unique among the social media sites discussed in this book, since the videos are the main source of content. When you find someone on YouTube, you have access to the most important information–his videos.

PRIVACY LEVELS AND ACCESS

Privacy is relatively simple on YouTube.

YouTube users have the option to make their posts public, which is the default and the most common setting; private, which restricts their visibility to invited users only; or unlisted, where anyone who has a link to the video can view it but the video does not appear in the search results or on a user's YouTube page.

Most videos are posted publicly. It is not a violation to watch unlisted videos if you somehow obtain a link to them. However, private videos will be difficult to access unless the video owner explicitly chooses you or invites you to watch.

CASE STUDIES
POLITICS

YouTube provides a place for people to share videos of people that the public might want investigated, especially in politics. One of the most high-profile revelations from YouTube came not from a politician's own channel, but from a video someone posted of him.

In the 2012 US presidential election, the *Mother Jones* magazine posted secretly recorded video footage of Republican candidate Mitt Romney speaking at a $50,000 per place fund-raiser. (Those two videos are still available on YouTube.[5]) In them, Romney is captured making controversial remarks. These videos came to be known as the "47%" because of the following quotes:

> *There are 47 percent of the people who will vote for the president no matter what. All right, there are 47 percent who are with him, who are dependent upon government, who believe that they are victims, who believe that government has a responsibility to care for them, who believe that they are entitled to health care, to food, to housing, to you name it. That that's an entitlement. And the government should give it to them ... And so my job is not to worry about those people—I'll never convince them that they should take personal responsibility and care for their lives.*

There was a strong response to the videos from both sides. Within the Republican party, the campaign was called "incompetent"[6,7] and "stupid and arrogant".[8] Obviously, opponents on the other side seized on the remarks as well. The political blog *FiveThirtyEight* showed Romney's poll ratings decline after the video aired,[9] though there is some question about the role the video played.

Regardless of its quantifiable impact, the incident showed how YouTube videos could reveal information about politicians that could shape the national dialogue.

CRIME AND MISBEHAVIOR

For a variety of reasons, many people enjoy posting videos of their bad behavior on YouTube. There are quite a few case studies of people being arrested for crimes or punished for bad behavior as a result of their YouTube videos that depict it.

In May 2014, *Michael Keith Maddox* of Piedmont, Alabama, was arrested for reckless endangerment as a direct result of the videos he uploaded to his YouTube channel.[10] The videos were mostly filmed from his dashboard and showed him ranting about cyclists, revving his engine, and speeding past them. In some instances where the cyclists appeared frightened as Maddox passed them, he laughed manically. He also makes passive threats in some videos, yelling, "Ride your little bicycle, you piece of crap! I'm going to hurt one of them one of these days. I can't help it." Maddox did issue an apology on Facebook for his "stupid" videos, but this did not prevent his arrest. His bond was set at $3000.

Another bad driving incident posted to YouTube led to an arrest. *Derek Kellett* was charged with reckless driving after he uploaded a video of himself running from the police on his motorcycle. The video, titled "Yamaha R6 Runs From Cops- Full High Speed Chase!!," shows him speeding, running red lights, weaving across lanes, and coming close to several cars, narrowly avoiding collisions. He was charged with five counts of reckless driving and released on a $2225 bond.[11]

Two teen girls from Ohio were arrested after their video of a fight, in which one threw a shovel at the other, hitting her in the head and knocking her to the ground, which was posted on YouTube.[12] Both were charged with disorderly conduct.

Adults are not immune from misbehavior caught on camera. Second-grade teacher *Thomas Hammer* was caught on a video, later uploaded to YouTube, where he threatened to hit a skateboarder over the head with the said skateboard. He was initially faced with both felony and misdemeanor charges. When the felony charge was dropped and he was allowed to return to work at his school, parents demanded he be fired. At the time of writing, his case is still being considered.[13]

CONCLUSIONS

YouTube is a video-sharing social media site and one of the most popular sites on the web. It has over a billion unique visitors per month. The videos themselves provide the main investigative insight on YouTube, and although videos can be made private, most are public. As video sharing becomes more popular online, sites like YouTube become increasingly valuable sources of information, both through videos people post of themselves and through videos posted by others that depict the target.

NOTES

1 Duke, Alan. 2014. "Timeline to 'Retribution': Isla Vista Attacks Planned over Years." CNN. May 27. http://www.cnn.com/2014/05/26/justice/california-elliot-rodger-timeline/.

2 [This video is no longer on YouTube, but a copy of it is available from *The New York Times*.] "YouTube Video: Retribution." 2014. The New York Times. May 24. http://www.nytimes.com/video/us/100000002900707/youtube-video-retribution.html.

3 Varandani, Suman. 2014. "California Police Knew Of Elliot Rodger's Disturbing Videos Days Before His Shooting Spree But Did Not Watch Them." International Business Times. May 30. http://www.ibtimes.com/california-police-knew-elliot-rodgers-disturbing-videos-days-his-shooting-spree-did-not-1592327.

4 Purcell, Kristen. 2013. "New Data Show Increases in Both the Percent of Adults Who Post and Who Watch Videos Online." Pew Research Center's Internet & American Life Project. October 10. http://www.pewinternet.org/2013/10/10/new-data-show-increases-in-both-the-percent-of-adults-who-post-and-who-watch-videos-online/.

5 Jones, Mother. 2012. "Full Mitt Romney Fundraiser Video Part One (36:39)." YouTube. September 8. https://www.youtube.com/watch?v=Ge03Sys8SdA and https://www.youtube.com/watch?v=rBj0joyCeag.

6 Noonan, Peggy. 2012. "Time for an Intervention." The Wall Street Journal (Peggy Noonan's Blog). September 18. http://blogs.wsj.com/peggynoonan/2012/09/18/time-for-an-intervention/.

7 Brooks, David. 2012. "Thurston Howell Romney." The New York Times. September 17. http://www.nytimes.com/2012/09/18/opinion/brooks-thurston-howell-romney.html?ref=davidbrooks&_r=1&.

8 Wallace, Chris. 2012. "Gibbs Defends Administration's Response to Libya Attack; Gov. Walker: Romney Needs to Show 'Fire in the Belly.'" Fox News. Fox News. September 23. http://www.foxnews.com/on-air/fox-news-sunday-chris-wallace/2012/09/23/gibbs-defends-administrations-response-libya-attack-gov-walker-romney-needs-show-fire?page=4#p//v/1856228251001.

9 Silver, Nate. 2012. "Sept. 27: The Impact of the '47 Percent.'" The New York Times. September 28. http://fivethirtyeight.blogs.nytimes.com/2012/09/28/sept-27-the-impact-of-the-47-percent/.

10 Schmitt, Angie. 2014. "Infamous YouTube "Run 'em in a Ditch" Driver Arrested in Alabama." Streetsblog USA. May 23. http://usa.streetsblog.org/2014/05/23/infamous-youtube-run-em-in-a-ditch-driver-arrested-in-alabama/.

11 Field, Carla. 2014. "Motorcyclist Posts YouTube Videos of Evading Police, Is Arrested." WYFF. May 30. http://www.wyff4.com/news/motorcyclist-posts-youtube-videos-of-evading-police-is-arrested/26250416#!WCcw2.

12 Zennie, Michael, and Joel Christie. 2014. "BOTH Girls in 'Shovel Fight' Video Are Arrested for Disorderly Conduct." The Daily Mail. May 13. http://www.dailymail.co.uk/news/article-2627439/BOTH-girls-infamous-shovel-fight-video-arrested-disorderly-conduct-revealed-brawling-BOY.html.

13 Chu, Hanna. 2014. "Parents Want Cielo Vista Elementary Teacher Fired for Controversial Skateboard Video." ABC7.com. May 20. http://abc7.com/news/parents-want-teacher-fired-for-skateboard-vid/69568/.

Forums and question and answer sites

17

Long before Facebook, Twitter, or even "old" social networking sites (like Myspace and Friendster), there were internet forums. In fact, Usenet, one of the first manifestations of this, came about in 1979—over a decade before the World Wide Web was invented.

DESCRIPTION OF *FORUM-* AND *Q&A*-STYLE SITES

Forums, at their heart, allow people to post topics and for others to reply. Discussions are usually grouped together by topic. A spin-off of the internet forum is the question and answer site. People certainly post questions and look for answers within forums. However, there are sites dedicated to question asking and answering, usually with less support for sustained discussions and more support for highlighting the best answer.

There are thousands of these sites. While some are general purpose, many are dedicated to a particular topic. Communities can (and often do) form within these forums. The result is that, if you can locate a target on one of these sites, the content of his or her posts and interactions can provide great insight into them, including their interests and personality.

The basic premise of forums is that someone starts a discussion thread, with a question, image, link, etc., and others reply. Figure 17.1 shows an example discussion about cooking for dogs taken from the forum section of dogster.com. Each post is shown in its own box, with a picture, name, and other info to the left. The posts also have a date and time when they were posted. This type of configuration is commonly seen across most forums.

Question and answer sites have a similar structure. Figure 17.2 shows a question and answers from the popular site Yahoo! Answers.

Users can also maintain profiles on the site. These may be simple, like a list of posts they have made, or only a name and date they joined. They can also be long and detailed, similar to a Facebook profile, with pictures, personal information, likes and dislikes, and more.

As an example of more extensive profiles available on these sites, consider Ask. fm, a question-answer site dedicated specifically to asking people questions about themselves. A person's profile contains their answers to all the questions people have asked them. Figure 17.3 shows Malcom's Ask.fm profile.

FIGURE 17.1

An example discussion from the Dogster forums.

FIGURE 17.2

A question and answers shown on the Yahoo! Answers site.

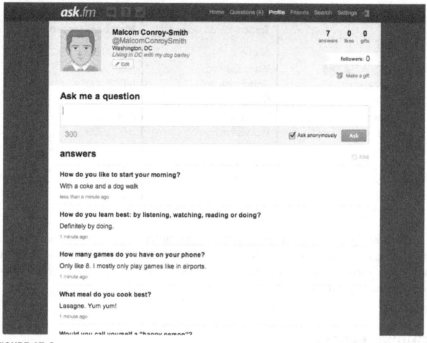

FIGURE 17.3

Malcom's profile on Ask.fm, which includes his answers to all the questions people have asked him about himself.

MAJOR FORUMS AND QUESTION AND ANSWER SITES

As mentioned above, there are thousands of internet forums. Some are public and easy to find and others are quite private, known only to their members. Some are free and open to join and others are restricted to approved or invited members only.

The ten most popular forums[1] in Table 17.1 show the diversity in number and topic. Also, note that even the largest of these forums is much smaller than any of the social networking websites we have looked at.

Question and answer sites tend to have more general topical focus (though it could be argued that they are just forums with a question and answer topic). Ask.fm is among the most popular of these, with 125 million registered users. The site trends young, with most users in their teens or early twenties.

Yahoo! Answers is also very popular. The exact number of users is hard to define, since anyone with a Yahoo! account for any reason has a Yahoo! Answers account by default. However, Quantcast[2] estimates it has about half the number of visits each month that Ask.fm receives.

Table 17.1 The Ten Most Popular Online Forums

Name	Topic	Members (approx.)
Gaia Online	Anime	27,000,000
Major League Gaming	Video Games	8,500,000
Bodybuilding.com	Bodybuilding	8,000,000
Ultimate Guitar	Music	6,000,000
XDA-Developers	Technology	6,000,000
Stack Overflow	Programming	3,000,000
PistonHeads	Cars	2,500,000
Forums—Slickdeals	Consumer advice	2,000,000
Ubuntu Forums	Ubuntu	2,000,000
City-Data.com	Cities	1,700,000

For investigation purposes, it is certainly worth looking for people on some of these large sites, particularly the question and answer ones. However, a more effective strategy is often to find forums that focus on specific interests of your target and then look for the target there.

FINDING PEOPLE

Because there are so many forums and question and answer sites, there are a number of strategies to use when looking for people. We will look at two major categories of search:

- A *wide search*, when you don't know what sites a target might participate in
- A *narrow search*, within specific forums

WIDE SEARCHES

When you don't know where you might find a target, Google searches may be your first best bet. If you have a known username for the target, simply searching for that username and the word "forum" will often turn up results. Since most forums have the word "forum" somewhere on the page, including the word in the search will narrow down results. This Google search is particularly effective when the user has a distinctive username; one that is a common word is less likely to be effective.

As an example, a search for "`malcomcsmith forum`" turns up a few false results and links to posts Malcom has made on goldenretrieverforum.com (Figure 17.4).

You may find accounts for a user on multiple forums this way. That alone can be an interesting insight into a target's life. You can potentially learn where they live, what their hobbies are, and what issues matter to them.

Note that not all forums are included in Google's search results, so you may not find all the forums a user participates in this way.

FIGURE 17.4

Searching for `malcomcsmith forum` on Google returns a link to Malcom's page (and links to his posts) on the Golden Retriever Forum.

NARROW SEARCHES

Google can also be useful for finding forums dedicated to particular topics that may interest a target. Searching for the term "forum" with any given topic is likely to turn up at least one forum result. Then, you can search for a user within that forum.

Question and answer sites have mixed search capabilities. Yahoo! Answers has basically no functionality to search for a user. A Google search restricted to the answers.yahoo.com domain may help you find a user. However, Yahoo! Answers does not have usernames—user profiles are shown with a name only (e.g., "Bob"), and they are usually first names. This makes it difficult to get a unique search result for a person. However, if the user has a unique name they might use on the site, a Google search like the following may work:

```
site:answers.yahoo.com "Malcom Conroy-Smith"
```

Ask.fm, on the other hand, has a search feature that lets you search by first and/ or last name, username, or email address, or if you connect through a Facebook or

Twitter account, you can search for anyone in your friend or follower list. Figure 17.5 shows the Ask.fm search interface. You can get to it by clicking the "Search" link at the top right.

Forums run on many different platforms. Most websites do not implement the forum component of their sites from scratch; they usually install existing forum software on their servers. The two most popular forum software packages are *vBulletin* and *phpBB*. You do not need to know about these to conduct an investigation, but their popularity means that knowing how to search and interact with each can be useful when working with many different forums online.

If you encounter a forum that uses either of these packages to run their forums, they may have the following search features. However, server operators can adjust the code and turn off some features. Also, some sites may require you to be registered and logged in before search options become available. Thus, consider these guidelines for the search capabilities that may be present.

vBulletin

vBulletin includes an advanced search option that lets you search for users through a variety of attributes. You can search by email, the username they use on the service and sometimes their username on other services (like Skype or Yahoo!), location, and even in the "biography" text a user has written about himself or herself. You can even search by IP address, the unique numerical address (e.g., 192.168.0.1) that identifies each computer on the internet. Figure 17.6 shows the advanced user search options as described in the vBulletin manual.

Again, not all sites will make all these options available.

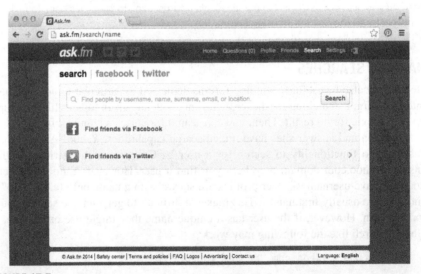

FIGURE 17.5

The Ask.fm search interface.

FIGURE 17.6

The advanced search option on vBulletin-powered forums.

phpBB

phpBB also has an advanced search option to find users. It too includes search by username on the site and on other services, as well as search by email and IP address. Figure 17.7 shows the phpBB advanced search that may be available on some forums running this software.

GENERAL SEARCH TACTICS

In addition to these advanced user searches, the social searches described for many other social media sites can also be effective in forums. If you can locate a friend of the target, you may be able to look at that person's "friends" list on the forum and identify the target in that list. In general, you can see a list of friends for any person on the forum, though this may be restricted unless you are logged in as a forum user. Searching these lists may turn up the target.

Use this form to search for specific members. You do not need to fill out all fields. To match partial data use * as a wildcard. When entering dates use the format YYYY-MM-DD, e.g. 2004-02-29. Use the mark checkboxes to select one or more usernames (several usernames may be accepted depending on the form itself) and click the Select Marked button to return to the previous form.

Username:		Joined:	Before ▾
E-mail:		Last active:	Before ▾
ICQ:		Posts:	Equal to ▾
AIM:			
YIM:		Posted from IP/domain:	
MSNM/WLM:		Group:	▾
		Sort by:	Joined date ▾
			Ascending ▾

Reset   Search

FIGURE 17.7

The phpBB advanced user search interface.

An important note: *As described above repeatedly, many forums restrict your ability to search and view information if you are not a logged in user. While registration is usually quick and relatively anonymous, many forums show users a list of people who have visited their profile pages. Thus, your browsing through profiles will not necessarily be anonymous.*

OBTAINING DATA

Each forum and question and answer site is likely to have different information available about users, but they follow a similar structure in providing it.

First, you can get to a person's profile either through search (discussed above) or by clicking on their name next to a post they have made. Figure 17.8 shows an example post by Malcom. His username and picture are above the post. Clicking his username would take you to his profile page.

FIGURE 17.8

A post by Malcom on a forum. Clicking his username above the post would take you to his profile page.

Other sites may have the username and photo off to the left or right of the main post text.

Profiles are likely to contain some personal information, like name, location, and the date the person joined the site. They often have additional data specific to the topic of the site. For example, the popular forum at Bodybuilding.com has options to include information about bodybuilding goals, body fat percentage, photos, weight history, and supplements being used. Each forum may have its own personalized profile information. Profiles often have a list of posts a user has made.

The posts themselves are great sources of insight, though it requires more work to get that insight than simply reading attributes from a profile. The posts will let you see how the target interacts online and may also contain text about his interests, movements, and activities.

CASE STUDIES

Investigators have used postings from forums and question and answer sites in a number of ways.

CASE STUDY 1

One case is that of *Adel Daoud*, an 18-year-old man arrested as part of an FBI sting in Chicago.[3] FBI agents provided him with a fake bomb and arrested him after he tried to detonate it outside a Chicago bar. He came to their attention through his posts on Yahoo! Answers. These allegedly included talk of violent jihad, and, according to *The Chicago Sun Times*,[4] he posted "Hmm. WELL on a personal scale i hate Shiites, Christians, Atheists and then Jews."

He also is alleged to have had a private chat in which he said he wanted to be a martyr and that he wanted to make a bomb. The posts he made online, especially the public posts on Yahoo! Answers, were a core part of the evidence brought forward so far in his legal proceedings.

CASE STUDY 2

In a gruesome case, *a 16-year-old Japanese girl* was arrested after posting on the popular Japanese forum 2channel about murdering her 15-year-old friend and classmate.[5]

The Japan Times reports that she started a thread titled "I have ended up killing" that included the message, "Oh no, blood keeps pouring out even though I have wiped it away many times."[6]

She also allegedly uploaded photographs of the dismembered body of her friend. Her posts went up late on a Saturday night and prompted a police investigation. The girl was arrested hours later and charged with murder on Sunday.

CASE STUDY 3

Not to be outdone, a British man was arrested after befriending a 14-year-old girl on a fetish-oriented internet forum and plotting to kill and eat her as part of a cannibalism fetish. He had posted on the board that he already had consumed "a woman aged 39 and a 5-year-old."[7]

CASE STUDY 4

Internet forums also helped catch a man who, in 2009, threatened to kill the then-President-elect Barak Obama.[8] The man, *Steven Joseph Christopher*, had previously threatened to assassinate President George W. Bush.

In January 2009, he posted several times on an alien- and UFO-oriented internet forum at alien-earth.org about his plots. Below is the text of three such posts released by the Department of Justice, who removed some of the racial slurs.

ok we have 6 days until my Presidential Assasination.

Yes, I have decided I will assassinate Barack Obama. It's really nothing personal about the man. He speaks well, has a loving although controlling wife and two cute daughters. But I know it's for the country's own good that I do this. And I'm not racist either, my family is a little, but isn't all Italian and european families? I mean how many times have you heard the word (racial slur) in the comforts of your home? I have a lot, and it really bothered me and I would confront them about it. No, it's not because I'm racist that I will kill Barack, it's because I can no longer allow the Jewish parasites to bully their way into making the American people submit to their evil ways. How many of you Obama supporters are now disappointed after some of his arm-twisted Jewish appointee decisions??? Make's you think he's not really in charge (which he isn't). No it's the same old, same old filthy (expletive) (racial slur) who are poisoning America, who have murdered thousands of innocent lives on 9-11-01, and are thinking that they are going to get away with it again.

Barack, I view more as a sacrificial lamb, but the sacrifice MUST take place. He had good intentions, but like the Steve Taylor song goes, "a politician next door, swore, he'd set the Washington arena on fire, thinks he'll gladiate them, but they're gonna make him a liar."

So, I'm stuck here in Mississippi, and I'll need bus fare or some way of getting to Washington. I don't own a gun, so maybe someone can give me one. And I'll need a leak in the secret service to get a close up shot, somewhere close to the podium, since I've never fired a gun, so I need to get an easy shot off. Wattdysay fellas? Any help?

You all know we can't live with the jewscum anylonger, dont cha? You got a better solution? I'm all ears.

Stevie

RE: ok we have 6 days until my Presidential Assasination.

Why is your heart so wicked?

I can get away with actually murdering Barack Obama OR just threatening to do it.

hth

To those who still think I'm a nobody, who antagonize me, who seek for my capture and arrest......

I wll have you found, arrested and executed, if you push me too far.

Christopher made the threats on January 11, 15, and 16. Secret Service agents read the posts and used them to track down the man's IP address, which they used to determine the place he was staying. He was arrested on January 16, the same day as his last threat. He was eventually convicted and sentenced to three years in federal prison.[9]

CONCLUSIONS

While any individual online forum or question and answer site is smaller than most social networking websites, they can be excellent sources of insight when investigating a target. There are forums for just about every imaginable interest online, and active participants may have thousands of postings. Profile information can also be extensive, but the text of the posts themselves is the most valuable data. It not only may describe crimes or plots but also may give a detailed picture of a person's beliefs, interests, movements, and the way they interact with others.

Not only may Google searches help find evidence of a target posting on a forum, but also it may be productive to first identify forums where a target might post and then search for them there. Policies vary from forum to forum, but some will require you to have an account and be logged in before you can search or access posts and profile data. Furthermore, users may be able to see when you have visited their profile if you are logged in while browsing.

NOTES

1 "List of Internet Forums." 2014. Wikipedia, the Free Encyclopedia. Accessed August 23. http://en.wikipedia.org/wiki/List_of_internet_forums.

2 "Quantcast: Measure+Advertise." 2014. Accessed August 23. https://www.quantcast.com.

3 Smith, Allan. 2014. "The FBI Targeted A Vulnerable 18-Year-Old As A Potential Terrorist." Business Insider. http://www.businessinsider.com/adel-daoud-targeted-as-a-potential-terrorist-2014-7.

4 Janssen, Kim. 2014. "Feds: Alleged Terrorist Was Prolific User of Yahoo Answers." The Chicago Sun-Times. http://www.suntimes.com/news/metro/28324511-418/alleged-terrorist-was-prolific-user-of-yahoo-answers-feds.html#.U_dwxktnKpa.

5 Chan, Aleksander. 2014. "Japanese Student Arrested for Killing and Dismembering Her Classmate." Gawker. http://gawker.com/japanese-student-arrested-for-killing-and-dismembering-1612354375.

6 Kyodo, Jiji. 2014. "Police Probe Possible Link between 2channel Postings and Sasebo Killing." The Japan Times. http://www.japantimes.co.jp/news/2014/07/28/national/crime-legal/police-probe-possible-link-online-postings-and-sasebo-killing/?utm_source=rss&utm_medium=rss&utm_campaign=police-probe-possible-link-online-postings-and-sasebo-killing#.U_dw10tnKpb.

7 Staff Writers. 2014. "Axe-Wielding Nurse in Plot to Eat Teenage Girl." The Australian. http://www.theaustralian.com.au/news/world/axewielding-nurse-in-plot-to-eat-teenage-girl/story-fnb64oi6-1226997999438?nk=6fa452c86fec4a57464962be9963159f#.

8 Talbott, Chris. 2009. "Steven Joseph Christopher Charged With Threatening Obama On The Internet." The Huffington Post. http://www.huffingtonpost.com/2009/01/16/steven-joseph-christopher_n_158703.html.

9 Gates, Jimmie E. 2009. "Man Who Threatened Obama Sentenced." The Clarion Ledger. http://archive.clarionledger.com/article/20091106/NEWS/91106033/Man-who-threatened-Obama-sentenced.

Other networking sites

18

Earlier in this book, we looked in depth at the major social media and social networking sites online. While these are your best chance to find an arbitrary target, there are thousands and thousands of other social networks online. Some are standalone sites, like Myspace, which serve a general audience. Others are integrated into other applications, like Yelp, which focuses on reviews of businesses but which has a social network feature as well. These sites can be great places to find information about a target. Indeed, if a target is an active participant, it is possible that you will actually find more information about him or her on one of these smaller social networks. The communities that form there tend to be more trusted exactly because they are smaller, and this can lead to freer sharing of information.

In this chapter, we will look at some of these networks. Our goal will be to identify common features and attributes in them, so if you come upon any new network in which your target is a participant, you will have general guidelines to follow to find him.

CHINESE SOCIAL NETWORKING SITES

There are many social networking Web sites that are not particularly popular in North America and Western Europe, but that have large user bases in other countries. We won't cover those in depth in this book, but it is worth looking at the Chinese market as an example. It has several networks that rival the size of Twitter and Facebook.

QZONE

With 650 million users, Qzone is the most popular social platform in China. In addition to making friends, users can post text entries, like blog posts, photos, and music. They can also read and comment on friends' posts.

RENREN

Renren is a traditional social network platform that started off as a near clone of Facebook for the Chinese market. With nearly 215 million users, it is quite popular in China, especially among college students. It has many of the features of a traditional social network, including profile pages and friend lists. It is also very popular—and makes much of its income—as a gaming platform.

Sina Weibo

Often called "Weibo" (pronounced WE-boah) for short, this site is a microblogging platform ("weibo" means "microblogging") that is similar to Twitter with some aspects of Facebook mixed in. It is very popular in China, where other popular sites like Twitter and Facebook are blocked. Estimates of its user base vary wildly, from 10 million core users to over 500 million registered users. Weibo itself claims 130 million active users[1]. It is also a platform where users express concerns with the government, within the allowed confines.

Chinese censorship limits what can be posted on Sina Weibo. The general type of content is similar to what is found on Twitter: Posts have a 140-character limit and hashtags and @mentions are commonly used. The content of posts is closely monitored, however, and posts can be filtered and deleted if they contain certain keywords or links. Accounts with offending material are often deleted. As an example of the extent of this censorship, on June 4, the anniversary of the Tiananmen Square protests that were quashed by the Chinese military, Sina Weibo blocked any posts that contained the words "today," "tonight," "June 4," and "big yellow duck"[2]. This latter block was because the famous picture of a man standing in front of a line of Chinese tanks during the protest had been circulating where the tanks had been replaced with rubber ducks; the image was created in response to Chinese censorship (see Figure 18.1).

Figure 18.2 shows an example profile page from Sina Weibo. You can see it closely resembles a Twitter page, with a background image and profile picture on top, followed by a list of posts underneath.

Chinese law states that internet companies are required to ensure that people register with their real names. The Chinese government also closely monitors what people post on social media and puts considerable investigation into people who post information unfavorable to the government.

Political cartoonist Wang Liming was arrested in 2013 for "rumor mongering," a common charge used to detain people for their social media posts. On Weibo, he forwarded a post about a grandmother who was holding her dead grandson, who had starved in a flooded region of the country. He was detained for "suspicion of causing a disturbance," according to Reuters[3]. Maya Wang, an Asia researcher for Human Rights Watch, was quoted by the media outlet, describing this type of arrest as the communist party trying "to dampen the effectiveness of the internet to embarrass the government and press it to change."

Wang is not the only one. In 2014, 81 people were detained and 4 arrested for similar reasons, "us[ing] social network services to fabricate and spread rumors, or forward rumors published on foreign Web sites," according to police[4].

OTHER SITES

There are many popular social networking sites with millions of users. Some of these are general interest sites and others are dedicated to a particular topic.

FIGURE 18.1

In protest to Chinese internet censorship, this image was created, replacing the tanks in the iconic photo from the Tiananmen Square protest with rubber ducks. The photo was later banned on Chinese internet sites and the words "big yellow duck" were also censored.

This section will look at Ning, a roll-your-own social networking site; Myspace, once the most popular social networking site on the Web, which still has tens of millions of users; and three examples of popular topic-specific social networking sites: Yelp, Goodreads, and Ravelry.

Note that these are simply interesting examples of other social networking sites; they were not chosen because they are more likely to reveal information about an arbitrary target. Hopefully, the discussion of each will paint a picture of general strategies for finding information across a wide range of sites.

NING

As social networks became increasingly prominent online in the mid-2000s, people were starting up their own networks all the time. Some were imagined as potential competitors to the big social networking sites, like Myspace and Facebook. Others were designed to support a specific community of users who wanted a more tailored experience than was available through a big networking site.

FIGURE 18.2

A user's page on Sina Weibo. Note that even without understanding the Chinese text, it is easy to identify the structure of the site as very similar to Twitter.

Ning was created to fill this latter need. It is a platform on which anyone can create their own social network. Users can register a social network and Ning hosts the site and provides the software and support to make it run. Within each site, users have an experience much like on any social networking site. They register for accounts; create profiles; blog; share photos, videos, and updates; and interact in discussions with other users.

Networks on Ning come and go. Some are created and used and then fade away. Others remain strong and have persisted for years. Over its life, estimates indicate that there have been roughly 2 million Ning sites created and that there are in the neighborhood of 100,000 active networks. Some of those have over 1 million users. Others have a tiny user base of less than 100 people. Overall, Ning claims to have 60 million active users across its sites[5].

Figure 18.3 shows an example of a user profile (for our example user, Malcom) on a Ning site. One of the more popular sites hosted on the platform is DIY Drones, a site dedicated to amateur UAV (short for "unmanned aerial vehicle") building with nearly 57,000 members. This page shows Malcom's profile within DIY Drones. On the left of Malcom's profile page is basic information about him, including his demographic information and friend lists. The center column shows posts and comments he has made within the community.

The design of individual Ning sites may vary, but they often use a common template for the overall structure. DIY Drones does this; see Figure 18.3.

To find someone on a Ning site, you can search for them using their name in the search box at the very top right of the page. Another feature of interest to find someone is the "Members" link on the navigation bar toward the top of the page (the third option from the right in Figure 18.3). This provides a full list of members of that site with links to their profile pages. Figure 18.4 shows the Members page for DIY Drones.

Ning does not provide a searchable list of all their sites or users. Thus, if you are looking for a target, you cannot simply search for them across all Ning platforms. However, if you encounter a Ning site, you will be able to identify it by a "Powered by Ning | Mode Social" banner at the very bottom of the page. If you see that, you know you should be able to find a member list and expect a certain type of profile.

FIGURE 18.3

A Ning profile page on the network DIY Drones.

FIGURE 18.4

The "Members" page of a Ning Web site.

One final note: Ning site creators can control the privacy for their sites. This might mean that you cannot access information within a Ning site without having an account. Unlike many larger social networks, registrations for Ning sites may be held for approval to ensure you are an interested and valid member of the community.

MYSPACE

In the early days of social media, Myspace was an important player. Before Facebook came on the scene, it was the dominant social networking site. In the mid-to-late 2008s, after losing much of its user base to Facebook, the site went through several transformations. The "new" Myspace profile page is shown in Figure 18.5.

Even though the site has been through many iterations, users who had accounts in the early days still have accounts on the new version of the site. In fact, Myspace took advantage of this to entice users back to the site by emailing them old photos of themselves that they had posted on the site long ago[6].

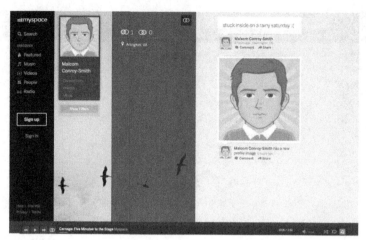

FIGURE 18.5

Malcom's Myspace profile page.

Myspace now has about 36 million users. To find people on the site, you can search by their actual name or a common username using the search box toward the upper left (see Figure 18.5).

Because the Myspace audience tends to be younger, many stories of people being investigated through the site relate to interaction with younger people. In 2009, a South Carolina swimming coach was arrested for contributing to the delinquency of a minor. Using fake accounts he created on Myspace, he befriended two 13-year-old girls and enticed them to send him sexually suggested photos[7].

He is not alone. A Los Angeles-area man was arrested after he also created fake profiles on Myspace between 2009 and 2014, which he used to have sexually explicit conversations with underage girls. He sent and received explicit photos with the teens and tried to arrange meetings[8]. According to the charges, he did meet with some of the girls, resulting in charges of committing lewd acts upon a child.

Not to leave those two men in small company, yet another man, a Jacksonville Florida man collected sexually explicit photos from over 200 underage girls by posing as a teenage boy on Myspace[9]. After receiving the photos, he threatened the girls, claiming he would post the photos online unless they sent him more. He was arrested and charged and will soon face trial.

YELP

Yelp started off as a question-answering site but quickly became a place for reviewing restaurants and local businesses. It is now extremely popular and powerful in that space. The site has tens of millions of reviews, and a study showed that a one-star rating change on Yelp could lead to a 5-9% change in business for a local company[10]. That power has led companies to carefully monitor their ratings and reviews. Some companies also monitor the people who write them (more on that shortly).

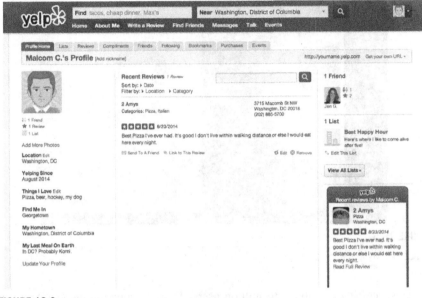

FIGURE 18.6

Malcom's Yelp profile page.

First, let's look at an overview of the site. Yelp has over 130 million unique users each month. Figure 18.6 shows Malcom's Yelp profile page. It has his personal information in the column on the left, his reviews in the center (currently, there is only one), and a list of friends and groups on the right.

Yelp can provide interesting insights into a person's habits and location. By looking at all the places a person has reviewed, you can get a sense of the neighborhoods they spend the most time in and cities they visit often. You can also find the types of venues they care about. One user may review a lot of bars and restaurants, while another may review playgrounds and children's activity centers.

To find people on Yelp, first click the "Find Friends" tab that is under the search boxes at the top. There, you can search for people by name or by email address. Furthermore, if you log in with a Facebook account, Yelp can search for your Facebook friends in their network. If you cannot locate a target this way, a social search is possible. As mentioned above, people's friend lists are public and browsable, so if you can find an associate of the target, you may be able to locate the target through this list.

Because Yelp has become a powerful influence on people's interest in businesses, it has also become a place where people can be punished for their reviews. One story that made headlines is that of an inn that told wedding parties that they would be charged $500 for every negative review a guest left for them on Yelp[11]. The venue was inundated with bad reviews in response to the story, as outraged Web users made their feelings known. However, there are many stories of people being specifically targeted for their comments.

One article details case after case of people writing negative reviews and threatened with lawsuits[12]. A woman was threatened with a suit after writing a negative review of a car repair shop; a dentist threatened to sue a patient for a bad review. Some suits were dropped, but not all. A woman in Virginia wrote a negative review of her contractor, who in turn sued her for $750,000. He was awarded $250,000[13]. The trial was complicated—there appeared to be lies in the Yelp review, including accusations that the remodeler stole jewelry from her home. Eventually, the reviews were taken down and both sides walked away without being awarded any damages.

However, many businesses who may want to file suit cannot, because Yelp users are anonymous in many cases. A California bankruptcy lawyer wants to sue a user for defamation as a result of a negative review, but that user's real identity is not known. Instead, the lawyer is suing Yelp in an effort to compel the company to turn over the true identity of the user[14].

GOODREADS

For readers, social media has always been a place to share thoughts about the books they are reading. Goodreads was put together for people to share those books and their thoughts about them and to keep lists of books to read later.

The social network on the site helps people see what books their friends have added to the lists along with ratings and reviews of books they have finished. It also has discussion boards for individual books or for online reading groups.

The site has around 650,000 users—very small compared with the mammoth social networking sites discussed earlier in this book, but quite large for a topic-specific social network.

Figure 18.7 shows Malcom's Goodreads profile page. It includes some basic demographic information and lists of books he has made along with ratings and reviews.

If you have an account, you can find people in the "Friends" section of your profile page. They can be searched by name or email address. The site also supports importing friends or contacts from Gmail, Yahoo! Mail, Facebook, and Twitter. People's friend lists are public, so it may be possible to find a target through an associate's account.

If the books a person is reading are of interest, Goodreads can be a useful source of information. You can find a person and see all the books they have read or plan to read.

RAVELRY

If the target of your investigation is a knitter or crochets, you will probably find him or her on Ravelry. With 4 million users, it is among the largest of the topic-specific social networking sites online.

Figure 18.8 shows Malcom's profile on Ravelry. It has basic demographics along with site-specific information on the right.

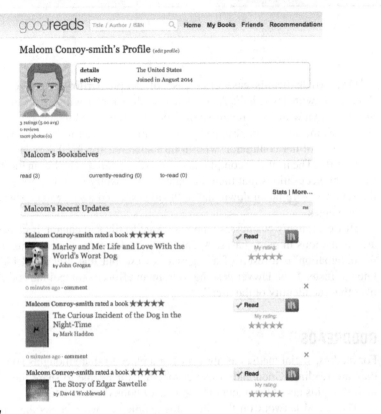

FIGURE 18.7

Malcom's profile on Goodreads.

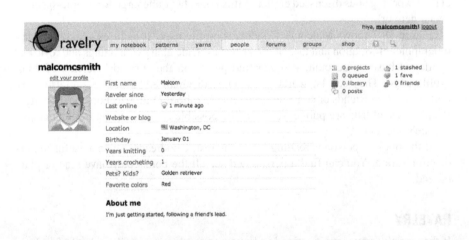

FIGURE 18.8

Malcom's profile on Ravelry.

Users on Ravelry post knitting and crocheting patterns and discuss projects. There are active forums on the site as well. An individual's forum posts can be found by clicking on the number of posts shown in the right of their profile (e.g., in Figure 18.8, Malcom's profile says "0 posts" at the bottom of the first column of links on the right).

The people search section of the site allows you to find people by username or full name. Users' friend lists are also public (e.g., in Figure 18.8, Malcom has "0 friends" shown on the right), allowing for social searches for a target.

Essentially, this site would be useful for a target whom you might investigate through an online forum about knitting. It provides additional information through the projects and friends that are part of the site.

CONCLUSIONS AND GUIDELINES

It is totally possible that your investigation target is not much of a reader and is not a knitter. The target may not post restaurant reviews and may have never set up a Myspace profile. However, looking at all these different sites can lead to a set of guidelines that can be useful when investigating on one of the many smaller social network sites:

1. *Finding people works in ways similar to those discussed for other networks*: Knowing a target's username and email address can help if they have a common name or if they use a pseudonym on a site.
2. *Social searches are effective on almost every site*: If you can't find the target, try searching through his or her associates. Friend lists are often public and browsable.
3. *Content is king*: The most valuable information you find on these sites will not be the basic profile information (which tends to be limited to demographics or data specific to the site's topical focus), but the things people say in discussions, posts, and comments. These can reveal a lot about them (their preferences and their behavior, in particular).
4. *Look broadly for social networking sites*: There is valuable information to be found even on smaller sites, and there are thousands of them. Know your target's interests and look for what's out there online to attract them. If you can locate them in a smaller network, you are likely to find a lot of good data.

NOTES

1 Li, Zoe. 2014. "Weibo's Core Users Number 10 Million." CNN. http://edition.cnn.com/2014/04/10/business/china-weibo-user-base/.
2 Tatlow, Didi Kirsten. 2014. "Censored in China: 'Today,' 'Tonight' and 'Big Yellow Duck.'" The New York Times. http://rendezvous.blogs.nytimes.com/2013/06/04/censored-in-china-today-tonight-and-big-yellow-duck/.
3 Wee, Sui-Lee. 2013. "Interview: Freed Chinese Cartoonist Refuses to Be Cowed by Internet Crackdown." Reuters. http://in.reuters.com/article/2013/10/23/china-cartoonist-idINDEE99M03420131023.

4 France-Presse, Agence. 2014. "85 People 'arrested or Detained' as China Steps up Clampdown on Internet Rumours." South China Morning Post. http://www.scmp.com/news/china/article/1570034/85-people-arrested-or-detained-china-steps-clampdown-internet-rumours.

5 Kern, Eliza. 2013. "Remember Ning? Once-Buzzy Social Network Has Relaunched Again as a Publishing Platform." GigaOm. https://gigaom.com/2013/03/25/remember-ning-once-buzzy-social-network-has-relaunched-again-as-a-publishing-platform/.

6 Wagner, Kurt. 2014. "Myspace Is Embarrassing Users With Old Photos to Win Them Back." Mashable. http://mashable.com/2014/06/01/myspace-old-photos/.

7 Lurye, Rebecca. 2014. "Bluffton Man, Former Swim Instructor, Arrested on Voyeurism Charge." The Island Packet. http://www.islandpacket.com/2014/07/31/3236678/bluffton-man-former-swim-instructor.html.

8 Moreno, John A. 2014. "Cypress Man Accused of Using Social Media to Contact Underage Girls for Lewd Acts; More Possible Victims Sought." KTLA 5 News. http://ktla.com/2014/07/26/cypress-man-accused-of-lewd-acts-with-underage-girls-more-possible-victims-sought/.

9 Micolucci, Vic. 2014. "St. Johns County Man Accused of 'Sextortion.'" News 4 Jax. http://www.news4jax.com/news/st-johns-county-man-accused-of-sextortion/27368888.

10 Luca, Michael. 2011. "Reviews, Reputation, and Revenue: The Case of Yelp.com." Working Knowledge: The Thinking That Leads (Harvard Business School). Michael Luca. http://hbswk.hbs.edu/item/6833.html.

11 Griswold, Alison. 2014. "Hotel Fines Guests for Negative Yelp Reviews: Don't Stay at Union Street Guest House." Slate. http://www.slate.com/blogs/moneybox/2014/08/04/hotel_fines_guests_for_negative_yelp_reviews_don_t_stay_at_union_street.html.

12 "People Are Getting Sued for Doing This One Thing Online." 2014. The Kim Komando Show. Accessed September 13. http://www.komando.com/tips/11733/people-are-getting-sued-for-doing-this-one-thing-online/all.

13 McAlister-Holland, Deb. 2014. "5 Easy Ways to Get Sued Over Online Content & Social Media." Business 2 Community. http://www.business2community.com/social-media/5-easy-ways-get-sued-online-content-social-media-0969797#!bNnbAV.

14 Roxas, Gabriel. 2014. "Yelp Reviewer Sued for Libel by Natomas Lawyer." News 10 ABC. http://www.news10.net/story/news/local/natomas/2014/07/29/lawyer-sues-reviewer-lawyer-natomas/13341389/.

Social media sharing

19

In addition to the many sites dedicated to supporting social networking as their main purpose, there are plenty of sites that allow social interaction around users sharing media like photos, videos, and music. In all cases, the social component of these sites comes from people being able to follow others who post things a person finds interesting.

The content people share on these sites can reveal a lot of information as we have already seen in the chapters about Instagram and YouTube. In this chapter, we will look at some of other popular sites in these categories and what kind of data is available.

PHOTOS AND VIDEOS

It used to be that video sharing was uncommon because the bandwidth required to upload video and download it was too taxing. However, smartphones with cameras that take photo and video, generous data plans, and Wi-Fi access have made it much easier to do.

As a result, sites that used to be restricted to photo sharing now also support video sharing, and there are a number of sites dedicated entirely to sharing videos.

FLICKR

Flickr is one of the most popular of these sites, with close to 90 million users. People can upload and view other people's pictures on the sites. Each user's personal page is a photo stream that shows all the pictures they have uploaded. Figure 19.1 shows an example of a user's photo stream. Users can tag images and add locations.

Anyone can click on any picture, like it, or comment on it.

Users can create limited profiles that include their name, location, occupation, and contact information if the user chooses to share this. You can find this profile by clicking the "…" on the right at the bottom of the user's header image, as can be seen in Figure 19.1.

Users can also create social connections to one another by following people whose pictures they are interested in. Many photos and videos on Flickr are public, but users can make them private or restrict them to different groups of friends.

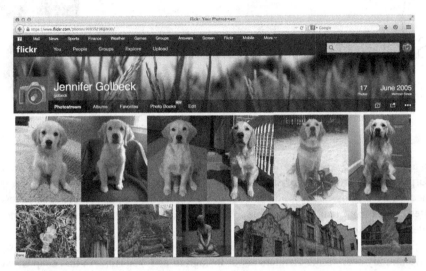

FIGURE 19.1

An example of a Flickr user's photo stream.

For an investigation, Flickr images can be interesting sources of information about the kind of events a person attends, the types of places they tend to go, and the subjects that interest them.

PHOTOBUCKET

Photobucket has 100 million registered members and stores photos and videos. It operates with many features similar to those Flickr offers. Users can create short profiles, follow others, and maintain a photo stream with their pictures and videos. There are privacy controls that users can set, so some images may be publicly visible and others are protected.

Photobucket makes money by selling prints of the photos people upload. It is also a common site used to store photos used online for business websites, blogs, and auction sites like eBay. Thus, the types of photos people upload are much more varied, with less personal content than one might expect.

VINE

Vine is a social video sharing app used on mobile devices. It has about 40 million users and is growing very quickly.

Users create six-second video loops that can have captions. Profiles are very limited and basically have a name, profile photo, location, and a short descriptive sentence. The main thing you can find on a user's Vine homepage is a series of videos he has created. Users can like videos or comment on them.

All Vine posts are public, and they are often shared on other social media sites, like Twitter. Thus, if you suspect a target might be posting to Vine, you can see if they link to any videos on Twitter, Facebook, or other sites. This might help you locate their Vine profile more easily. You can also search for people by their real name on Vimeo.

Figure 19.2 shows the view of a Vine video on an iPhone. The username is at the top, and this links to the user's profile page.

While you might think that it is hard for people to reveal too much in a six-second video, Vine played a role in the investigation of an Australian student. In August, 2014, 23-year-old Chris Lane was jogging in Oklahoma where he was studying on a baseball scholarship. He was shot, and despite witnesses' attempts to revive him, he was declared dead on the scene[1].

FIGURE 19.2

A video on Vine.

Three teens were arrested for the murder, and one claimed they did it "just for the fun of it." In their investigation of the boys, police found a Vine video posted by James Edwards, the youngest of the accused who was only 15 years old[2]. The clip shows him brandishing a weapon (a still from this Vine video is shown in Figure 19.3). Another investigation on social media found photos of guns and money on the suspects' Facebook pages, shown in Figure 19.4.

The teens are currently facing charges of first-degree murder and are being held without bond. They are set to go to trial in April 2015.

FIGURE 19.3

A still from a Vine video showing a murder suspect brandishing a weapon. His face is blurred here for privacy.

FIGURE 19.4

Two additional photos from the suspects, taken from their facebook pages.

VIMEO

Vimeo is a video-sharing site with many features similar to YouTube. It has 22 million registered users and 100 million visitors each month. Users can upload videos and follow other people whose videos they like. They can also restrict the privacy of their videos. You can search for people by their real name or email address on Vimeo in the main search box.

Like on YouTube, the content people post is used in investigations. Though Vimeo is less popular, it, too, has been cited in cases. One such case is that of a French teen who posted an aerial video of the city of Nancy that he took with a remote-controlled drone[3]. The video collected hundreds of thousands of views before it was ordered to be removed and the teen was investigated. French law requires drone operators to have the equivalent of a light aircraft license, because officials fear they could injure someone if they crashed. This video maker did not have that license, so he was arrested and charged with "endangering lives." The videographer eventually pled guilty and was fined $550[4].

MUSIC

There are many sites for listing music preferences and listening to music. Some of these have social components. This section looks at a couple of the most popular social music sites online.

Last.fm

Last.fm is a site that recommends music and allows users to keep track of their favorite artists and songs. They have around 50 million users. Figure 19.5 shows a Last.fm profile page for Malcom, which includes his library—a list of songs and artists. Profile information includes name, gender, and location. Users can also participate in discussions, and those posts can be tracked from the profile page as well.

There are privacy settings on Last.fm, though most profile information is public. You can search for people on Last.fm by their real name or by username. While sites like this are unlikely to have a lot of information about people's activities, they do yield a lot of insight about people's interests and preferences.

SoundCloud

While Last.fm allows people to curate music they like that other people have created, SoundCloud lets people upload and share their own audio files. In the same way YouTube and Vimeo let people upload video, SoundCloud supports uploads of audio, both music and spoken word. The site has roughly 40 million users.

Figure 19.6 shows Malcom's profile page on SoundCloud. It includes the audio files he has uploaded. Users can comment on audio files and follow users who they find interesting. You can search for people by their name or username on SoundCloud in the search box shown at the top of Figure 19.6.

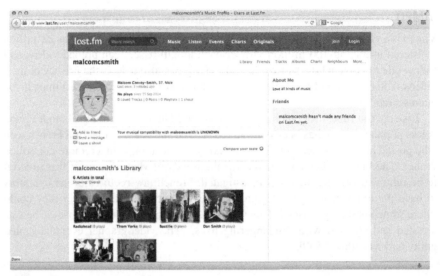

FIGURE 19.5

Malcom's Last.fm profile page.

FIGURE 19.6

Malcom's SoundCloud profile page.

We have seen many stories of people being investigated for their posts on social media. SoundCloud offers an interesting anecdote about a user leveraging the site to share results of his own investigation. Posting under a pseudonym, a Turkish user used the site to share audio files of secretly recorded phone conversations of the prime minister talking with others[5]. The calls discussed illegal and corrupt activity. In response, the Turkish government blocked access to the site entirely.

CONCLUSIONS

As with the smaller social networking sites we looked at, smaller media sharing sites for photo, video, or music can also reveal useful information about users, their preferences, and their social interactions. The types of investigations you can conduct on these sites are similar to what you would do on their larger cousins like Instagram and YouTube. While it may be less likely that you will find any specific individual on these sites, if you *do* find them, these sites can be an excellent source of information.

NOTES

1 http://www.theblaze.com/stories/2013/08/19/student-randomly-shot-dead-by-gang-of-teens-just-for-the-fun-of-it-police-say/.
2 http://www.theblaze.com/stories/2013/08/20/these-are-the-three-teens-arrested-and-suspected-of-murdering-student-chris-lane-for-the-fun-of-it/.
3 http://www.hdwarrior.co.uk/2014/02/17/teenager-gets-arrested-in-france-for-flying-a-drone/.
4 http://www.nydailynews.com/news/world/video-french-teen-fined-illegally-flying-drone-article-1.1801628.
5 http://www.spin.com/articles/soundcloud-service-outage-turkey-banned-prime-minister/.

Online dating

20

INTRODUCTION

Online dating websites are a specific type of social media designed for people to find romantic partners and friends. The industry is extremely popular. There are roughly 54 million single Americans, and 41 million people have tried online dating. Ten percent of Americans—and ≈40% of single Americans—have used an online dating service.

On dating sites, people create profiles for themselves. The personal information in these profiles is quite extensive. Sites have dozens of personal attributes and hundreds of questions that people use to describe themselves. These include basics like age, race, height, and favorites (books, movies, music, etc.), along with other personal information, like smoking and drinking habits, interest in having kids, dietary preferences and restrictions, and religion. Figure 20.1 shows basic profile information from the online dating site okcupid.com.

Most sites also have options for users to answer questions that give additional insights into their personalities and preferences. OkCupid allows users to answer as many questions as they wish. Figure 20.2 shows one of these questions.

Although this personal information can be useful for investigation, people aren't always honest in their dating profiles. Over half of online daters believe that someone has seriously misrepresented themselves in their profile. Men most often lie about age, height, and income; women most often lie about weight, physical build, and age.

MAJOR ONLINE DATING SITES

There are dozens of dating sites. Some are intended for a wide audience. Others are dedicated to specific demographics (e.g., Christian Mingle, JDate, or Gay Friend Finder) or interests (e.g., Adult Friend Finder, a swinger-oriented site).

If you know your target has a particular interest, it is worth checking out related dating sites. However, for your average target, the major websites are most likely to yield results. Some of the most popular sites in the U.S. are as follows:

- **Match.com:** With 35 million unique monthly visitors, Match.com is one of the most popular dating sites. People can sign up for free, but generally pay a subscription in order to communicate with others.

My self-summary 🖉		My Details 🖉	
I'm an empty essay... fill me out!		Last Online	Online now!
		Orientation	Straight
What I'm doing with my life 🖉		Ethnicity	—
I'm an empty essay... fill me out!		Height	—
		Body Type	—
I'm really good at 🖉		Diet	—
I'm an empty essay... fill me out!			
		Smokes	—
The first things people usually notice about me 🖉		Drinks	—
I'm an empty essay... fill me out!		Drugs	Never
Favorite books, movies, shows, music, and food 🖉		Religion	—
I'm an empty essay... fill me out!		Sign	—
		Education	—
The six things I could never do without 🖉		Job	—
I'm an empty essay... fill me out!		Income	—
I spend a lot of time thinking about 🖉		Relationship Status	Single
I'm an empty essay... fill me out!		Relationship Type	—
		Offspring	—
On a typical Friday night I am 🖉		Pets	—
I'm an empty essay... fill me out!		Speaks	English
The most private thing I'm willing to admit 🖉			
I'm an empty essay... fill me out!			

FIGURE 20.1

The basic profile information section of online dating website OkCupid.

- **Zoosk:** Targeted to younger users, with 70% of users under 35. There are an estimated 12 million unique monthly visitors to the site. It runs on desktop computers and mobile devices (including Android and iPhone devices).
- **OkCupid:** A very popular free dating site with around 11 million monthly users. This site has a special focus on quizzes used to match people. Figure 20.2 shows an example of one question in the quizzes.
- **eHarmony:** With roughly seven million unique monthly users, this paid site focuses on matching people through compatibility testing using an extensive questionnaire. The main site does not allow same-sex couples. They also refuse some people after they complete the long profile questionnaire.
- **Tinder** is a relative newcomer to the online dating scene, but it is increasingly popular. It's a service accessed through an app on mobile devices. Users browse the photos and profiles of other people online near them (see Figure 20.3). They indicate people whose profiles they like. If that person likes back, they are able to text with one another.

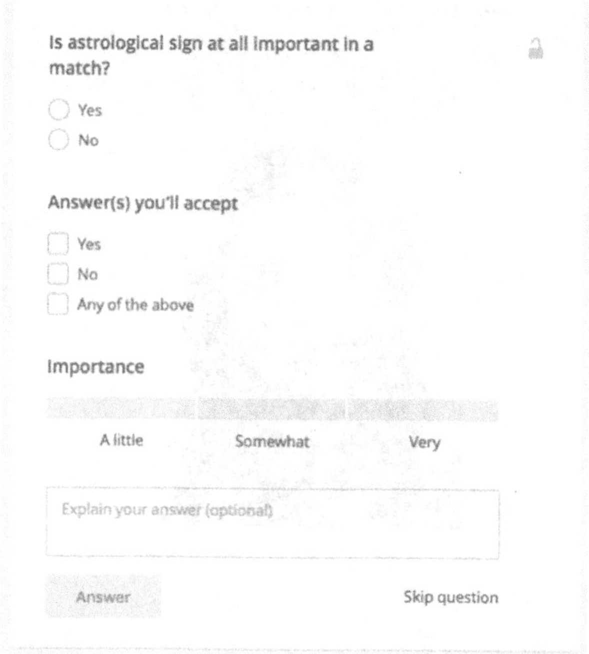

FIGURE 20.2

An example question from OkCupid.

FINDING PEOPLE
BY BASIC AND ADVANCED SEARCH

Most online dating sites have extensive search functionality. The most basic search functionality includes gender, age, and location of the target. Most sites also have advanced search functionality, which allows filtering results according to many personal attributes and interests.

Figure 20.4 shows the search page from OkCupid. A number of search options have already been entered, and the "Advanced" search options allow the user to choose attributes (like religion, education, drug use, pets, languages, or astrological signs, among many others) to filter the results.

BY EFFECTIVE SEARCH STRATEGIES

Remember that people often lie about themselves on online dating sites. Therefore, you may wish to search for a wider range of ages, body types, and income levels. In addition, some people leave parts of their profile blank; for example, many choose not to share their income level. If you search for a specific income level, users who

FIGURE 20.3

A profile page from Tinder. This image is a promotion profile for the show *The Mindy Project*, but represents the average kind of information on a Tinder profile.

haven't specified one will usually not appear in your search results. Thus, keeping the search as broad as possible will yield more results to review, but may increase the chances of finding a target.

BY EMAIL OR USERNAME

You may also search for people by email address or username. Usernames from other social media accounts are good candidates to try here, though people often hide their real names in their online dating profiles—often specifically to keep interested people from finding them elsewhere online.

Tinder is an exception to this rule: it does not offer searching for individuals. Anyone within range of your current location may come up, and you can only communicate if you both have liked one another's profiles.

FIGURE 20.4

An example search page from OkCupid, including a long list of advanced search options that a user can choose from to narrow the results.

FIGURE 20.5

A search option on OkCupid that allows search by username.

OBTAINING DATA

If you can find a target on an online dating website, you will usually find a wealth of personal information. All the attributes a person can search by, as shown in Figure 20.4, are listed on a user's profile page. There are also often short personal essays on a profile page, along with photos. Figures 20.6 and 20.7 show samples of a condensed profile on Match.com and a full profile on OkCupid, respectively. Note the long lists of personal attributes.

WHAT YOU WON'T FIND

At the same time, for privacy and safety, dating sites try to keep users somewhat anonymous. Full names are never shown; rather, a username or a first name and last initial are usually shown instead. Addresses, contact information, and other personal data (which could allow someone to track down someone else) is also kept off these sites.

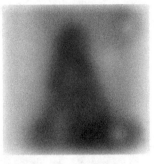

Height:	5' 10" (177 cm)
Body Type:	Slender
Ethnicity:	Black / African descent
Relationships:	Never Married
Have Kids:	No
Want Kids:	Definitely
Drink:	Never
Smoke:	No Way
Religion:	Muslim / Islam
Politics:	Some other viewpoint
Education:	Bachelors degree
Occupation:	Financial / Accounting / Real Estate
Income:	No answer

FIGURE 20.6

A sample summary profile of a Match.com user.

RECENT ACTIVITY

Another common feature on dating sites is to display when a user last visited the site. This can help you learn how often a user is checking in and how frequently they interact on the site.

PROFILE VIEW NOTIFICATIONS

An important thing to keep in mind when using online dating sites to investigate a target is that, in most cases, people can see who viewed their profile. Nearly every site requires you to have an account and to be logged in to search for others. When you visit someone's page, the site typically logs your visit, and shows that person a list of everyone who's viewed their profile. Some sites, like OkCupid, have options to browse anonymously. However, in general, you should expect a visit to someone's page to notify them with a link to your profile.

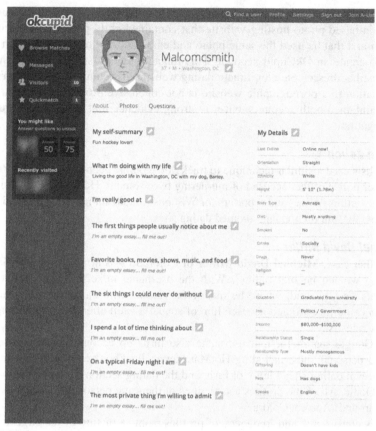

FIGURE 20.7

Example user Malcom's OkCupid profile.

CASE STUDIES

There are many cases where profile information from online dating sites has been useful to better understand a target, to locate them elsewhere online, or even catch them misbehaving.

ARRESTS AND INVESTIGATIONS

There are many stories of people being arrested where information from their online dating profiles was used to discover more information about them or to confirm their identities.

John Baylo

In June 2014, Christian Radio Host **John Baylo** was arrested in Michigan on child pornography charges[1]. He allegedly met his victim through another man, Ronald

Moser. Police used known screen names for Ronald Moser to find his account on a Russia-based photo hosting website that contained child pornographic images. They found that he used the same photo and email address from the Russian porn sites to create an OkCupid account. This linkage, though screen names, photos, and email addresses on a legitimate dating website that contains a lot of personal information to a pornographic website is not conclusive proof that the same person maintained both accounts, but it is strong evidence that would justify further investigation.

Steven Zelich

Journalists used a similar technique to track down online accounts of Steven Zelich, a former police officer accused of murdering two women[2]. He was reported to have met his victims online, and reporters for Wisconsin radio station WTMJ found three accounts for him on bondage-themed dating sites.

Michael David Miller

In another case, **Michael David Miller** of Colorado was arrested for sexually assaulting women he met online[3]. With the username mike22486, he maintained accounts on OkCupid, where he met some victims who came forward. Another woman came forward and accused him of sexual assault after they met through an ad on Craigslist.

A Google search for that username also turns up accounts on several adult-themed personal sites, including HotMatch.com, Fuckbook.com, along with more mainstream dating sites Plenty of Fish, and the dating section of the online marketplace Oodle. All of the profiles use pictures of the same person and list his location in (or around) Aurora, Colorado.

This consistency and frequency of profiles paints a picture of the target's interests, and also serves as a starting point for further investigation into his communications and contacts.

CONCLUSIONS

Online dating websites generally have extensive profile information about people, including their personal attributes and self-descriptive text. Millions of single people, especially in the US, have tried online dating and have profiles on at least one sight. The most popular dating sites have millions of users, but there are dozens of other sites designed for users with narrower interests.

It is rare to be able to browse profiles on dating sites without being logged in. While many sites allow you to create a free profile to search and browse others' profiles, viewing them is usually logged, and notifies the profile's owner. Therefore, during investigations, you should be careful about how you use these sites, especially if you want to keep your searches private.

NOTES

1 http://www.mlive.com/news/grand-rapids/index.ssf/2014/08/man_accused_of_setting_up_chil.html.

2 http://www.620wtmj.com/news/local/Zelich-waves-right-to-preliminary-hearing-requests-new-judge-271419811.html.

3 http://www.thedenverchannel.com/news/local-news/michael-miller-accused-of-sexually-assaulting-woman-he-met-on-dating-website-appears-in-court.

Analyzing networks

21

So far in this book, we've addressed how to collect information that people post on their social media profiles. After collection, there may be useful things to learn from that information as is. But if you want to go further, then the information must be analyzed.

There are many kinds of analysis, but a particularly useful one is *social network analysis:* the analysis of social connections a person has with others. Social network analysis (or *SNA*) involves studying the structure of people's connections—especially things like who is most important or influential in the network and which groups of people are closely connected.

This chapter will introduce basic concepts in SNA and describe some available tools for conducting it. These are more advanced techniques than those covered so far.

INTRODUCTION

Before learning any terminology or technical details, we can begin with an intuitive first example of what can be done with SNA.

First, recall that in almost all social media sites, people have friends or other social connections. In doing SNA, we look at the connections among the target's friends. For example, if Alice is friends with Bob and Chuck, we would consider whether or not Bob and Chuck are friends with one another.

VISUALIZATIONS

Much of the analysis involves using pictures (called *visualizations*) of a social network. Each circle in the image represents a person. If two represented people are friends on the social media site, then they are connected by a line.

A SIMPLE VISUALIZATION

Consider the simple example of Figure 21.1. The three circles represent three people, labeled Alice, Bob, and Chuck. Lines from Alice to Bob and from Alice to Chuck indicate that she has connections to both of them. Conversely, since no line exists between Bob and Chuck, we know they are *not* connected.

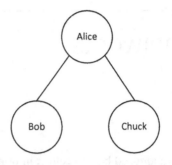

FIGURE 21.1

A visualization of a small social network. This shows that Alice has connections to Bob and Chuck, but that Bob and Chuck do not have a connection to one another.

Most social network visualizations are much larger than this. At those scales, patterns tend to emerge.

A COMPLEX VISUALIZATION

Take a look at Figure 21.2. It will seem complex at first but should be clear with a bit of explanation.

This picture shows all the followers of a specific target on Facebook. The lines that connect two dots indicate that the people have a social connection. In this case, since it is a Facebook network, a line between two dots means that the two people are friends. The target is not in the picture, since we know the target would have a line connecting him or her to every other dot. Remember that although the dots/circles are smaller than in Figure 21.1, each one still represents a person here.

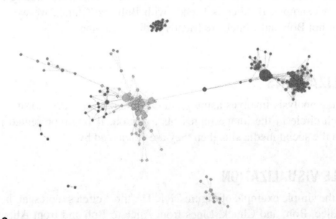

FIGURE 21.2

A visualization of a more complex network. As before, each dot represents a person and each line connecting two dots indicates that those people have a social connection.

Sometimes, when the dots are really close together, you can't see a line between them. On the other hand, the closer the dots are to one another, the more strongly they (and their friends) are connected. Thus, even if you can't see a line between very close dots, there's often a connection between those overlapping dots.

The color coding in the image is used to indicate which people are most tightly grouped together. You'll also notice that some dots are bigger than others. The size indicates the influence that person has in the network. Both the groups of nodes and the importance rankings are things that can be calculated by tools that produce these visualizations, and we will see how that works later in the chapter.

Learning from the Visualization

Proceeding only from the picture in Figure 21.2, we can draw some conclusions. (Recall that the dots are people and the lines are social connections.) First, this target has very distinct groups of friends. The red group toward the top of the image and the green one at the bottom are totally disconnected from everyone else. Only one person connects the blue and purple groups on the right with the larger yellow group on the left. If we put names on the dots, we would know which people are part of which group, who is most influential, etc.

SNA allows us to generate these pictures and make calculations about people's role in the social network. The rest of this chapter will explain the basic terminology and computations of SNA, along with the software available to help you collect and analyze this data.

TERMINOLOGY

If you choose to apply any SNA to your targets, there are some terms that are important to know.

NODES, EDGES, AND GRAPHS

People in your network are called *nodes*. Nodes are represented by the circles/dots in the image shown in Figure 21.1. The relationships between people, shown as lines connecting the nodes in Figure 21.1, are called *links* or *edges*.

A group of nodes and edges make up a *social network*. This is also called a *graph* or *social graph*.

Nodes and edges can have information attached to them. For example, nodes represent people, so they could be labeled with the names of the people they represent. Edges can also have labels. This could describe the type of relationship people have (e.g., family, friend, and coworker), or it could be a numeric value that describes how often people interact with one another or how strong their relationship is.

You can use any labels you want on nodes and edges if it makes the network more informative.

EDGE DIRECTIONALITY

Edges can also have a direction.

An *undirected* edge generally means that the people connected by the edge know one another. For example, on Facebook, when Bob adds Chuck as a friend, Chuck has to approve it. The friendship relationship on Facebook implies that both people want the social connection. However, that is not always the case. For example, on Twitter, Bob may follow Chuck, but Chuck may not follow Bob back. In that case, we would want to represent that the following relationship only goes one way.

A *directed* edge is usually drawn with an arrow head pointing in the direction of the relationship. If there are some directed edges in a network, *all* the edges should have a direction indicated, even if they are mutual. Figure 21.3 shows a couple ways of drawing these edges. In this case, A has a directed edge to B, while A and C have a mutual relationship. The graph on the left shows a double-headed arrow between A and C indicating their relationship. This can also be drawn with two arrows that show each direction, like in the graph on the right.

With any network (directed or undirected), there are common features that are helpful to consider. Figure 21.4 shows a sample network that we will use to think about these concepts. The network in Figure 21.4 is undirected.

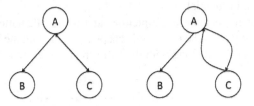

FIGURE 21.3

Two ways of drawing directed networks. The graph on the left has a one-way relationship from node A to node B and a bidirectional relationship between A and C indicated by a two-headed arrow. The same is shown on the right, but two edges connect A and C.

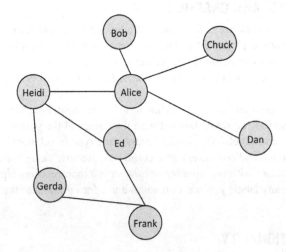

FIGURE 21.4

A sample network with 8 nodes and 8 edges.

PATHS

A *path* is a series of edges connecting two nodes. For example, though Ed and Alice do not have an edge connecting them (there is not a direct relationship), there is a path from Ed, to Heidi, to Alice. Paths have lengths, which are measured in the number of edges you have to traverse to get from one person to the next. In the path from Ed to Alice, the shortest path between them has a length of 2 (one edge from Ed to Heidi and another from Heidi to Alice).

From Frank to Chuck, there are two shortest paths: the first step can go to either Ed or Gerda; then, the second step goes to Heidi, then to Alice, and then to Chuck. The path length is 4.

Shortest path length is a very important property in SNA. It helps you understand how closely two people are connected. If the shortest path connecting two people is very long, it is unlikely that they may ever interact or influence one another. Two people with a path of length 2 between them mean that it's more likely they will have some interaction.

NODE DEGREE

People may have many friends or few. In a network, the number of connections a node has is called a *degree*. In Figure 21.4,

- Alice has the highest degree: 4 (connections to Heidi, Bob, Chuck, and Dan);
- Dan has a degree of 1 (only one connection to Alice); and
- Frank has a degree of 2 (connections to Gerda and Ed).

If you have a directed network, nodes also have an *in degree* and an *out degree*, which correspond to the number of edges coming in (with arrows pointing at the node) and going out (arrows pointing away), respectively.

Egocentric Networks

It is not possible to look at the full Facebook network of 1.4 billion people. It is too big and it is unlikely to yield many interesting insights from looking at the whole thing. However, one way we often look at social network data is through an *egocentric network*. This is a social network focused around one individual. The egocentric network for Alice will consist of Alice's friends' any edges that exist between her friends.

In Figure 21.4, Alice has four friends: Heidi, Bob, Chuck, and Dan. There are no edges directly connecting any of them to one another, so Alice's egocentric network would have only 4 stand-alone nodes.

In social media, egocentric networks are often much more complex and interesting. For example, Figure 21.2 is actually a visualization of the author's egocentric network on Facebook. The colored clusters represent different groups of friends. The yellow group in the center is work friends. The blue group toward the upper right is family and the purplish group next to that is high school friends. The large blue node connecting family and high school friends is her brother. The green group isolated at the bottom is her hockey team, and the red group at the top is a group of internet friends who met on a forum.

Clusters

This egocentric network also highlights another important concept for analyzing networks: *clusters*. Clusters are groups of nodes that have many connections between them and are more tightly grouped than others. There is no real technical definition of a cluster, but they are easy to see when looking at a picture of the network, like in Figure 21.2.

This chapter will primarily focus on egocentric networks—specifically, a target's egocentric network. The analysis will reveal information about the target's social circles, the people important in the target's life, and those who have the most influence among the target's friends.

ANALYSIS

One of the most interesting things we can do when analyzing a social network is to determine which nodes are most important. There are a number of ways to do this, and each measure tells us about importance in a different way. In this section, we will look at the most popular measures of node importance, but we will not go over the details of how to calculate these values. If you use a network analysis program (discussed later in this chapter), it will calculate those values for you.[1] Thus, the important thing to take from this section is to recognize the names and meanings of each measure.

CENTRALITY

Centrality is the term used to describe the collection of measures that indicate how important a node is. There are a number of ways to calculate centrality, but we will focus on four major methods: **degree centrality**, **closeness centrality**, **betweenness centrality**, and **eigenvector centrality**.

Degree Centrality

Degree centrality is the simplest centrality measure to compute. Recall that a node's degree is simply a count of how many social connections (i.e., edges) it has. The degree centrality for a node is simply its degree. A node with 10 social connections would have a degree centrality of 10. A node with 1 edge would have a degree centrality of 1.

Sometimes, a SNA program will convert those numbers into a 0-1 scale. In such cases, the node with the highest degree in the network will have a degree centrality of 1, and every other node's centrality will be the fraction of its degree compared with that most popular node. For example, if the highest-degree node in a network has 20 edges, a node with 10 edges would have a degree centrality of 0.5 ($10 \div 20$). A node with a degree of 2 would have a degree centrality of 0.1 ($2 \div 20$).

For degree centrality, **higher values** mean that the node is more central. As mentioned above, each centrality measure indicates a different type of importance. Degree centrality shows how many connections a person has. They may be connected to lots of people at the heart of the network, but they might also be far off

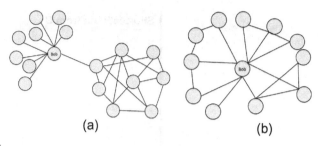

FIGURE 21.5

Two networks where "Bob" has a degree of 9. In (a), he is on the periphery of the main network. In (b), he is right in the middle.

on the edge of the network. For example, in Figure 21.5, both nodes labeled "Bob" have the same high degree (i.e., lots of social connections, 9 in this case), but the two roles they play are very different. The one on the right is very central and the one on the left is peripheral. These show that while degree centrality accurately tells us who has a lot of social connections, it does not necessarily show who is in the "middle" of the network.

Closeness Centrality

Closeness centrality looks for the node that is closest to all other nodes. Recall that a path is a series of steps that go from one node to another. Closeness centrality for a node is the average length of all the shortest paths from that one node to every other node in the network.

To see how it works, we can do a simple example with the network in Figure 21.6. Let us determine the closeness centrality for node D and for node A. Start by computing the average shortest path length of node D. Next, we need the distance from D to every other node in the network. It has a distance of 1 to each of its direct friends: C, E, and H. The following table shows all of the shortest path lengths for D.

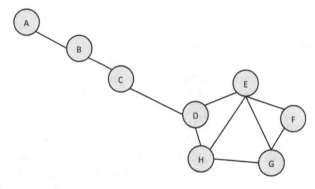

FIGURE 21.6

A sample network.

Node	Shortest path from D
A	3
B	2
C	1
E	1
F	2
G	2
H	1

The average of those shortest path lengths is

$$\frac{(3+2+1+1+2+2+1)}{7} = \frac{12}{7} = 1.71$$

We divide it by 7 because there are 7 other nodes. Thus, the closeness centrality for node D is **1.71**.

We do the same process for node A. The table below has all the shortest path lengths.

Node	Shortest path from A
B	1
C	2
D	3
E	4
F	5
G	5
H	4

Here, the average shortest path length is

$$\frac{(1+2+3+4+5+5+4)}{7} = \frac{24}{7} = 3.43$$

Thus, node A's closeness centrality is **3.43**.

In the case of closeness centrality—unlike with degree centrality—*smaller* values mean that the node is more central, because it means that it takes fewer steps to get to other nodes. So, since D's value of 1.71 is smaller than A's value of 3.43, D is more central.

Closeness centrality corresponds the closest to what we see visually. Nodes that are very central by this measure tend to appear in the middle of a network. A node with strong closeness centrality also tends to be close to most people. In an investigation, that means the person will be in a good position to hear from most friends of friends. They will be a good source of secondhand information since it can reach them quite easily.

The final two centrality measures are more complicated in their calculation, but they also offer additional insights.

Betweenness Centrality

Betweenness centrality is a widely used measure that captures a person's role in allowing information to pass from one part of the network to the other.

For example, consider Bob in Figure 21.5 (A). He is the critical mode that allows information to pass from the cluster on the right to all the individual people he knows that were shown on the left. All information passing to and from those notes on the left must go through Bob if it is going to reach anyone else.

Thus, Bob is very important to the flow of information through this network. This is what betweenness centrality captures. Technically, it measures the percentage of shortest paths that must go through the specific node. The computation of this is quite complex, but every network analysis software tool will compute it for you. The important thing to know is that betweenness is a measure of how important the node is to the flow of information through a network.

In an investigation, a node with high betweenness is likely to be aware of what is going on in multiple social circles. For example, in Figure 21.2, the large blue node in the upper right connects the blue group to the purple group. It is the only node that does so. Thus, talking to this large blue node with high betweenness is likely to yield insights about what both groups are doing and what is going on between those two groups.

Eigenvector Centrality

The final centrality measure is *eigenvector centrality*. It measures the influence that a node has in a network. Again, the computation is quite complex, but any software package you use will compute it for you. (Interestingly, this measure is very similar to what Google uses to rank web pages by importance.)

A node may have a low-degree centrality—and maybe even weak closeness centrality and betweenness centrality—but it can still be influential. Although a node that is central by one measure is *often* central by several other measures, this is not necessarily always the case.

Figure 21.7 shows centrality according to the four measures we have looked at. Red nodes are very central according to the given measure, and blue nodes are not central. Notice how there are large differences among the four pictures of the same network.

In summary, in an investigation, it is worth taking a look at anyone who has high centrality according to any of these measures. It's important to remember what each measure of centrality means:

- **Degree centrality** shows people with many social connections.
- **Closeness centrality** indicates who is at the heart of a social network.
- **Betweenness centrality** describes people who connect social circles.
- **Eigenvector centrality** is high among influential people in the network.

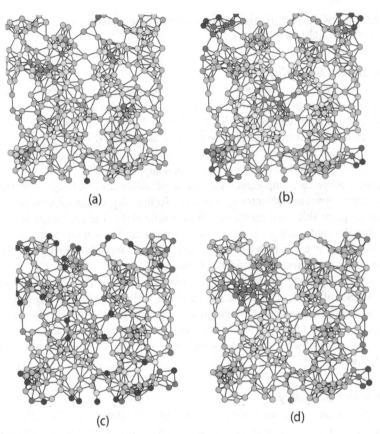

(a)   (b)

(c)   (d)

FIGURE 21.7

This is the same network shown four times. Color coding indicates centrality according for different measures. Red nodes are more central and blue nodes are less central. Version (a) is degree centrality, (b) uses closeness centrality, (c) shows betweenness centrality, and (d) is eigenvector centrality. This visualization is adapted from Claudio Rocchini.

OBTAINING SOCIAL NETWORK AND DATA

For anyone—of any skill level—obtaining data about the social network is often the most challenging part of the process. Although social networks can be encoded by hand, social media networks often have hundreds or thousands of people in them, with thousands or tens of thousands of edges, making hand encoding impossible.

Fortunately, there are tools available online and built into network analysis tools that will grab the social network for a target user and allow you to save it in a format that an analysis tool can open. Those tools are constantly evolving and changing, and new ones are becoming available.

In the next chapter, we will look at popular and stable tools that are likely to be available to you. Those tools will also allow you to analyze social networks.

In addition to computing the centrality measures described above with other statistics, these tools create *visualizations*. The images in Figures 21.2 and 21.7 are network visualizations. It is essentially a picture of the network. Nodes are shown as dots and edges are lines connecting them. There are many automated techniques for arranging the network into patterns that highlight important features, like clusters and important nodes.

The next chapter will also illustrate how to get started with these tools, including how to calculate some of the statistics mentioned here and how to create a visualization. But before we get to the details of how to get the data and create a visualization, let's look at some examples of what you should look for in a visualization and what it means in the context of an investigation.

EXAMPLE ANALYSES

To see how this analysis could work in an investigation, this section will present several example networks and walk through some of the insights that come from looking at them.

EXAMPLE 1

Start by looking at the network in Figure 21.8. (This network is contrived for illustrative purposes, not created from real-world data.) We will treat it as the egocentric network of a target (i.e., each node is a person the target knows). The edges connect which of those people know one another.

The nodes in Figure 21.8 indicate additional information as follows:

- Color indicates betweenness centrality (higher betweenness nodes are darker).
- Size indicates degree centrality (higher-degree nodes are larger).

Each node is labeled with a letter to make discussion easier.

What are some things we can learn about the target from looking at this network?

First, remember that this is an egocentric network. It shows only people who are connected to the target. The edges indicate which of the target's connections know one another. For example, since node Z and node S are connected in the network, that means that the target knows both Z and S and they know one another.

With that in mind, the groups at the top and bottom become very interesting. At the bottom, node Z is connected to six people (T, U, V, W, X, and Y) who are not connected to anyone else. Since this is an egocentric network, that means that the target and node Z know all these people, but they do not know anyone else in the social circle. This probably implies that the target and Z have a special kind of relationship where they are together when they meet other people. There is no way to know what kind of relationship, but spouses would be one example where we

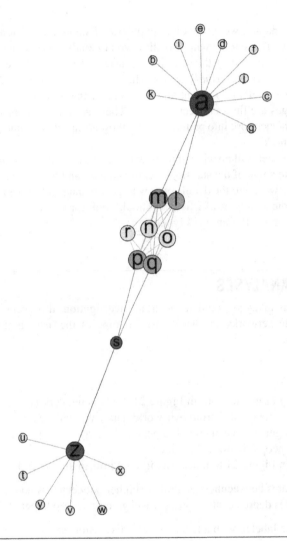

FIGURE 21.8

A sample egocentric network of a target. Color indicates betweenness centrality, with darker nodes being more central. Size indicates degree centrality, where larger nodes have higher degree.

might see this. If the target and node Z are married, it is likely that, as a couple, they would have met people together. The nodes connected to Z could be six people they had met as a couple.

Even more interesting is the fact that at the top of the network in Figure 21.8 is *another* node with which the target had a similar relationship. Node A is connected to 9 other nodes that are not connected to anyone else in the network. Could this be another romantic relationship for the target, where the couple is meeting different people? Could it be a business partner and could this part of the network reflect business contacts that the partners have met together? We can't tell that from the network, but the fact that the target has these type of relationships means that both node A and node Z would be interesting people to look to for more information.

There is also a tightly connected cluster of people in the middle of the network, and node A knows two of these people as well. While this group is very tightly connected, it is not uncommon to see groups like this in egocentric networks. It usually reflects a tight group of friends or coworkers who are all connected to one another. Since, basically, everyone in this group knows everyone else, it makes it interesting that only two of the nodes know node A. Does that mean these two nodes (M and L) are connected to another part of the target's life? Do they hold a position of special privilege? Why would they know node A when no one else in the tightly clustered group does? This makes nodes M and L interesting for a couple reasons: first, because there are these open questions about their relationship with the target and, second, because they can likely provide more insights into the target's relationship with node A.

Node S is also connected to two people in this cluster: P and Q. But node S has only one other connection—Z.

This also raises a few questions. First, what does it mean that node Z does not know anyone in the central cluster? If node Z has a special relationship with the target, why is Z in the dark about people with whom the target obviously has a close relationship?

It also leads to questions about node S. Is S like the other singleton nodes known by the target and node Z, and it just happens that S knows other nodes in the main cluster? Or do the target and node S have a special relationship where node S is connected to the target's main group and the group connected to node Z.

EXAMPLE 2

Now, let's consider a larger network that is more typical of what you might find when looking at a target's social media network. Figure 21.9 shows the egocentric network for a Twitter user.

There are two major features of this network that pop out in the visualization:

- First, there is a large, tightly grouped cluster shown in red that has some connections to the large central group but is mostly separated.
- Second, there is a very large blue node in the center cluster. It has a thick black border added to make it easier to see in this visualization. This node happens to connect the red cluster to the main part of the network.

Understanding who these groups and individuals are will provide insight into what the relationships are in this network.

We can begin by focusing on that large node. It has high betweenness (indicated by the large size) because many shortest paths pass through it. Essentially, this node

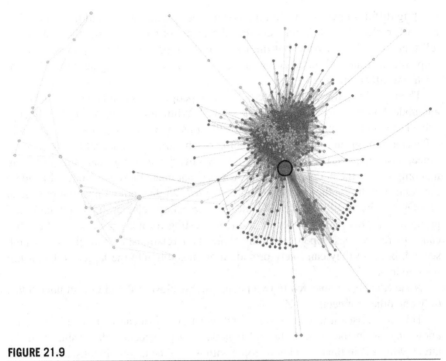

FIGURE 21.9

An egocentric network for a Twitter user. Color indicates the community where our analysis tool guesses each person belongs to. Size indicates betweenness centrality.

connects the main part of the network with the red cluster. Thus, we know that both this node and the target, who is not shown in the network, know one another and that they both know two groups of people: the red group and the main group including blue, green, orange, and purple nodes.

The next step is to understand what makes the red cluster unique. This is not something we can deduce just from looking at the visualization. Instead, we need to look at who the people are whom these nodes represent. On social media, that means finding the accounts of people in the cluster and looking for common patterns. When there are hundreds of nodes, as in this case, you can start by picking a handful to examine to see if patterns emerge. In this example, we would do that by displaying or finding the usernames of some nodes in the red cluster and going to their profiles at http://twitter.com/«username».

These users are not revealed here to protect their privacy, but an analysis would show that the users in the red cluster almost exclusively post in Japanese and are located in Japan. Users in the main cluster, on the other hand, are primarily English speakers. Thus, our target (and the large blue node in the center) appears to have connections to a community of Japanese users in addition to their main contacts who speak English.

In many people's social media networks, you are likely to find clusters like this, and they will often share a distinguishing trait. It may not be something as obvious as language. You may have to probe deeper into their profiles to see where they are from, what they topics are that they discuss, or what other personal attributes they have in common.

NOTE

1 If you're interested in learning how to do this analysis in a more mathematically technical way, the author recommends you read her other book, Analyzing the Social Web!

How to use NodeXL

22

Derek Hansen[1] and Marc Smith[2]
[1]Brigham Young University, Provo, UT, USA
[2]Social Media Research Foundation, Belmont, CA, USA

GETTING STARTED WITH NODEXL

Network data is inherently different than traditional datasets and require specialized software to analyze and visualize. New tools, such as NodeXL, are making network analysis increasingly accessible, particularly to nonprogrammers. NodeXL is a free add-in for Microsoft Excel, supported by the Social Media Research Foundation. In this chapter, we'll introduce the basics of using NodeXL. For a more comprehensive treatment, see *Analyzing Social Media Networks with NodeXL: Insights from a Connected World.*

INSTALLING AND NAVIGATING

Users of recent versions of Windows and Office can run NodeXL. The application is downloaded from http://nodexl.codeplex.com. Once installed, type "NodeXL" into the start menu and choose "NodeXL Excel Template." This will open a blank NodeXL workbook file, which includes a custom NodeXL menu ribbon as shown in Figure 22.1. The menu provides access to all NodeXL features, which are organized into meaningful groups such as Data, Graph, Visual Properties, and Analysis. Network data is stored in Excel worksheets, while the graph pane displays the network visually as shown in Figure 22.1.

Each NodeXL workbook file (which ends in .xlsx like all Excel files) includes a single network. Within each file, there are several specialized worksheets, which each contains data associated with different dimensions of a network. For example, the **Vertices** worksheet includes a row for each person (i.e., node) in the network as shown in Figure 22.1. Additional information about each person is shown in the many columns to the right of the person. For example, the number of followers and tweets associated with each user in Figure 22.1 are shown. Other columns show the visual properties of a node (e.g., its color, size, and shape), labels, and centrality metrics that help identify how "important" a person is in the network.

The **Edges** worksheet includes a row for each link, tie, or connection between two entities along with related information. For example, the first row of Figure 22.2 shows that Twitter user bostontweetup mentioned ga_boston in a tweet posted 1 Dec,

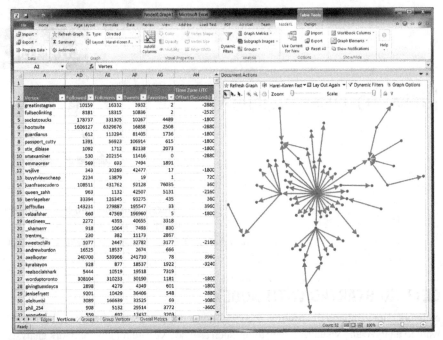

FIGURE 22.1

NodeXL worksheets (left), graph pane (right), and custom menu (top) in Excel showing Twitter data.

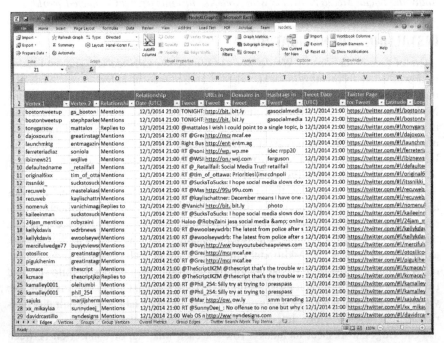

FIGURE 22.2

NodeXL Vertices worksheet and graph pane showing data from Twitter.

2014 at 21:00, along with other information. Other columns show information such as the visual properties (e.g., thickness and style) and labels associated with each edge.

Additional worksheets contain additional information about the summary of overall network metrics, the composition of groups (i.e., clusters of related nodes), and the summary of textual analysis of text content. The following sections explain how to capture social media network data similar to this example and introduce the techniques needed to gain insights into network data by calculating appropriate network metrics and creating meaningful visualizations.

COLLECTING NETWORK DATA

Although network data is at the core of social media sites, these services do not always make it easy to extract. NodeXL helps collect social media network data by providing data importers that automatically grab data from popular social media sources such as Twitter, email, YouTube, and Flickr. Additionally, third-party data importers (which can be installed separately) allow users to import data from other sources such as Facebook and MediaWiki (see http://nodexl.codeplex. com/wikipage?title=Third-Party%20NodeXL%20Graph%20Data%20Importers). Network data can also be manually entered, copied in from another spreadsheet, and imported from another network analysis tool (e.g., GraphML file) or from the NodeXL Graph Gallery (found at http://nodexlgraphgallery.org), which features collections of NodeXL network datasets available for download.

Importing Twitter Search Data

To import tweets that contain a certain keyword or phrase, choose the NodeXL > Data > Import > From Twitter Search Network menu option from the NodeXL menu ribbon. This will open the import dialog shown in Figure 22.3. This feature can create a network of Twitter users who recently used the keyword(s) you specify ("social media" in this example). Twitter users will be connected to each other based on mention and reply-to relationships as shown in Figure 22.2.

The search term(s) that you want to map and measure can be entered in this dialog along with other options as desired. By default, the importer only grabs the latest 100 tweets, which should be increased to as much as 18,000 for more popular items. Twitter's data access rules and restrictions limit the amount of data you can download, particularly for follow relationships, as described in the "More about this option" section. Additionally, only recent data is collected—anywhere from a few hours to about a week depending on the popularity of the topic. The first time you use the NodeXL Twitter importer, you will need to authenticate with Twitter as described in the checkboxes in the lower left corner of Figure 22.3. Selecting the "Expand URLS in Tweets" option will convert shortened URLs into their underlying form.

After clicking OK and waiting for the network data to download from Twitter, NodeXL will populate the Edges and Vertices worksheets with the basic network data and the additional Twitter statistics shown in Figures 22.1 and 22.2.

Other NodeXL network importers work in a similar way, although the networks they create differ depending on the types of connections supported by the social media

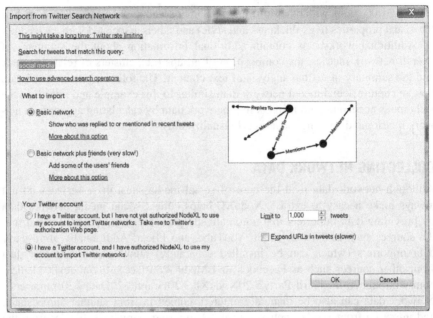

FIGURE 22.3

Twitter Search Network importer with limit changed to 1000 tweets and the search phrase "social media" entered.

platform. For example, the YouTube Video Network imports a network where the nodes are YouTube videos and the edges connecting them are generated based on the number of people who comment on both videos (or the number of category tags they share).

Importing a Sample Facebook Ego Network

The remainder of this chapter will use data from one of the author's anonymized Facebook ego network. In other words, it shows the relationships among all of one of the author's Facebook friends (though their names have been changed to the most popular baby names of 2014). You can find the Sample Facebook Ego network on the NodeXL Teaching Resources web page, which also links to other resources that may be of interest: https://nodexl.codeplex.com/wikipage?title=NodeXL%20Teaching%20 Resources. Once downloaded to your desktop (or other "trusted" location on your computer), open a new NodeXL file and choose NodeXL>Data>Import>From NodeXL Workbook Created on Another Computer. This will create a local copy of the NodeXL network data file, which you can then navigate to and open.

Alternatively, you can import your own Facebook ego network after installing the Social Network Importer for NodeXL plug-in (see http://socialnetimporter.codeplex. com for download and installation instructions). There are three different Facebook importers that extract networks from Facebook Fan Pages, Groups, and personal Friend networks. To import your personal ego network, use the default settings in the From Facebook Personal and Timeline Network importer.

After importing the sample file or your own network, change the Graph Type to Undirected. To do this, find the Type: drop down in the Graph portion of the NodeXL ribbon and select Undirected. Facebook Friendship relationships must be mutual or "undirected." When analyzing other networks, such as Twitter follow networks, the network Type should be set to Directed, which will assure that arrows appear on network edges to indicate a relationship that starts with one person and ends with another.

ANALYZING NETWORKS

NodeXL includes several tools to help analyze network data, which are available via the Analysis section of the NodeXL menu ribbon. This section introduces the most commonly used features including a guide to creating groups of nodes based on network clustering algorithms and calculating common social network analysis metrics such as those described in the prior chapter.

CREATING GROUPS OF NODES

It is often useful to identify network groups or collections of nodes that belong together. Groups can be created based on different techniques in NodeXL, which are available via the Groups drop-down menu in the Analysis section of the NodeXL menu ribbon. One technique is to create groups based on a shared attribute of the vertices (e.g., Facebook users that share the same gender and Twitter users that are in the same time zone). Another technique, illustrated in this section, is to create groups based on the network structure itself.

As illustrated in the prior chapter, there are often subsets of nodes that are highly connected to one another, which are only loosely connected to other nodes or subgroups in the network. This will become apparent as we calculate network-based groups, called clusters in NodeXL, in the Sample Facebook Ego network file. The sample Facebook file includes all of one of the author's Facebook friendship interconnections. The author is not shown in the graph itself, since he would be connected to all other nodes, making it unnecessarily cluttered. The focus instead is on the shared connections among his friends.

Once you have opened the file, choose the "Group by Cluster" option in the NodeXL>Analysis>Groups drop-down menu, which will open a window similar to that shown in Figure 22.4. There are several clustering algorithms (also called "community detection algorithms") to choose from, each of which will give slightly different results. Trial and error can help identify the one that creates the most meaningful groupings. For now, use the Clauset-Newman-Moore algorithm and make sure to check the box, which will create a single group that includes all nodes that are disconnected from all other nodes. This can help keep graphs with many isolated individuals less cluttered.

Once the clustering algorithm calculation completes, you will be taken to the Groups worksheet shown in Figure 22.5. Each row on the worksheet shows a

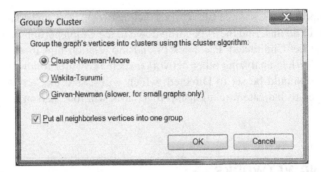

FIGURE 22.4

Group by Cluster options.

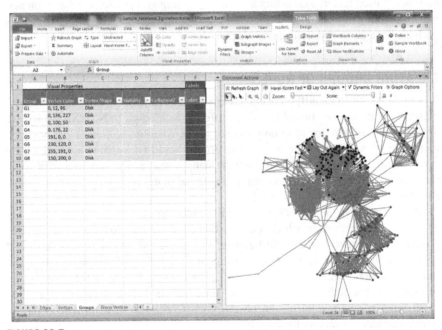

FIGURE 22.5

Groups worksheet showing eight different groups (G1, G2, … G8).

different group (named G1, G2, G3…) each of which is given a default color and shape, which becomes visible when the NodeXL > Graph > Refresh Graph menu option is selected. Clicking on one of the rows will highlight all of the nodes in that group. Labels can be entered in the label column (see Figure 22.5). Do not change the group names themselves (e.g., G1), since changing them will break the group functionality. Labels only show up if the network visualization is configured to show each group in a separate area on the graph pane, as described later in this chapter. NodeXL can automatically calculate network metrics for each group as described in the following section.

In the Facebook social network, the groups created and shown in Figure 22.5 correspond to different groups of the friends of one of the authors. For example, G1 consists of one of the author's family and friends, G2 includes friends from graduate housing, G3 includes work colleagues, and so forth. To be clear, the network clustering algorithm knows nothing about the individuals' attributes (e.g., where they went to graduate school). It creates groups based solely on which nodes are densely connected to one another in distinct clusters. Labels, such as "work colleagues," can be applied only by someone who knows the network and can interpret it.

The list of which nodes are included in each group is stored in the NodeXL Group Vertices worksheet. For example, in the sample file, we see that Becket, Tucker, and many others are part of G1 since they are next to G1.

CALCULATING NETWORK METRICS

Many commonly used network metrics can be calculated using NodeXL. Choose Graph Metrics from the Analysis portion of the NodeXL ribbon to open the dialog shown in Figure 22.6. This shows a list of all possible metrics that can be calculated including the centrality metrics described in the prior chapter (e.g., Degree, Closeness, Betweenness, and Eigenvector Centrality), Overall Metrics (described in the table at the bottom of the dialog), and Group Metrics. For moderately sized networks, you can Select All to calculate all of them and then decide which to use later.

The various network metrics are displayed on the appropriate worksheets. For example, the centrality metrics, which are calculated for each individual node, are displayed on the Vertices worksheet in a set of columns labeled Graph Metrics. Likewise, the Group Metrics are displayed on the Groups worksheet. The Overall Metrics that describe the entire network graph are displayed on their own Overall Metrics worksheet. If Twitter search network top item metrics were calculated (on imported Twitter data), they will also show up on their own worksheet.

The meaning of network metrics differs depending on the specific dataset you are analyzing. For example, in the Sample Facebook Ego network dataset, the degree centrality metrics (found on the Vertices worksheet) can be interpreted as the number of shared friends that the person has with the author. Betweenness centrality helps identify bridge spanners—that is, individuals who uniquely connect to otherwise disconnected groups. For example, Lena has a high betweenness centrality because she was the only friend connected to work colleagues and graduate housing friends.

Sorting by Network Metrics

A useful strategy for identifying the most "important" individuals in the network is to use Excel's built-in sort feature. For example, navigate to the Betweenness Centrality column on the Vertices worksheet and choose "Sort Largest to Smallest" from the

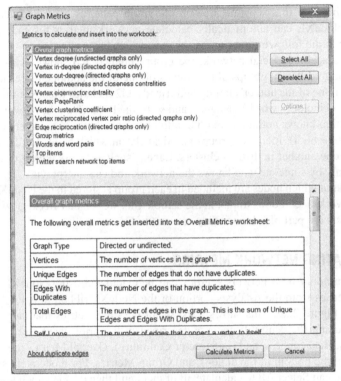

FIGURE 22.6

Graph Metrics dialog after choosing Select All.

drop-down menu found within the title cell. This will sort the entire table so that the vertices with the highest betweenness centrality will show up at the top of the table and those with the lowest will be at the bottom as shown in Figure 22.7. Note that eigenvector centrality in NodeXL is calculated as 1/(average shortest distance) so that higher numbers indicate that the node is more central to the network (i.e., has a shorter average path distance to all other nodes).

VISUALIZING NETWORKS

Networks are complex structures, and to fully understand them, it is often useful to visualize them. Network metrics give only a partial picture, just as summary statistics like the average and standard deviation only give a partial picture of a distribution. Sometimes, a picture really is worth a thousand words—or numbers. NodeXL provides a very sophisticated and highly customizable network visualization toolset that is briefly introduced in this section. Features associated with network visualization are found in the Graph and Visual Properties sections of the NodeXL menu ribbon and the top of the graph pane itself.

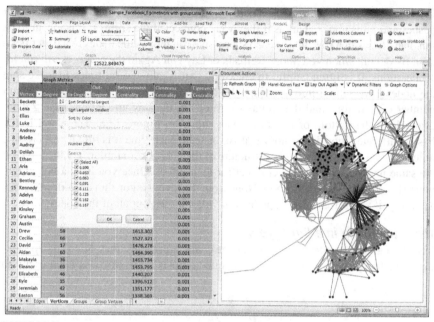

FIGURE 22.7

Sorting on betweenness centrality from largest to smallest to identify bridge spanners.

DISPLAYING AND LAYING OUT NETWORKS

To visualize a network in NodeXL, simply click on the Show Graph/Refresh Graph button in the NodeXL graph pane or menu ribbon. This will place the vertices on the graph pane and show the edges between them. If it is a directed network, such as an email network, then it will state that the Type is Directed in the NodeXL ribbon and edges will include arrows. If it is an undirected network, such as a Facebook friend network, then no arrows will be shown. The network type can be changed at any time in the NodeXL ribbon menu.

Individual nodes can be moved by simply clicking and dragging them to a different location. Groups of nodes can be selected by drawing a rectangle around them or by right-clicking on a node and choosing Select Adjacent Vertices, which will select all nodes that are directly connected to the selected node. Groups of selected nodes can be moved all at once. When a node is selected in the graph pane, it is highlighted in red, and its corresponding data in the Vertices worksheet are also selected. It is often useful to fine-tune layouts in order to reduce unnecessary edge crossings or nodes that are obscured by other nodes or edges.

Choosing a Layout Algorithm

There are a number of different "layout algorithms" that determine the position of nodes on the graph pane. NodeXL allows you to choose which layout algorithm to use as shown in Figure 22.8. The first two options are typically best for large social media datasets (including the Sample Facebook Ego network), though the

Circle layout can also be used effectively at times. The Fruchterman-Reingold layout pushes and pulls nodes apart as if they were connected via springs. It is meant to be run many times in a row, where each successive run moves the nodes to a better position. By default when you Show, Refresh, or Lay Out Again the graph, it will run for 10 iterations. It is often helpful to click Lay Out Again several times to make sure the nodes have settled into a reasonable location. You can also change the default number of iterations and the "repulsive force" in the Layout Options dialog that's available at the bottom of the drop-down shown in Figure 22.8. The Harel-Koren Fast Multiscale algorithm is not iterative. Instead, each time it is run, it will create a unique layout, though the overall structure of the network is similar. Try these out on the same network and you'll get a feel for their effect. Once you have a layout that you're happy with, you can choose None from the layout algorithm drop-down menu. That way, if you refresh the graph later, it will not relayout all of the nodes.

Using the Group in a Box Layout

Visualizing large or dense networks can be challenging since they often end up looking like a hairball. To help gain insights into complex networks, it is often useful to

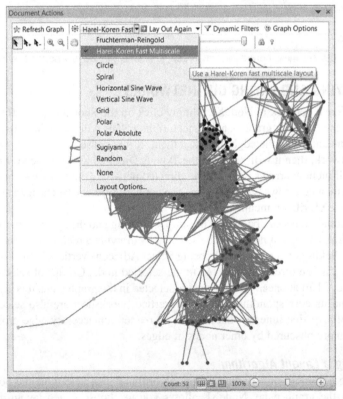

FIGURE 22.8

Graph pane with the layout algorithm drop-down expanded.

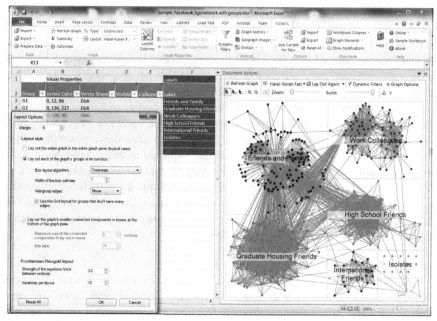

FIGURE 22.9

Group in a Box layout with group labels and Layout Options dialog shown.

visualize each connected component (i.e., subnetwork that is not connected to other nodes in the network) or cluster of nodes in its own section of the graph pane. This is called the "Group in a Box" layout, since it assigns a different group into its own box as shown in Figure 22.9, which displays the Sample Facebook Ego network. To recreate this layout, choose Layout Options from the layout algorithm drop-down menu on the graph pane, which will open up the Layout Options dialog shown on the left-hand side of Figure 22.9. Choose "Lay out each of the graph's groups in its own box" and check the box that says "Use the Grid layout for groups that don't have many edges." Click OK and refresh the graph to see the changes take effect. Labels that have been entered into the Groups worksheet, as shown in Figure 22.9, will now appear at the center of each group box. Play around with some of the other options, such as the box layout algorithm and intergroup edges in the Layout Options menu to see some alternatives.

VISUAL PROPERTIES

Each node and edge has a number of visual properties such as color that can be used to create more meaningful and readable network graph visualizations. The available visual properties for each edge are found on the Edges worksheet and include Color, Width, Style (e.g., solid, dashed, and dotted), Opacity, and Visibility (e.g., if the edge is shown at all). Nodes can be styled on the Vertices worksheet by changing their color, shape (including geometric shapes and images and labels, which pull image or label data from other columns), Size, Opacity, and Visibility. The Groups page also has columns for Vertex Color, Vertex Shape, Visibility, and Collapse (which will combine all nodes in a group into a single large node).

Data can be entered into the visual properties cells in several ways. Some columns such as Shape have a list of preset options that become available in a drop-down menu once you click inside of a specific cell. To choose a color, click into a cell and click on the color picker icon in the Visual Properties section of the NodeXL ribbon. After choosing a color, the red, green, and blue values or the official name of the color will populate the cell. Notice that tool tips drop-down when the mouse hovers in these cells to explain what values are expected in these columns. In addition to manually selecting values, Excel formulas can also be used. For example, if Facebook data is provided on gender in a separate column, a simple If formula could be written to change the color of the nodes to differ for males and females. However, the easiest way to change visual properties based on other data is to use the NodeXL Autofill Columns feature as described below.

Using Autofill Columns

The Autofill Columns feature in NodeXL automatically fills the Visual Properties data (or other columns such as Label or Tooltip) based on data stored in some other column on the same spreadsheet. To see how this works, click on the Autofill Columns button in the NodeXL menu ribbon to open the dialog (Figure 22.10). Next, click on the Vertices tab and choose Betweenness Centrality from the drop-down menu next to the Vertex Size: row and click Autofill button at the bottom. This will make nodes with a higher betweenness centrality a larger size helping to draw visual attention to them.

Notice that the Size column on the Vertices worksheet now has been populated with values ranging from 10 (for Becket) to 1.5 (for most of the nodes with a relatively small betweenness centrality). By default, a linear mapping is used. In other words, the largest betweenness centrality value (43,269) becomes 10, the smallest value (0) becomes 1.5, and something right in the middle would be mapped to a size right in the middle. As a result, since Becket has such a high betweenness centrality compared with the others, his circle becomes large (size 10) and all the others look incomparably small.

To create a more meaningful visualization, click on the arrow in the Options section (see right-hand side of Figure 22.10) next to the Vertex Size row and choose "Vertex Size Options…." This will open up the dialog shown in Figure 22.11, which allows you to change how size is impacted by betweenness centrality. Increase the maximum vertex size (To this vertex size) to 15 instead of 10. Next, check the "Ignore outliers" box. This will make it so that Becket's extremely high betweenness centrality (considered an outlier) will not be used to determine the size of all other nodes. It will be given the maximum size (of 15), but the next nonoutlier score (Lena's betweenness centrality of 12,522) will become the new maximum size when determining the size of all other nodes. Click OK and the Autofill button and look at the Size column on the Vertex worksheet. It should look like the one in Figure 22.12.

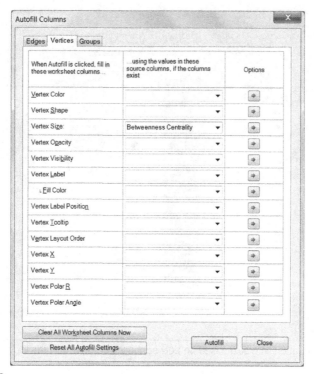

FIGURE 22.10

Autofill Columns dialog showing the Vertices tab and basing the Vertex Size based on Betweenness Centrality.

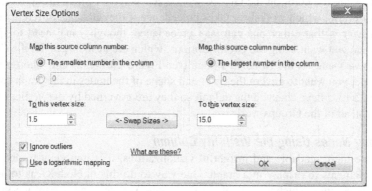

FIGURE 22.11

Autofill Column Vertex Size Options dialog.

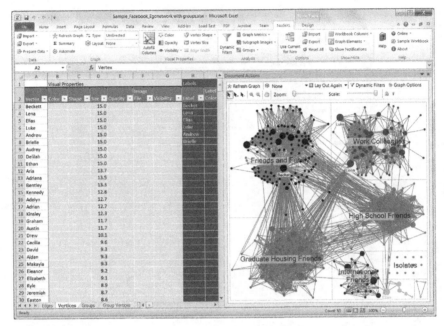

FIGURE 22.12

Network visualization with size based on betweenness centrality and the top six individuals with labels.

Choosing Between Group and Vertex Level Data Sources for Determining Vertex Color and Shape

A final warning is in order. As you may remember, both the Vertices worksheet and the Groups worksheet have columns that define the Color and Shape of vertices. For example, the color on the Vertices worksheet may be based on the gender of the person, while the color on the Groups worksheet indicates which group the person is a part of. So, which worksheet takes precedence if they indicate different colors? The answer is that either one can take precedence, though you'll need to specify which one you want using the Group Options, which are available under the Groups drop-down menu on the NodeXL ribbon (see Figure 22.13). Simply choose which worksheet you want to govern the color and shape of the nodes in the graph pane. In Figure 22.13, I have changed the default so they are governed by the Vertices worksheet instead of the Groups worksheet.

Filtering Nodes Using the Visibility Column

To create more readable and insightful visualizations, it is important to determine which elements to display in a graph. One way to do this in NodeXL is to use the Visibility column, which is available on the Edges, Vertices, and Groups worksheets.

The Visibility options on the Vertices worksheet are shown in Figure 22.14. To reduce clutter, only nodes with at least one edge connected to them are shown by default

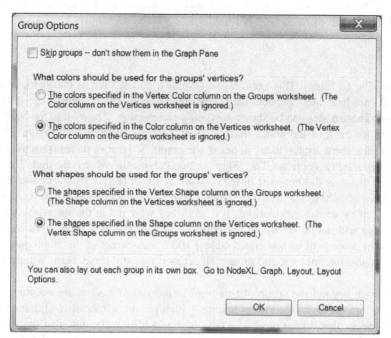

FIGURE 22.13

Group Options window configured so that the colors and shapes on the graph will be from the Vertices worksheet.

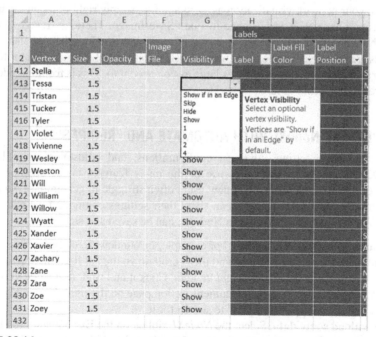

FIGURE 22.14

Visibility options on the Vertices worksheet.

(Show if in an Edge). This excludes any isolated nodes, such as Facebook Friends who do not have any connections to any other Friends in the sample ego network dataset. These nodes can be shown by typing or selecting "Show" into the Visibility column for each of the nodes that have no other connections (see Figure 22.14). Sometimes, there are too many nodes in the graph. To remove nodes from the graph pane, there are two options. The "Skip" option is typically what is desired. This will act as if the node did not exist in the network at all. In fact, if groups or metrics are calculated after Skip is selected for certain nodes, those nodes will not be included in the groups or metrics calculations. It is as if they were not in the spreadsheet at all. They also will not be shown on the graph. Alternatively, the "Hide" option simply makes the node (and its associated edges) 100% transparent in the graph pane. The layout algorithm, metrics, and groups all act as if it is still there, but it is simply not visible.

Though beyond the scope of this brief introduction, readers are encouraged to also explore the Dynamic Filters feature, which provides interactive sliders to hide certain nodes that do not meet selected criteria. Additionally, note that the Autofill Columns feature can be used to automatically set the Visibility column data based on some other data (e.g., if degree is below 2, Skip; otherwise, Show).

EXPORTING NETWORK VISUALIZATIONS

To save your network visualization as an image file, simply right-click on the image background and select Save Image to File > Save Image. There are Image Options available that can determine the size of the image and text for a header and footer. Images are best saved in a lossless format such as .png or .gif. The .xps vector format is also available, which will scale as large as you need it to. This is recommended for high-resolution printing (e.g., posters).

SIMPLIFYING NodeXL WITH AUTOMATE AND "RECIPES"

There are many settings, options, configurations, and adjustments possible in NodeXL. Expert users can make use of the many features in the application to achieve sophisticated results. But new users often struggle to get similar results. To save time for new users, experts can share their settings configurations with other users. All configuration changes in NodeXL can be saved and shared.

1. **Start a new NodeXL session**. For example, in Windows 7, click the *Start* button and then *All Programs* and then scroll down the list from the top until you see the *NodeXL Excel Template* item. Click it and wait until NodeXL is loaded; that is, you see the Document Action pane on the right. In Windows 8, click Start and type "NodeXL" to search for it.
2. **Download some data**. Select the *NodeXL* ribbon on the Excel menu's top line; then, in the *Data* section (the first one from the left), click the *Import* drop-down, and click on the *From Twitter Search network...* item in the menu. In the

box under "Search for tweets that match this query," type (say) "your query" (without quote marks). If you have a Twitter account but haven't used it in NodeXL before, you'll have to select the first radio button under "Your Twitter Account" and follow the steps to authorize NodeXL to use your account to import Twitter networks. To keep it quick, just leave the other defaults the way they are; you can play with them later. Click OK.

3. **Get a recipe from the NodeXL Graph Gallery**. Once you have downloaded network data, you have to change various NodeXL settings to fine-tune the network graph to get the results you want. An easy alternative way to do this is to copy a recipe file from a network graphs saved to the NodeXL Graph Gallery. Many of these networks have a link to the recipe used to create them (technically referred to as the "NodeXL Options file"). Scroll to the bottom of many NodeXL Graph Gallery pages, and click the link "Download the NodeXL Options Used to Create the Graph." Save this to a convenient folder, for example, the place where you keep your NodeXL data; you'll now have a file there called *WorkbookOptions-#####.NodeXLOptions*.

4. **Apply the NodeXL data recipe to your network data**. Returning to the NodeXL ribbon in Excel, in the *Options* section, click on *Import*. This opens a file open dialog; navigate to and open the file *WorkbookOptions-#####.NodeXLOptions* that you just downloaded.

5. **Automatically compute metrics and visualize the network graph**. Click the *Automate* button in the *Graph* section on the NodeXL ribbon. (You can deselect tasks if you wish by unchecking boxes, and you can change Options for those tasks by selecting a task and clicking the *Options...* button.) Click the *Run* button. (You may get an error message that reads: "This workbook can't be saved"; you can avoid it by following the instructions in the dialog box. Just click OK for now.)

6. **Explore the results**. The network graph will now be in Document Actions pane. If you don't see the pane, you can bring it back by selecting the *View* ribbon in Excel and clicking the *Document Actions* icon in the *Show* section. Click on the various worksheets to dig into the data that NodeXL has created about each edge, vertex, group, and the network as a whole.

7. **Export to NodeXL Graph Gallery**. NodeXL will summarize information about the network for you and can export the visualization and report to the NodeXL Graph Gallery. Click the *Export* drop-down in the *Data* section of the NodeXL ribbon and then click on the "To NodeXL Graph Gallery..." entry. Select the "I don't have an account" radio button, and provide a guest name; for now, just leave the defaults the way they are. (You can create an account on http://nodexlgraphgallery.org by clicking on the Create Account link in the top left-hand corner.) When Excel's finished churning (uploading may take a while; wait for the dialog box to disappear), go to the NodeXL Graph Gallery home page http://nodexlgraphgallery.org/Pages/Default.aspx; you should see your graph near the top of the page. Click on the thumbnail to go to the page.

Beyond the individual

23

This book has focused on how to find individual people and information about them on social media. However, it is worth dedicating one chapter to how social media can be used to understand groups of people. That could be organizations, communities, or people who share a common trait or demographic attribute.

What kind of things might an investigator want to know about a group? It depends on who or what you are investigating and what you want to know. If an organization is the target, like a terrorist group or organized crime syndicate, then any information you can find on the group might be useful. You can see how they are using social media, what their goals are, who participates, where they are posting from, etc. While large organizations (like al-Qaeda) may not be targets of investigation by anyone outside government groups, law enforcement has successfully used social media to investigate street gangs and other small organizations. Law firms have used social media to investigate disruptive groups' plan to sue. In these situations, any information can potentially be useful.

It may be that an individual person is a target, but you know he or she is an active member of an organization or community or a participant in an event. In that case, learning about the group the target is part of can help an investigator understand more about the target's life and world views. You can learn about the target's motivations, interests, activities (through association with group activities), and interactions. You can also learn who might be an influential person to contact if you are trying to reach out to or influence the target.

Finally, when you have an individual target in mind but you do not know much about him, it can be helpful to understand information about the demographic groups that the target is a member of. These can be broad categories, defined by age or race, or more specific categories, like people with the same profession or background. The characteristics common to the group may not necessarily describe your target, but they can provide insights about where to start looking for information specific to the target.

ORGANIZATIONS

All types of organizations have presences on social media, from small town community service groups to international terrorist organizations like al-Qaeda. As we will see in this section with a number of excellent examples of work done by individuals and groups, investigating the behavior of a group can lead to excellent insights that apply to individuals and that often lead to critical information about events. However, even when that connection to individually interesting behavior is not there, understanding a group that a target is a member of can lead to valuable insights about that target.

Note that this chapter is separating out formal organizations, addressed in this section, from communities and events that tie people together (discussed in the next section). In one sense, it is a somewhat arbitrary distinction. However, the line generally falls in a way that separates people who identify with a particular organization that may have a hierarchy from those who identify with an issue, event, or philosophy. Both of these "groupings" are interesting, but the way you approach them can differ.

In particular, when looking at organizations and their members, there may be a greater assumption that the actions endorsed or encouraged by the organization will be embraced by its members. Therefore, understanding the activities, motivations, and online statements of the organization can be valuable background for understanding an individual target.

TERRORISTS

Though not everyone might expect it, terrorist groups are extremely active on social media. Facebook, Twitter, YouTube, online forums, and other social media sites are all hosts to terrorist activity.

Gabriel Weimann of the University of Haifa asserts that 90% of organized terrorism online is conducted through social media.[1] They use it for recruiting, intelligence collection, and communication with the general public.

In earlier chapters, we saw examples of people who were investigated for their individual terrorist activity. Those people were recruited through the online social media activity of terrorist groups.

The Department of Homeland Security (DHS) created a report in late 2010 addressing this issue, titled "Terrorist Use of Social Networking Sites: Facebook Case Study". That report was restricted to dissemination among law enforcement, but copies of it are available online. This chapter relies on a version provided by Public Intelligence.[2]

The report summarizes terrorist use of Facebook as follows:

> As part of this trend, jihad supporters and mujahideen are increasingly using Facebook, one of the largest, most popular and diverse social networking sites, both in the United States and globally, to propagate operational information, including IED recipes primarily in Arabic, but in English, Indonesian, Urdu and other languages as well. While some tactical information is available on Facebook, the majority of extremist use of Facebook focuses on disseminating ideological information and exploiting the site as an alternative media outlet for terrorist propaganda. However, to a lesser degree, the site is used as a gateway to radical forums and jihadi sites with explicit radical agendas (and easily

downloadable operational information) and as a platform to promulgate some tactical and operational information.

Terrorist Use of Facebook:

- *As a way to share operational and tactical information, such as bomb recipes, AK-47 maintenance and use, tactical shooting, etc.*
- *As a gateway to extremist sites and other online radical content by linking on Facebook group pages and in discussion forums.*
- *As a media outlet for terrorist propaganda and extremist ideological messaging.*
- *As a wealth of information for remote reconnaissance for targeting purposes.*

—***Department of Homeland Security***
"Terrorist use of Social Networking Sites:
Facebook Case Study"

For each of the bullet points above, the report goes on to detail how terrorist groups are using the site. The report even appears to contain screenshots of some of their posts. Figure 23.1 shows an example post with instructions on how to make a bomb.

This report, from 2010, came quite early in the timeline of online social networks; Facebook was around one-third of its current size at that time. As social media has grown in popularity, so has terrorists' use of the sites. As described in the 2010 DHS report, that activity is largely used for outreach and propaganda and often appears in English to reach Western audiences.

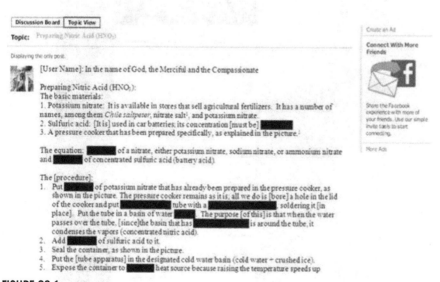

FIGURE 23.1

This Facebook screenshot is reported by Fox News to have come from a Department of Homeland Security report on terrorist use of Facebook. The post describes how to make a bomb.

Many major international terrorist groups have social media accounts, including al-Qaeda, ISIS, and the Taliban. Boko Haram, the Nigerian terrorist group well known for kidnapping over 200 school girls,[3] makes extensive use of YouTube to post videos of propaganda messages and even videos of mass executions (Figure 23.2).

As another example, the Taliban was active on Twitter from 2011 on. Figure 23.3 shows screenshot of their Twitter feed from May of 2014. Note that it is in English.

FIGURE 23.2

A still from a Boko Haram video posted online.

FIGURE 23.3

The Taliban Twitter feed. Note the tweets are in English.

FIGURE 23.4

The Taliban's English language website, used extensively in their social media posts.

You can see that each post has a link at the end to a news story. These link to the Taliban's English website, also used for propaganda. Figure 23.4 shows the top of the main page of the Taliban's website, which features strongly in their social media presence.

The Taliban's Twitter feed has since been shut down, and this is a common back-and-forth battle between terrorist groups and social media sites. The social media sites have policies against much of the language and intention that terrorist groups use. Thus, they eventually find the accounts of the terrorist groups and shut them down, but new accounts pop up.

And while the contents of these accounts are often disturbing, understanding the propaganda and messaging terrorist groups are putting out can be an excellent way to understand the group's (and thus its members') motivation and activities.

STREET GANGS

Street gangs also have a strong presence online, and indeed, a lot of interaction between rival gangs takes place online. In 2013, Ben Austin wrote an excellent article for Wired, "Public Enemies: Social Media Is Fueling Gang Wars in Chicago."[4] He describes the violence that has overtaken Chicago in the past few years resulting from the fractious street gang environment. He explains, through extensive examples, how gangs interact with one another and with rivals. With examples from Facebook, Instagram, and Twitter, he explains how gang members post photos of themselves with guns, drugs, and cash, unconcerned about whether parents, teachers, or police see the posts. The term "Facebook driller," describing a gang member who starts problems with rivals online, is not just introduced but demonstrated through examples that sometimes lead to real killings.

Austin's article is extensive and so thorough that I would like to reprint the whole thing here. Short of that, here is one excerpt that shows the role social media plays through one specific example:

> *Increasingly, disagreements that end in bloodshed have their origins online. The Chicago police department, which now patrols social media along with the streets, estimates that an astonishing 80 percent of all school disturbances result from online exchanges. At one point on Morgan Street, a 15-year-old joins us at the stone table. He calls himself Boss Nick, and he says he regularly posts pictures to Instagram of himself with guns. He doesn't care if the police or his teachers or really anyone sees it. He feels he has to let rivals know he is out there "with these poles." Boss Nick had been friends with Shondale Gregory, known as Tooka, a 15-year-old killed in 2011. Gregory was shot in the head, and rivals soon posted pictures of his corpse to Facebook, doctoring the image with horns and splattered brains. The Chicago police said that within minutes of the images' appearing on the site, 81 kids at Gregory's high school were suspended for fighting and an additional 200 students walked out. Gregory's clique of Gangster Disciples, which had called itself the St. Lawrence Boys for their block on the South Side, started referring to their turf as Tookaville and to themselves as the Tooka Gang.*
>
> *"All that 'cause of Facebook," Baskin's 20-year-old grandson says. "That's why Tooka blew up."*
>
> *—Ben Austin from*
> *"Public Enemies: Social Media*
> *Is Fueling Gang Wars in Chicago"*

Police have embraced this kind of investigation. Particularly for street gangs, investigating the entire group often leads to the arrests of individuals because of their participation. Consider one example from New York. Police arrested Melvin Colin for weapons and drug crimes and for murder. His Facebook page had some public material, but in his posts that were restricted to his friends only, he made many incriminating statements. Police were able to convince one of Colin's friends to give them access to those private posts.

Colin's lawyers appealed this, claiming he had an expectation of privacy, but the courts struck down that argument. The judge ruled that once Colin shared with his friends, the expectation that the information would remain private disappeared since the friends could do anything they wanted with the posts—including sharing them with police.[5]

Cincinnati also uses social media to track gang activity and has used it to break up street gangs. Officials there report that their officers, in partnership with the University of Cincinnati, use the social media posts to create and maintain a database of gang members and activities that officers can use in their investigations.[6]

COMMUNITIES AND EVENTS

As discussed in the chapter on "Forums and Question Answering Sites," many online communities find gathering places to discuss their activities. These communities may be in forums, but they can also coalesce around hashtags within certain social media sites. For example, many conferences and conventions have an agreed upon hashtag that people use when they tweet about the event. At ComicCon, an entertainment fan convention, people tweet with the hashtag #comicon or #sdcc. Communities may also have a hashtag they use to identify their social media posts, regardless of whether there is an event. For example, politically conservative Twitter users in the United States often use the hashtag #tcot (Top Conservatives on Twitter) to label their posts.

As with organizations, it can be useful to analyze what is going on within a community or around an event within social media. The content of the posts tells you what topics are of interest to the group, what is going on, what plans are being made, etc. The people within the groups and how they interact can tell you who is important and what role they play.

Recall the chapter on "Analyzing Networks" where we created visualizations of social networks. We can apply those techniques in this domain. Figure 23.5 shows a visualization of an online community. Each circle represents one person in the network, and a line connecting two circles shows those two people have interacted. In this visualization, larger circles indicate people who are more important in the community. The color of the circles indicates different subgroups.

Without a lot of other data, we can see there are three people who are quite important, represented by three large circles in the middle of the image (two purple ones and one green one). We can also see small pairs of people off to the sides who do not interact with everyone else. This kind of information can be very helpful when you are looking at a community online and want to learn more about who is important and who might be a good person to talk to in order to find more information.

One example of how some communities are monitored comes from the Southern Poverty Law Center, or SPLC. The SPLC is a civil rights organization, founded in 1971 as a law firm. The group sues on behalf of victims of hate crime and is noted for its success in battling white supremacist groups including the Ku Klux Klan.

As part of their activities, they monitor hate groups around the country for all kinds of activity. These groups leverage the internet as much as anyone, and so SPLC monitors the online and social media activity of hate groups.

In the realm of white supremacy, that includes monitoring the online forum Stormfront (see Figure 23.6). Ku Klux Klan leader Don Black established the site in 1995, and it is the first and one of the largest racial hate sites online.

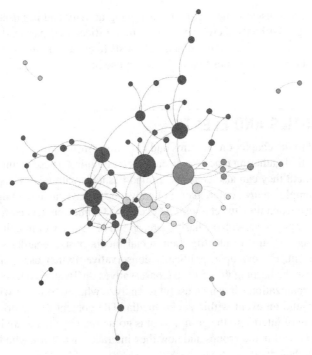

FIGURE 23.5

The network of a discussion group. Larger circles indicate people who are more important and lines connecting circles indicate two people who have interacted.

SPLC's Intelligence Report on the users is disturbing. They found that the site is a home for perpetrators of violent hate crimes. Author Heidi Beirich said "Stormfront is the murder capital of the racist internet."[7] Members of Stormfront were responsible for nearly 100 murders since 2009, and SPLC saw a marked increase in violence after Barak Obama took office as President.

The report[8] both profiles the killers and details many of their crimes. They begin with a general description of the Stormfront users who go on to kill:

A typical murderer drawn to the racist forum Stormfront.org is a frustrated, unemployed, white adult male living with his mother or an estranged spouse or girlfriend. She is the sole provider in the household. Forensic psychologists call him a "wound collector." Instead of building his resume, seeking employment or further education, he projects his grievances on society and searches the internet for an excuse or an explanation unrelated to his behavior or the choices he has made in life.

—"White Homicide Worldwide" Southern Poverty Law Center

It goes on to detail the progression from frustration to committing acts of violence as it plays out within the Stormfront site. It then looks at case after case of racially

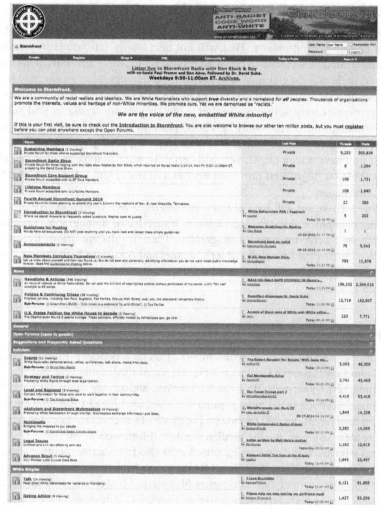

FIGURE 23.6

A portion of the forums at white supremacist site Stormfront.org. Note the variety of topics from site administration to white supremacy events to dating.

motivated murders committed by members of the site and details their participation on the site leading up to their crimes.

As disturbing as the contents are, the report is an excellent example of the value that comes from close monitoring of a community online. The authors track not just the content of posts, but the traffic rates to the site (which allows them to identify peaks of activity, like the one that followed in the immediate aftermath of the 2011 white supremacist mass killings in Oslo[9]), topics discussed, the relationship between discussions and other current events, and individual members of the site.

DEMOGRAPHICS AND SHARED TRAITS

Another way to look at groups in social media is to study the use, habits, and feelings of certain demographics. That will not necessarily tell you how your target will behave, since these tend to be broad groups with a lot of diversity within them. However, understanding common behavior for a demographic group may be useful in guiding your investigation. For example, we know that African Americans are disproportionately active on Twitter. Thus, if you are trying to find someone online in that group, Twitter may be a good place to start. As another example, we know teens use a variety of social media but have especially embraced Instagram. Thus, if you have a teen target, you will certainly want to look at all social media sources, but you might first turn your attention to Instagram where you could find richer information.

In this section, we will look at three groups: teens as a representative of an age-based demographics, African Americans as a race-based demographic, and family caregivers as a behavior-based demographic. These results are drawn from studies conducted by the Pew Research Center's Internet and American Life Project,[10] which focuses heavily on obtaining balanced and representative samples of people to conduct their research.

TEENS

Teens are very active users of social media. This data is drawn from an extensive report from Pew Research Center about teens, social media, and privacy.[11]

Among 12-17-year-olds, 95% use the internet, and among those, 80% are on social media. Facebook is the most popular site, used by 77% of teens who are online. A typical teen has about 300 friends on Facebook. Twitter is also popular, with 24% of online teens using it, and the median number of followers is 74.

Teens who are very active on Facebook tend also to be active on other social media sites. Those who have more than 600 Facebook friends are three times as likely to have a Twitter account and six times as likely to use Instagram. That means that if you have a teen target who is very active on Facebook, you should look for them on other sites as well.

Teen users share a lot of personal information. The vast majority (91%) have posted photos of themselves. Sharing a school and hometown is also extremely common (71% of teens have done these things). More than half share an email address, which can be used to search for them on other sites and which may reveal a possible username to search on other sites.

At the same time, teens are also concerned about privacy settings. Only 14% say their profiles are totally public. The rest have their profiles restricted to friends only or to friends of friends. Girls are much more likely to keep their profiles private than boys (70% vs. 50%). Some also try to mislead people with fake information to protect their privacy; 26% say they have posted some fake information for this purpose.

AFRICAN AMERICANS

Pew Research Center has also conducted research on racial demographic groups and their use of social media. In this section, we look at results from a study on African American users.[12]

The "digital divide" between black and white users has been with us for decades, and while it still exists, it is less prevalent on social media platforms. 87% of whites have internet access compared to 80% of blacks, but the numbers are much closer on mobile platforms, which are particularly popular ways to access social media. The divide vanishes with education; black college graduates and higher-income African Americans have the same level of internet access as their white counterparts.

African Americans have high levels of social media use; 73% use social media, and that jumps to 96% among teens (much higher than the overall average discussed in the section above). Twitter is especially popular. Among 18-29-year-old African Americans, 40% use Twitter, much higher than their white counterparts (28%).

Focusing on teens in this group, there are differences that emerge in social media usage. As mentioned above, many teens post false information to protect their privacy. This behavior is more prevalent among African American teens. Compared to 26% of teens overall who have posted false information, black teens are far more likely to do this, with 39% claiming to have done so. Black teens are less likely to disclose their real names on their social media profiles; 95% of white teens use their real names, while only 77% of black teens do.

FAMILY CAREGIVERS

In contrast to the more traditional demographic groups discussed above, in this section, we will focus on a behavior-based demographic group: family caregivers. This is one example of the wide range of behavior-based demographics who use social media in similar ways. Family caregivers are adults who help care for a loved one by doing chores, offering personal care, tending to finances, or regularly checking. Note that this demographic does not include parents raising children as caregivers. The majority of caregivers are taking care of an adult, while a small percentage take care of a child with significant health issues or care for multiple people. A full 30% of Americans qualify as caregivers. Information in this section comes from a Pew Research Center study on this group and internet use.[13]

We see typical internet access rates among this group, with 80% having access to the internet. They have a strong and active interest in medical information—88% report looking for this online, and many are conducting these searches on behalf of someone else. In terms of investigation, this does not speak directly to social media usage, but it might direct you to look at forums and online interest groups related to health issues if your target falls in this group.

Caregivers tend to look for personal connections online regarding health issues. Pew Research Center reports that 26% have looked for others with similar health concerns online, compared to 15% of people who are not caregivers. Caregivers are also significantly more likely to use social media sites in particular to follow other's health experience *and* to look for health information in general.

CONCLUSIONS

There is a lot of information available on social media to better understand organizations and communities of people. Similarly, there is excellent research done on how different demographic and interest groups use social media sites. Learning these insights about groups of people may not reveal exactly what a specific investigation target is doing, but it can provide valuable insight into where that target might be found online, how he or she is using social media as a member of that group, and what topics and activities are of interest. In addition, we saw in some cases that investigation of groups online can also lead to valuable intelligence about individuals within those groups who late become interesting.

NOTES

1 "Terrorist Groups Recruiting through Social Media." 2012. CBC News. http://www.cbc.ca/news/technology/terrorist-groups-recruiting-through-social-media-1.1131053.

2 The Department of Homeland Security. 2010. "(U//FOUO//LES) DHS Terrorist Use of Social Networking Facebook Case Study." Public Intelligence. https://publicintelligence.net/ufouoles-dhs-terrorist-use-of-social-networking-facebook-case-study/.

3 Winter, Jana. 2010. "Al Qaeda Looks to Make New 'Friends'—on Facebook." Fox News. Fox News. http://www.foxnews.com/tech/2010/12/09/facebook-friends-terror/.

4 Abubakar, Aminu. 2014. "Boko Haram Engaged in Talks over Kidnapped Girls." CNN. http://www.cnn.com/2014/09/20/world/africa/nigeria-boko-haram-kidnapped-girls/.

5 Austen, Ben. 2013. "Public Enemies: Social Media Is Fueling Gang Wars in Chicago." Wired. http://www.wired.com/2013/09/gangs-of-social-media/all/.

6 Kelly, Heather. 2012. "Police Embrace Social Media as Crime-Fighting Tool." CNN. http://www.cnn.com/2012/08/30/tech/social-media/fighting-crime-social-media/.

7 Graham, Gordon. 2012. "Cincinnati Police Using Social Media to Catch Criminals." Fox 19 News. http://www.fox19.com/story/19454817/cincinnati-police-using-social-media-to-catch-criminals.

8 "SPLC Report: Users of Leading White Supremacist Web Forum Responsible for Many Deadly Hate Crimes, Mass Killings." 2014. Southern Poverty Law Center. http://www.splcenter.org/get-informed/news/splc-report-users-of-leading-white-supremacist-web-forum-responsible-for-many-dead.

9 "White Homicide Worldwide." 2014. Southern Poverty Law Center. http://www.splcenter.org/get-informed/publications/White-Homicide-Worldwide.

10 "Massacre in Norway." 2014. CBS News. Accessed September 29. http://www.cbsnews.com/feature/massacre-in-norway/.

11 Madden, Mary; Lenhart, Amanda; Cortesi, Sandra; Gasser, Urs; Duggan, Maeve; Smith, Aaron; Beaton, Meredith. 2013. "Teens, Social Media, and Privacy." Pew Research Center. http://www.pewinternet.org/files/2013/05/PIP_TeensSocialMediaandPrivacy_PDF.pdf.

12 Smith, Aaron. 2014. "African Americans and Technology Use." Pew Research Internet Project. http://www.pewinternet.org/2014/01/06/african-americans-and-technology-use/.

13 Fox, Susannah; Brenner, Joanna. 2012. "Family Caregivers Online." Pew Research Internet Project. http://www.pewinternet.org/2012/07/12/family-caregivers-online/.

Inferring traits from profiles

24

The technology to do everything in this chapter already exists. Most of it is in the hands of lab researchers, and not available for commercial use. However, it is likely to become available in the very near future, and it will have a profound impact on the way we investigate people online.

So far, we have looked at what people are sharing on social media, what they say about themselves, who they interact with, where they post from, and what is reflected in their posts.

But it turns out that people reveal a lot more about themselves in those posts, including information they would prefer to keep private. This information is discovered using advanced computer programs or *algorithms*, which examine the huge amounts of data people share online and look for subtle patterns within it. From that, they are able to predict or infer a wide range of personal attributes (including things like sexual orientation, personality traits, drug and alcohol use, and political leanings). In some instances, they can even predict a person's future behavior.

This chapter will describe some of the work happening in this area and insights that may come within reach in the future.

Since these algorithms tend to be used on one particular site, the analysis is broken down by social media site.

TWITTER

Twitter is a great source of information for computer programs, because almost all of its data is public. Furthermore, most of it is text—and computer scientists know a lot about how to analyze texts.

Your words can reveal quite a lot about you, in more subtle ways than you think. The little words we use, which we could often dismiss as meaningless, are chosen unconsciously. Our unconscious choices reveal information about how our mind works. Research has shown that these words, called "particles"—which include pronouns ("you," "I," and "we"), prepositions, articles, and auxiliary verbs ("could," "should," and "may")—are inexorably linked to a person's personality, emotional state, and social identity.[1]

Computer scientists can use this by grouping words into categories and then analyzing people's social media posts to find connections between the word categories and individual traits. The analysis starts with a long list of words and each word's category. This is fed into an algorithm, along with a file that has text a person has written online; it could be, for example, a bunch of a person's tweets. The algorithm then compares that text to the lists of words and outputs a report. The report can then be used in statistical analysis to find connections between word use and personal attributes.

Here are some examples:

- As people get older, they tend to use more positive emotion words (like "happy" or "joy"), more future tense verbs, and fewer past tense verbs.
- Men tend to curse far more than women.
- People who rate higher in neuroticism (indicating they are less emotionally stable) tend to use more anxiety words (like "worry").
- Agreeable people tend to use more positive emotion words.
- People who are anxious use more explainer words (like "because" and "since").

The list goes on and on.

On Twitter, this kind of analysis has been used to predict social media users' big five personality traits.[2] The traits include

- whether someone is extroverted or introverted,
- their openness to new experiences,
- how conscientious they are (which deals with planning or procrastination),
- how agreeable they are, and
- their emotional stability (neuroticism).

Algorithms have been able to guess a person's scores on a big five personality test with accuracy of close to 90%. Similar techniques have been used to measure the strength of people's interpersonal relationships, too.[3]

TOOL: ANALYZEWORDS

Most of the computer programs that discover people's personality traits from social media only exist within the research community and aren't public available. However, there is one online tool you can use to analyze someone's Twitter personality right now. It's called AnalyzeWords, and you can find it at http://analyzewords. com. Enter your (or anyone else's) Twitter handle, and see a report of some high-level personality traits.

As an example, here are analyses of two Twitter accounts from AnalyzeWords: the author's account, and President Obama's account (Figures 24.1 and 24.2).

FACEBOOK

Because people share so much information on Facebook, there are numerous algorithms that use its data to infer user traits. None of these tools are currently available for public use. We will look at two studies that highlight the breadth and depth of information that such tools can uncover from Facebook.

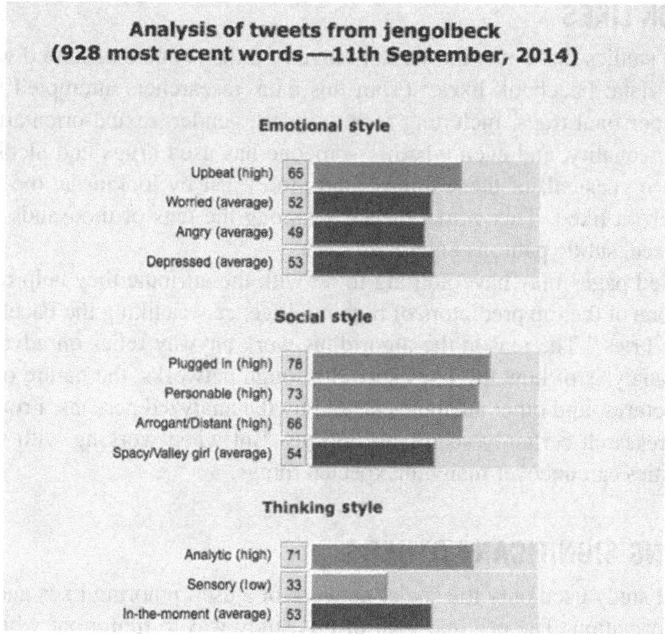

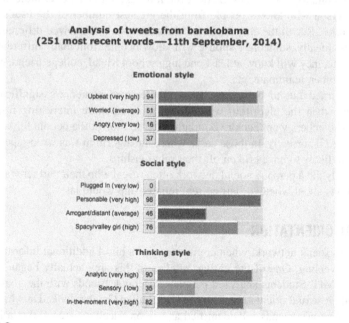

FIGURE 24.1

AnalyzeWords analysis of the author's tweets.

FIGURE 24.2

AnalyzeWords analysis of the President Obama's tweets.

FACEBOOK LIKES

One of the studies that cover the widest range of traits is one that started with a narrow set of data: Facebook likes.[4] From this data, researchers attempted to predict dozens of personal traits, including race, religion, gender, sexual orientation, intelligence, personality, and even whether someone has used drugs and alcohol. They were able to guess all of these things (and more) just by looking at the Facebook pages a person liked. This works because, among the tens of thousands of people they analyzed, subtle patterns emerge in likes.

The liked pages may have nothing to do with the attribute they help reveal. For example, one of the top predictors of high intelligence was liking the Facebook page for "Curly Fries." The reason the algorithms work anyway relies on advanced patterns and analysis of how the likes spread through networks, the nature of people's social structures, and other attributes shared by the analyzed persons. From the outside, this research certainly seems mysterious. But when working with very large data, statistics can uncover many unexpected things.

ANALYZING SIGNIFICANT OTHERS

A different study used only the social network of a user, ignoring likes and all other profile information. The original goal of this study was to figure out which person among all of a user's friends was that user's spouse or significant other.[5]

A first guess at how to do this might be to find the person who had the most friends in common with the user. However, it turns out that a better indicator is finding the person who knows people from the greatest number of the user's different social circles. Recall the chapter on network analysis that showed different clusters of friends. Ideally, someone's spouse will know people from many different groups; for example, they will know at least one high school friend, college friend, coworker, family member, teammate, etc.

This turned out to be a very good predictor of someone's significant other. However, when the algorithm was wrong, an even more interesting result came about. Researchers went back two months later to look at the people for whom they had guessed incorrectly. In those cases where the algorithm was wrong, people were 50% more likely to have broken off their relationships.

Not only did a person's social network often reveal who their partner was, but also it gave hints about whether their current relationship would last.

SEXUAL ORIENTATION

A person's social network, when combined with a bit of additional information, can also be revealing. One of the earliest studies in this area actually began as a class project at MIT. Students analyzed people's Facebook friends with the goal of determining their sexual orientation. Their project, called Gaydar, looked at what percentage of a person's friends self-identified as gay on Facebook (recall that a Facebook profile has a section where people can indicate their orientation). They found that, for men, they could draw a line regarding a percentage of gay friends. If someone had a higher percentage of gay friends, there was a good chance they were gay, too.

This relies on a principle we all know, often stated as "birds of a feather flock together." People tend to be friends with people who are similar to them more than would be expected if they chose friends randomly. This applies to not only sexual orientation but also wealth, education level, race, politics, and many other traits. While projects like Gaydar are not online, this insight can be useful in an investigation. If you find someone has, for example, many politically conservative friends, it would be logical to guess that they, too, might be conservative.

OFFLINE

Obviously, this book is concerned with social media, but these same techniques are being used offline. One example worth mentioning comes from big-box retailer Target.[6] In 2012, *The New York Times* reported a story of a 15-year-old girl who received coupons for baby items like diapers and bottles in a flyer sent by Target. Her father was very upset by this until two weeks later when his high school daughter told him she was indeed pregnant. Target found out before her parents did.

How did they do this? By analyzing her purchases. Target calculates a score for their female customers that not only guesses whether or not they are pregnant but also even attempts to pinpoint their due dates. They do this through analyzing patterns in what people buy.

As with some of the examples above, the patterns are not obvious ones. To find out someone is pregnant, it is not the purchase of a pregnancy test or of baby items that reveals it most clearly. Instead, strong indicators are things like buying more vitamins than normal, buying a large handbag, or buying a brightly colored rug.

If you saw those purchases in the checkout line ahead of you, it is unlikely that you would guess the woman buying them was pregnant. However, when considered in the context of data from tens of thousands of other customers, they happen to reveal a common attribute.

Target isn't the only company doing this kind of analysis, but this example reveals the kind of power that comes from analyzing the vast amounts of data in this digital age.

CONCLUSIONS

Computer scientists are actively developing technology that reveals all kinds of secrets about social media users. Although people say a lot online, there are things they want to keep secret, and that's becoming harder to do. From personalities to basic demographic information, a lot comes through in subtle or unconscious ways. When data from millions of people can be analyzed, statistical analysis and advanced computational techniques can detect patterns that indicate that a person has a particular attribute.

While most of this technology is not yet available to the public, it is coming in the next five to ten years. Some tools, like AnalyzeWords, are already available online. Technologies like this will become an increasingly important tool for social media investigation.

NOTES

1 Pennebaker, J.W., Mehl, M.R., Niederhoffer, K.G. 2003. Psychological aspects of natural language use: our words, our selves. *Annual Review of Psychology* 54(1): 547–577.

2 Golbeck, J., Robles, C., Edmondson, M., Turner, K. 2011. Predicting personality from twitter. In *2011 IEEE Third International Conference on Privacy, Security, Risk and Trust (PASSAT), and 2011 IEEE Third International Conference on Social Computing (Socialcom)* (pp. 149–156). IEEE.

3 Gilbert, E., Karahalios, K. 2009. Predicting tie strength with social media. In *Proceedings of the SIGCHI Conference on Human Factors in Computing Systems* (pp. 211–220). ACM.

4 Michal, K., Stillwell, D., Graepel, T. 2013. Private traits and attributes are predictable from digital records of human behavior. *Proceedings of the National Academy of Sciences* 110(15): 5802–5805.

5 Backstrom, L., Kleinberg, J. 2014. Romantic partnerships and the dispersion of social ties: a network analysis of relationship status on Facebook. *Proceedings of the 17th ACM Conference on Computer Supported Cooperative Work & Social Computing*. ACM.

6 Duhigg, C. February 16, 2012. How Companies Learn Your Secrets. *New York Times*. www.nytimes.com/2012/02/19/magazine/shopping-habits.html

An Example Investigation 25

Many of the investigation stories in this book are relatively simple: A target uses one social media site, and an investigator collects information through that site. With large sites like Facebook and Twitter, there is often a good chance a target will have an account, so this is a good strategy.

But some investigations are deeper and require more thorough methods. In this chapter, we will examine one such case. This is a step-by-step description of an actual investigation that I was asked to do. I am anonymizing the identity of the target for her protection, as she has not been arrested or charged with any crime. This story is intended to demonstrate the investigative process, including all the dead ends that led to the final insights.

THE TARGET

The target of this investigation, whom I will call "June Collins," is a woman who has an unhealthy interest (perhaps obsession) for a classic rock band. Her interest was especially focused around one band member in particular, whom I will call "Dan."

June maintains Facebook tribute pages to Dan. She travels around the country to see Dan's band and always has pictures taken with them. She also sends Dan emails and gifts. But it was when she showed Dan pictures she had taken of his house— a few hundred miles from where she lives—that she was brought to my attention. Dan was concerned that June's interest had escalated to a level where she might be dangerous.

THE BACKGROUND
INITIAL INFORMATION

The initial information I had for June included some screenshots of discussions she participated in, from her Facebook tribute page to Dan. In the discussions, she would occasionally post angry rants about other women who had an interest in Dan, especially if they posted a comment she disapproved of. She actively banned people from viewing the fan page (and her profile page).

Her true name was very common, so simply searching for her on the web was not likely to return good results. She also appeared to have several fake accounts that she used to post. The language used in the rants from these fake accounts was very similar to the language in June's own posts. Also, June's profile picture was a photo of her and Dan together, while the fake accounts' profile photos were beach scenes; no actual person was shown. While this is not evidence of anything by itself, it might suggest that someone did not have a personal profile photo to upload.

THE INVESTIGATION

Facebook, Part I: Finding an "In"

I began by visiting the Facebook fan page for Dan. Since the fan page was public, I found a few posts by June. These linked back to her Facebook profile page. She had her privacy settings turned on quite high, so I could not find any information about her from her page. In fact, I could not even send her a friend request, since we did not have any friends in common. (This is a Facebook setting people can choose to protect themselves from "spam" friend requests.)

I decided to start by sending friend requests to active members of the fan page. I assumed that some of them would be friends with June, which thus allows me to send her a friend request. I became a fan of Dan's page myself and sent the friend requests. I did not include any messages with these requests; there was no deception. I simply befriended people who actively posted in the community, particularly people who had liked or commented on things June had posted.

Within an hour, one member had accepted my friend request. He was friends with June, so I could now send June a friend request. This would show up as a request from someone who had a friend in common with her.

Other Social Networks, Part I

While I waited for her to respond to my request, I began searching for her in a number of different ways on the web.

I started with her Facebook username, which was something like June.collins.4121. However, this did not turn up anything outside of Facebook. I also saved a copy of her Facebook profile picture and did a Google image search for matching pictures, in case she had used it on other profiles. However, that returned no results either. I searched for forums or forum posts centered around Dan's career, hoping to find posts by June. No luck.

I went to both Twitter and Pinterest and searched for her by name. Since I had a photo of her from Facebook, I hoped I would be able to identify her visually in a profile picture. This did not turn up any accounts that I could identify. I also searched on Pinterest for boards dedicated to Dan, thinking she might have maintained one of these, but there were not any. I even looked at photos of Dan posted on Pinterest, but there were not too many. I was able to check out each one and confirm that, as far as I could tell, it had not been posted by June.

On LinkedIn, there were over 350 people with June's name. I went through the list by hand, looking for people in her known home state of North Carolina. I found one woman who did not have a profile photo. She was a fourth grade teacher. I then searched for her and the name of her school. This Google search eventually leads to a Facebook page for her church that, in turn, linked to her Facebook profile. It was not the June I was looking for. I went through a few more dead ends before hitting page 8 of the search results, where I found a profile with her photo on it. It was the same person in the Facebook photo.

Unfortunately, this page did not provide much more information. She listed no places of employment, and her connections were not visible. All that showed were interests in freelance writing and photography. Using a nonpersonal account, I sent her a LinkedIn connection request.

Other Social Networks, Part II: First Success

However, since she had a different profile photo on LinkedIn than she had on Facebook, I did another Google image search for photos. This time, I looked for those that matched her LinkedIn picture.

I was rewarded with four hits, all on the internet forum "Find A Grave." This site is dedicated to locating grave sites of celebrities and people's ancestors. The first hit was for June's profile page on this forum. It included a rambling and somewhat patronizing message, instructing people on what was "respectful and appropriate," which was very much in line with her tone on Facebook.

The site provided a list of her ancestors and links to many pages she created and maintained, which described the graves of her relatives. The comments on her profile page also indicated that she has asked several people to transfer control to her for pages that they had created for graves of her relatives.

This was actually an important insight, even though it did not have anything to do with Dan. The fact that she used a condescending, demanding tone in her posts and that she overreached her bounds in a need to control things on this grave-oriented website indicated that her behavior was typical of her personality and not restricted to her interest in Dan (Figure 25.1).

June did have a username on Find A Grave that was not simply her name. Unfortunately, this name was also extremely common—something many different people would use across sites. Still, I tried searching for the username along with Dan's name and his band's name on Google, but there were no promising results.

Facebook, Part II: Fake Accounts and Friends

Back on Facebook, I looked for a couple of the fake accounts that Dan suspected June of maintaining. One had disappeared, but one was still active. Using the screen grabs, I was able to match photos from the deleted account with photos on the active fake account. Both used the same beach scene on their profile pages. Again, while this is not necessarily evidence of anything, it suggested a possible connection between the two pages. I checked to see if the active fake account was friends with June, but I could not see a connection there (possibly because there was none or possibly because of June's privacy settings).

By this point, June had logged on and accepted my friend request. Now, I could see all her posts, photos, and profile information. Browsing through her photos and

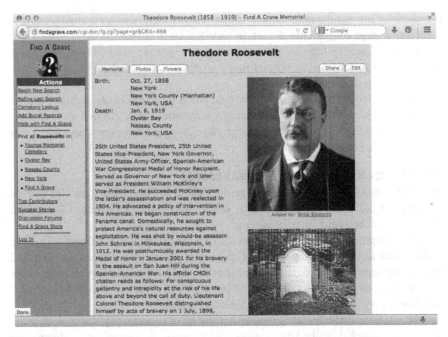

FIGURE 25.1

An example page from Find A Grave, a site where users maintain pages about people and their grave sites.

status updates, it became clear that she was obviously a serious fan of Dan and his band, but she also mentioned other bands. She also mentioned her interest in tracking down the grave sites of famous actors and her family members, echoing what I found on the Find A Grave forum.

Facebook, Part III: Findings

About half her posts detailed her trips to see Dan's band or other bands perform. She talked about breaking down in her car when she heard one band member was retiring. The other half of her posts were both melancholy and somewhat self-righteous. Examples include

- "How frustrating it is when you're the only person who can see how evil and sneaky someone is and everyone else is blind to it,"
- "Sometimes it's better to be alone nobody can hurt you," and
- "A successful woman is one who can build a firm foundation with the bricks others have thrown at her."

Her profile included links to her Twitter and YouTube pages. Her YouTube channel was dedicated to a totally different artist, featuring tributes to him and videos of him performing.

Her Twitter handle included Dan's last name in it, but her tweets were protected. I sent a follow request to her from the Twitter account that matched the Facebook account she had already approved. To gain her trust through mutual interests, I tweeted a link to a video from Dan's band, so she would see it if she checked out my profile.

Other Social Networks, Part III

As I waited to see if she would respond, I used her Twitter handle as a username in another Google search. This username was more unique. It turned up June's Pinterest account (with her real name attached to that Twitter handle). The account had only one photo posted, and it was of a band in the same genre of Dan's band (but not Dan's band itself).

It also turned up a single post on the weight loss site MyFitnessPal, which did not have anything to do with Dan.

At this point, I had a pretty clear picture of June's activities. She had not replied to my requests to connect on LinkedIn or Twitter, but I felt like the other sources had provided enough background to draw my conclusions.

INVESTIGATION RESULTS

After reviewing all the information available about June on Facebook, Twitter, YouTube, LinkedIn, and the forum site Find A Grave, I was able to draw a few conclusions about June.

First, she ties a lot of her identity into her fandom for bands in general and Dan's band in particular. She is definitely a big fan of Dan himself as well. She follows the band around the country and posts about them frequently on a number of platforms. However, Dan (and his band) is not her only focus; she talks about other bands and maintains fan pages for them, too.

She is also a lonely person who does not seem to be happy with her life. She does not have a career, and her posts suggest she is divorced and unhappy being single. She gets angry with people for perceived small slights and responds with long, angry rants and often completely cuts these people out of her social media life. Many of her posts are preemptively defensive, warning people about the potential consequences if they get in her way. Yet, she has no power to actually do anything to anyone who "crosses" her, except to block them.

Taken together, it seems that June's few interests form the core of her personal identity. Her confidence is low, and she holds on to these interests with fierce intensity. At the same time, it seems that she has never done anything to anyone who hurt her except to complain about it or hide from them.

In addition, she had interests beyond Dan and did not post anything especially creepy about him. Her enthusiasm seemed unhealthy, but not dangerous. Thus, as a result of the investigation, I reported back to Dan that nothing on social media indicated he had to worry about June.

CONCLUSION

This investigative process is typical of what I do when I'm looking for information about someone online. It shows the different types of social media to look at, the various and repeated Google searches for profile photos and usernames that can turn up previously undiscovered accounts, and techniques for gaining access to information restricted to a person's online friends.

Not all the techniques will be right for every investigation. In particular, you may have rules that prohibit you from friending people from fake accounts. However, most of what I did here required no interaction with the target. It is also important to recognize that many searches I did failed to find any useful information. That is typical of these searches—though usually, as in this case, you will eventually turn up information on someone who is active online.

Glossary

A

Algorithm The process or series of steps that a computer program follows to achieve its goal. In this book, we look at algorithms that read in social media information and output analysis of that data.

B

Blog Originally an abbreviation of "web log," a blog is a type of online diary. This technology was one of the early steps in the rise of social media on the web.

C

Centrality A measure of how important a person is in a social network.

Check-in When a user logs their presence at a location, it is called a *check-in*.

F

Facebook The most popular social networking website, with over 1.4 billion users. The site allows people to connect to friends, send messages, and share content.

Following Creating a one-way social connection on a social media website, generally so the follower can see content posted by the person they follow.

Forum A website that supports discussions, where people usually post questions or start topics and others respond.

Foursquare A social media site where users log their location, generally at restaurants, stores, and other venues.

Friending Creating a mutually recognized relationship with another person in a social media site.

Friendster An early social networking website. While it is still active, it has shifted to be more of a gaming website and is not a popular social network today.

G

Geotagging Adding location information, like GPS coordinates or a place name, to a post.

Google+ Google's social networking website, which allows people to connect with friends, organize them in groups called "circles," share content, and chat.

Graph Another term for a network (see *Social network*).

H

Hashtag A keyword or phrase (with no spaces), prefixed with a # character. They can be considered a specific type of *tag*. Examples of hashtags are #dogs or #socialmedia. These are used to label posts, often so other people interested in the topic can find them.

HTML (hypertext markup language) The computer language used to create web pages.

I

Instagram A photo-sharing platform that runs on mobile devices and supports sharing pictures, often altered with artistic filters.

IP address Internet Protocol (IP) address, which is a numeric code in the form of 192.168.0.0, that uniquely identifies each computer on the Internet. While IP addresses may change, a person connecting from a fixed computer, like a desktop or laptop that remains connected in the same location, is likely to have a relatively consistent IP address that can be used to track them.

L

LinkedIn A professional social networking website, dedicated to helping people maintain and create business relationships.

M

Metadata Data about a person, update, or other data online. This can include things like the date and time of the update, the location where it was posted, and the platform or tool used to post it.

Microblog A type of social media website where users post short updates. In contrast with a traditional blog that allows longer posts, it is often essay-length.

Myspace One of the leading social networking websites in the early-to-mid 2000s, Myspace's popularity was usurped by Facebook. It is still popular, usually ranking among the top 15 most visited social media sites.

P

Pinterest A social media site designed around sharing photos, organized on "boards" that have a consistent theme.

Post A message, photo, or other pieces of content that a person puts on social media.

S

Screen name See *Username*.

Script Computer code that runs on a server or in a browser, allowing for websites to be personalized or interactive.

Server A computer that contains the code for a website, including the HTML code for pages and any scripts used to run services.

Social network A social network describes a collection of people and their connections with one another.

Social networking website A social media site where a major focus is on allowing people to create profiles and connect with friends or acquaintances.

Status update A short post, which could also contain links, photos, or videos, that a user posts on a social media site. It often is about what the user is doing or thinking or something interesting they have seen.

T

Tag A label added to a post or photo on social media. The tags can make the post easier to find, since people can search for the tags.

Tumblr A microblogging website, frequently used to share gifs and other images.

Tweet An update posted to Twitter.

Twitter A microblogging website where people post short updates limited to 140 characters.

U

Username The name a person uses on a website or service, often the name they use to log in.

V

Visualization A picture of a social network, where people are often represented as small circles and their relationships to others are shown as lines connecting them.

Y

YouTube The most popular online video-sharing website, where users can view, comment on, and upload video.

Index

Note: Page numbers followed by *f* indicate figures and *t* indicate tables.